D1278271

Build Your Own Pentium™ Processor PC and Save a Bundle

2nd Edition

Aubrey Pilgrim

McGraw-Hill

New York   San Francisco   Washington, D.C.   Auckland   Bogotá
Caracas   Lisbon   London   Madrid   Mexico City   Milan
Montreal   New Delhi   San Juan   Singapore
Sydney   Tokyo   Toronto

McGraw-Hill

*A Division of The **McGraw·Hill** Companies*

©1996 by The McGraw-Hill Companies, Inc.

pbk   7 8 9 10 FGR/FGR 9 0 0 9 8 7

hc   2 3 4 5 6 7 8   9 FGR/FGR 9 0 0 9 8 7 6

Pentium is a trademark of Intel Corporation. Other product or brand names used in this book may be trade names or trademarks. Where we believe that there may be proprietary claims to such trade names or trademarks, the name has been used with an initial capital or it has been capitalized in the style used by the name claimant. Regardless of the capitalization used, all such names have been used in an editorial manner without any intent to convey endorsement of or other affiliation with the name claimant. Neither the author nor the publisher intends to express any judgment as to the validity or legal status of any such proprietary claims.

Library of Congress Cataloging-in-Publication Data

Pilgrim, Aubrey.
   Build your own Pentium processor PC and save a bundle / by Aubrey Pilgrim.—2nd ed.
     p.   cm.
   Prev. ed. published under title: Build your own Pentium processor PC.
   Includes index.
   ISBN 0-07-050183-1 (hc : alk. paper)   ISBN 0-07-050184-X (pbk. : alk. paper)
     1. Pentium (microprocessor)   2. Microcomputers—Design and construction.   I. Pilgrim, Aubrey. Build your own Pentium processor PC.   II. Title.
QA76.8.P46P55   1995
621.39'16—dc20   95-32910
                                                  CIP

McGraw-Hill books are available at special quantity discounts to use as premiums and sales promotions, or for use in corporate training programs. For more information, please write to the Director of Special Sales, McGraw-Hill, 11 West 19th Street, New York, NY 10011. Or contact your local bookstore.

Acquisitions editor: Brad Schepp
Editorial team: Jim Gallant, Editor
              Susan W. Kagey, Managing Editor
              Joanne Slike, Executive Editor
              Joann Woy, Indexer
Production team: Katherine G. Brown, Director
              Rhonda E. Baker, Coding
              Rose McFarland, Desktop Operator
              Janice Ridenour, Computer Artist
              Toya B. Warner, Computer Artist
Design team: Jaclyn J. Boone, Designer   WK2
            Katherine Lukaszewicz, Associate Designer   050184X

To the computer

Most people don't think about it, but in just a few short years, the computer has enriched and changed the lives of all of us. I have no doubt that computer technologies have grown faster than any other industry in all of recorded history. No other technology has had the impact on our lives as has the computer. It has made possible medical research and breakthroughs that would have been impossible without the computer. With the aid of computers, we were able to put a man on the moon. Thanks to the computer, shuttle space flights are now routine. The computer can also do many of the mundane, boring, and repetitive jobs, so it has given us more freedom to do other more enjoyable things.

In spite of all of the things the computer can do today, it is nothing compared to what it will accomplish in the next few years. We are truly living in the best of times. The times are going to be even better tomorrow.

Acknowledgments

I want to thank editor Brad Schepp of McGraw-Hill for his suggestion that I write a book on the Pentium computer. He and the other editors at TAB/McGraw-Hill have been a great help.

I also want to thank my son, James Aubrey, for his help in research and for doing the line drawings.

Contents

Introduction

 Easy to assemble

If you are like a lot of people I have talked to, you might say, "I couldn't assemble something as complicated as a computer. Especially one as sophisticated and powerful as a Pentium." But believe me, you can do it.

Even though the Pentium is more powerful than some minicomputers, it is very easy to assemble one. You need only plug a few components together. The only tool you need is a screwdriver for a few screws.

The ancient XT computer processed data at 0.75 million instructions per second (mips). The 66-MHz Pentium can perform 112 mips, the 120-MHz and 150-MHz Pentiums can more than double this figure. So the Pentium is over 300 times faster than the XT. Yet, there is very little difference in the assembly of an XT and the fastest Pentium.

 # How this book can help you

This book shows you what is inside a Pentium computer and how easy
it is to build your own. If you plan to buy a Pentium instead of building
your own, this book can still help you. There are thousands of options
and different components that can be installed and used with the
Pentium. This book is not just about assembling a computer. There are
individual chapters about each of the major components with detailed
information about the components and the options that you may have.
There are also some short reviews of essential software that you will
need. Software is as important as the computer. Chapter 16 contains
some tips that can save you hundreds of dollars on essential software.

 # Compatibility

The powerful Pentium can run all of the software that was developed
for the original PC and any other PC software developed since the first
IBM PC was introduced. Software that will take full advantage of the
Pentium's many capabilities is still being developed.

The Pentium is also compatible with all of the billions of dollars worth
of hardware developed since the first PC. New hardware is constantly
being developed that can take better advantage of all it has to offer.

 # No special skills required

Computers are very easy to assemble. Anyone can do it. You don't
need to do any soldering, wiring, or electronic testing. Computers are
made up of components that are just connected together. Many
components plug into the motherboard; others, such as printers and
mice, use cables.

I built my first computer, an XT, in early 1984. By today's standards, it
was a very simple machine. I had very few options and very few
vendors from which to choose. Today there are hundreds of new

products and vendors. I spend most of my waking hours just trying to keep up with the industry, the new products, and the new technology.

If you compare the old XT to the Pentium, it is about like comparing a covered wagon to an 18-wheel semi. The XT CPU had 29,000 transistors and operated at 8 megahertz (MHz). The Pentium has 3.1 million transistors and operates from 60 to 120 MHz. By the time you read this, there should be CPUs on the market that operate at 150 to 180 MHz.

Even though the Pentium is a vastly superior product, it still uses the same basic components as the old XT. These basic components such as disk drives, keyboard, and plug-in boards, have been very much improved over the original XT components. Since it uses the same basic components, it is no more difficult to assemble a powerful Pentium computer than the lowly XT.

Again, you won't need any special tools. A couple of screwdrivers and a pair of pliers should be all you need.

 # Plug and Play

Up until recently, it has been plug and pray that it will work. But new standards are being formulated to make it a lot easier to add components to a computer. They call the new standard *Plug and Play*.

Assembling a computer is very easy. But adding to it may cause some problems. Most motherboards have eight slots that can be used to plug in various boards. Plugging in a board is easy. The hard part is configuring it to make it work. I have had much more trouble installing and using things like a mouse, a modem, fax board, sound card, or CD-ROM than I ever had building a computer.

When a board is plugged into one of the slots, depending on what kind of board it is, it must be configured to use one of the 16 interrupt request (IRQ) lines, and it must be assigned a specific address in memory. Usually jumpers are used to short out certain sets of pins on the board. The board might also have small switches that must be set.

No two components may have the same IRQ or memory address. If the board is not configured properly, or if it conflicts with the setting of another component in your computer, it will not work. I recently tried to install a CD-ROM. It came from the factory with the memory address set for 0340 hex. It would not work. It had five different sets of pins on the board for changing the memory address. I misplaced the documentation that came with the board, so I tried blindly setting it at different locations. Each time the setting was changed, the software had to be told what it was. I finally gave up and called the vendor, and he faxed me a sheet with the settings. More than 90 different combinations were possible with those five sets of pins.

Boards and components built to the new standards have onboard firmware that scan your computer and determine which components are already installed at the various IRQs and memory addresses. It then either automatically configures itself or lets you configure it for the best possible setting.

Plug and Play might not be available on some hardware. It will be available on most all new systems that are released. The release of Windows 95 will also make the Plug and Play a lot easier.

Plug and Play will make life a whole lot easier. If this had been available years ago, I might not have nearly as many gray hairs.

 # Technophobia

Dell Computer did a survey that was reported in the November 1993 issue of the *Computer Shopper*. The survey discovered that 55% of people have a fear of new technology. The company coined a new term to describe this phenomenon—*technophobia*.

I must admit that I get a twinge of technophobia myself at times when I see some of the new products. But I worked in the electronic industry for more than 30 years before I retired. So I am not quite as afraid of the new technologies as some people might be. I know how simple and easy it is to put a computer together. There is nothing to fear about assembling a computer. If you follow the simple instructions and photos, you will have no problems.

Falling prices

It happens to me all the time. I go out and buy a product, and the very next day I see a newer or better product on sale for a much lower price. You will have about the same problem when you decide to build or buy a system. When the 486 first came out, the CPU chip cost almost $1000. You can buy the same CPU today for less than $100.

It is not only the CPU prices that are falling, hard disk drives, motherboards, modems, printers, keyboards, and most plug-in boards are being practically given away. The prices have not come down much on two of the items that we need very much, monitors and memory. Monitors are difficult to manufacture and require a lot of intensive labor. The newer computers and software need lots of memory. The demand for memory has depleted the supply, and I'm sure you know all about supply and demand.

 # Making the decision

We can never have perfect knowledge. Time is a continuum and as each second passes, new factors enter into whatever it is that you are trying to decide on. When I have to make a decision, I gather as much information as I can in a reasonable amount of time, then do it. Just like everybody else, I am wrong sometimes. But I think it is better to be wrong sometimes rather than to agonize and never make a decision.

The technology is evolving very fast, so you may decide to wait for a faster and more powerful component or system. Another reason to wait is to take advantage of the falling prices. I guarantee that if you wait until tomorrow, the item will be faster, more powerful, and less expensive.

So the longer you wait, the more you will save, and the better the system you will get. I also guarantee that no matter how long you wait to buy it, there will be a newer, faster, more powerful, and less-expensive item on the market before you get your unit home. But you should also consider that the longer you wait, the more of the great benefits of the powerful Pentium that you will be missing out on.

The 60-MHz Pentium that I put together just a short time ago for the first edition of this book is a very powerful machine, but it is now obsolete. I am not a bit sorry that I went ahead and built it at that time. I have had some very good service from it and it will continue to give good service for a long time. But I am also putting together a faster 100-MHz system even though Intel will have their much faster and more powerful CPUs on the market very soon. Even the P6 will be on the market in just a short time.

One other piece of good news is that we no longer have to depend on Intel for our CPUs. The AMD Company, Cyrix, and NexGen are all manufacturing Pentium-type CPUs that are as good as, or even better than, Intel's. The competition forces prices down and provides newer and better products. When it comes to assembling a computer, it doesn't matter too much who made the CPU that is on the motherboard. The assembly instructions in this book apply to all brands. They all go together the same way.

 # How much can you save?

By doing it yourself, you can save from $100 up to $1500 or more. It is difficult to determine exactly how much you can save. The reason is that there are so many different vendors and so many different components. The one thing that makes the computer so versatile and valuable is the very large number of options that are available. The cost, and how much you save, depends on how well you shop and the type of components you want in your computer. For instance, you need a keyboard for your computer. You can buy one for as little as $15 or pay as much as $150. In most cases, the $15 keyboard does just about everything that the $150 keyboard does. You will find just about the same wide price range for each component that goes into your computer.

It is somewhat like the clothing business. You can go to a high-class store and pay as much as $1000 or more for a tailor-made suit. Or you can go to a discount store and get one off the rack for about $150. Both suits accomplish their basic purpose, that is, to hide your nakedness.

Frankly, I don't pay that much attention to clothes. Unless I could see the label, I probably would not be able to tell the difference between a $1000 suit and one from a discount store. It's the same with computers. A computer with an IBM, Compaq, or Apple label on it does not compute any better than a no-name computer with an equivalent configuration. If you cover up the labels, you probably would not be able to tell the difference between them. The big difference is that the no-name computers cost about half as much as the big-name computers.

So the amount that you save depends primarily on you and what you want in your computer. Every manufacturer and assembler has to make some profit in order to stay in business. If you assemble a Pentium and use the exact same components that a vendor would use in a preassembled unit, you might save from $100 to $500. This would be the vendor's profit that he needs to pay overhead, rent, and for labor to assemble the unit.

But consider this: If you buy a unit that is preassembled, it might not have the exact components in it that you want or need. There are many ways that a vendor can cut corners in order to increase his profit. For instance, the monitor might have a 0.39 mm dot spacing. This is the amount of space between two dots of the same color on a monitor screen. You should get one with at least a 0.28 mm spacing. If a modem is included, it might be an older obsolete model. The modem board should also include a fax on it.

A recent article in one of the major computer magazines compared several brand name computers with no-name clones. In almost every case, the clones performed as well as or better than the brand names.

The capacity of the power supply is very important. You should not even think of running a Pentium with less than 200 watts—250 or 300 would be even better. Three of the brand-name computers that were compared by the computer magazine had 150-watt power supplies and one had a 110-watt supply. The computer works best if it is only using from 25 to 75 percent of a power supply's maximum output. It doesn't hurt to have a larger power supply than what you actually need. It is something like having a 400-horsepower engine in your automobile.

You might never need it but it is nice to have. A 250-watt power supply would only cost a few dollars more than a 150-watt supply. But some vendors do almost anything to save even pennies.

The point is that if you do it yourself, you can include the items that you want. If you do it yourself, you also receive a bonus that money can't buy, the experience of doing it yourself. You will learn firsthand what is in a computer. It will remove most of the mystery of how it works. And it will give you a great feeling of accomplishment.

 # An alternative to the Pentium

Depending on what you want to do with your computer, you might want to build a computer based on the PowerPC RISC-type CPU. IBM is a changed company. A short time ago, you could not buy parts for a PS/2 or any of IBM's proprietary systems. If you needed a new BIOS or hard drive, it had to be replaced by an authorized dealer. IBM now sells to end users almost anything that it has, including PS/2 components and any component that goes into the PowerPC. IBM is a big company. Call (800) IBM-4YOU if you want to find a particular item. I have a bit more to say about the RISC-type machines in Chapter 4.

Other good alternatives to the Intel Pentium are the NexGen 586, the Cyrix M1, and the AMD K5. Still another alternative might be the latest 486DX4 CPUs. The 100-MHz 486DX4 does just about everything the 60-MHz Pentium does but is a bit less expensive.

 # Green computers

You will see lots of computers and components advertised as being *green*. The green refers to the Environmental Protection Agency Energy Star guidelines. The green components use less energy than similar components used in the past. Computers, printers, and other peripherals use a lot of energy. Often they just sit there burning up kilowatts without doing anything. Many products are now being designed to go into a sleep mode when not being actively used. For

instance, laser printers use a fuser that heats the toner to fuse it to the paper. The fuser might draw 300 watts or more all of the time that the printer is on. Some printers can now place the fuser into a sleep mode where it draws about 30 watts. It takes a few seconds for the fuser to heat up again when you need to use it, but it can save a lot of energy, which is good for the *green environment*. Since I know that you are a good person who wants to help our country and its environment wherever possible, I'm sure that you will look for the green components. Besides being environmentally correct, an energy efficient green PC system can save you a few greenbacks.

 # Chapter contents

Chapter 1 talks a bit about the powerful Pentium and why you need it. Chapter 2 is a discussion of the overall components that make up a system. Chapter 3 has photos and detailed instructions for the assembly of a Pentium.

In Chapter 4, I discuss the different types of motherboards that are available. I also talk about how to upgrade an older computer. Chapter 5 discusses memory, why you need it, how much you need, and the type that you need. In Chapter 6, I discuss the floppy disks and drives. In Chapter 7, I talk about the hard disks that you need. In Chapter 8, I discuss the necessity of backup and how it can be accomplished. Chapter 9 discusses the various types of input devices that you need, such as the keyboard, mice, and scanners.

In Chapter 10, I talk about how monitors operate and the various types. I discuss communication devices such as modems, fax, and online services in Chapter 11. In Chapter 12, I talk about the various types of printers. In Chapter 13, I talk about CD-ROM and some multimedia applications. Chapter 14 discusses some of the sound and MIDI applications that can be used on your Pentium.

Chapter 15 discusses presentations, networks, and some of the other applications for the Pentium. Chapter 16 lists some of the essential software that is needed to run your Pentium. I also show you how you can save hundreds of dollars on the essential software that you need

by buying surplus software. This chapter alone can pay for this book many times over. Chapter 17 lists some of the sources for Pentium products. Chapter 18 lists some of the troubleshooting techniques that can help you when things go wrong. I've also included a comprehensive glossary.

I often see articles in magazines about products without any mention of a telephone number or address for the vendor. Throughout this book, when I mention a product, I list a telephone number.

 # Advancing technology

It is absolutely amazing that just a few years ago we thought that the 386 CPU with 275,000 transistors was the ultimate chip. Then, when the 486 came along with 1.2 million transistors, it was almost unbelievable. But now we have the Pentium with 3.1 million transistors on a chip just slightly larger than the 486. Intel has recently introduced the P6 that has 5.5 million transistors. That isn't the end. At this very moment, Intel is working on the next generation CPU that will have about 10 million transistors. They have stated that they will have CPUs with over 100 million transistors in the near future.

When you have lots of transistors on a chip, there is a possibility that some will be defective. Intel takes the defective chips and makes them into key chains. Figure I-1 shows 386, 486, and Pentium chip key chains. Call (800) 523-9009 for an Intel catalog. Figure I-2 shows a Pentium chip before the top cover is installed on it. Figure I-3 shows the functions of the main sections of the Pentium CPU.

Figure I-4 shows the Intel P6 with 5.5 million transistor in the CPU on the left and 16 million transistors in the 256K cache on the right.

Figure I-1

Key chains made from a 386, a 486, and a Pentium CPU chip. The 386 has 275,000 transistors, the 486 has 1.2 million, and the Pentium has 3.1 million transistors.

Figure I-2

A Pentium CPU chip before the top cover is installed.

Figure I-3

How sections of the Pentium CPU are dedicated.

Figure I-4

The P6 CPU with 5.5 million transistors and 16 million transistors in the 256K cache on the right.

What should you build or buy?

The answer is simple. Build or buy the most powerful and fastest computer you can possibly afford. The faster and more powerful it is, the longer it will last before it becomes obsolete.

The powerful Pentium

THIS chapter discusses the Pentium chip and why you should have a Pentium computer.

A simplification of how a computer works

Along with the 3.1 million transistors in the CPU chip, there are many other chips located on the motherboard and on plug-in boards. A computer does work by causing the transistors to turn on and off.

Transistors can be used as switches, much as a light switch. When we flip a switch on, electricity flows through the lamp. If we place a small voltage on the base of a transistor, we can turn it on or off quickly and automatically. By turning the voltage on and off with the transistors, we digitize the voltage and break it up into small chunks. By using just two transistors, we create four different types of output. The first would be with both transistors off, which would be 00. With one on and one off it would be 10. With the first one off and the second one on, it would be 01. With both of them on, it would be 11. If we used four transistors, we could create 16 different outputs and with eight transistors 256 different signals can be created. With 32 transistors, 4,294,967,296 different signals could be produced.

So how do we get those transistors to work for us? We use software that instructs the computer to turn the transistors on and off to

perform the various tasks. Although most software is something that is written, when it is typed into the computer from a keyboard, it generates electrical pulses that turn those little transistors on and off. When the software is loaded in from a disk, the magnetic flux of the disk is converted to electrical pulses that are identical to those created by the keyboard. The end result of all software applications, no matter how it is input to the computer, is to cause on and off voltages that control the transistors.

Ordinarily, the more complex the software and the more transistors available, the more work a computer can accomplish.

A couple of computers were developed in the early 1940s, but we had no transistors in those days. The computers used thousands of vacuum tubes and cost millions and millions of dollars. It took several large rooms to house one of these computers. It could perform fewer functions than a present-day, two dollar calculator. Technology has come a long, long way since the advent of the transistor.

System clock

The computer has a real time clock and calendar that keeps track of the date and the time. But the computer also has a system clock that is much more precise than the real time clock. Everything that a computer does is precisely timed. The timing is controlled by crystal oscillators. The computer carries out each instruction in a certain number of clock cycles. On some of the early systems, the clock was fairly slow. Even so, it often took several clock cycles to perform a single instruction.

The 486 was able to perform an instruction in a single clock cycle, even though the clock frequency was faster than any PC ever before. The Pentium has again raised the performance so it can do two instructions in a single clock cycle. The fastest 486 can perform 57 million instructions per second (mips). The 66-MHz Pentium can perform 112 mips.

Figure 1-1 shows a Pentium motherboard and some of the chips and sockets for chips and plug-in boards. There are six slot connectors for plug-in boards. The two at the top are also Video Electronic Standards Association local bus (VLB) slots. At the left end of the board are sixteen very fast static RAM (SRAM) chips used for memory cache. The white slots at the bottom right are for single in-line memory modules (SIMM) of dynamic random access memory (DRAM). Near the center is the large white Pentium CPU. In the upper center, just below the VLB slot, is the system BIOS chip with the white cover. There are several other very large scale integrated (VLSI) chips on the board.

Figure 1-1

A Pentium motherboard that shows some of the slots, sockets, and chips.

⇨ The Pentium

The Pentium has 3.1 million transistors in its CPU. It is more powerful than some early mainframes. The 66-MHz Pentium is capable of performing 112 million instructions per second (mips). Some of the reduced instruction set computers (RISC) type CPUs are

capable of over 150 mips, but the Pentium is the first complex instruction set computer (CISC) system that can do over 100 mips. Intel has now introduced a 120-MHz Pentium CPU and by the time you read this there will be a 150-MHz and a 180-MHz version on the market. These CPUs will match the performance of most of the RISC computers.

Some RISC type computers might be less expensive than the Pentium. One reason is because the RISC CPU has fewer transistors and costs less to manufacture. There are several different RISC CPUs and Intel has at least a half dozen Pentium CPUs. At the time of this writing, a comparable RISC CPU costs about half what an Intel Pentium CPU costs. But as Intel manufactures more of Pentium chips, the yield that they get from each batch will become greater and the costs will go down. Another reason for Intel to lower the prices on their CPUs is that they now have some competition from AMD, Cyrix, and NexGen.

The RISC computer might cost less to buy, but it will cost more to operate because it requires special software and hardware. At this time, there are very few manufacturers of RISC motherboards for end users. IBM and a few other companies are manufacturing them for original equipment manufacturers (OEM). There are many Pentium motherboard manufacturers for OEMs and end users. The competition will keep the prices fairly reasonable. The Pentium can run all present software. Lots of new software that will take full advantage of the 64-bit bus is still being developed at this time.

The 64-bit bus

The Pentium can handle data over a 64-bit bus externally, but can process it 32 bits at a time internally. Being able to handle 32-bit data internally, makes it compatible with software written for the 32-bit 386 and 486 CPUs. The Pentium can operate at 60 MHz and 66 MHz. Eventually there will be 64-bit software available to take full advantage of the Pentium.

The 64-bit bus allows 8 bytes of data at a time to be transferred back and forth to the RAM. Operating at 66 MHz, the Pentium can

transfer data at a rate of 528MB per second (8 bytes × 66 MHz). A 486 operating at 33 MHz over a 32-bit bus can transfer data at a rate of 132MB per second (4 bytes × 33 MHz).

Even with a 64-bit bus, the dynamic RAM (DRAM) might not be able to feed data to the CPU fast enough to keep it busy. So most systems will have a fast cache system. The cache RAM will be made of static RAM (SRAM). It is much faster than DRAM. Quite often a software program causes certain parts of data to be looped in and out of memory. The cache memory stores this most often used data and is able to feed it to the CPU in a very short time. Many of the newer motherboards are using a newer type of DRAM called Extended Data Output or EDO DRAM. The EDO DRAM allows faster access and output than the standard DRAM.

The powerful Pentium allows graphics and CAD programs to run much faster. It also allows full-screen motion pictures to run. The Pentium is ideal for running the 32-bit Windows 95, Windows NT, and OS/2 applications.

Since not too many applications can take advantage of the 64-bit bus, some companies have designed motherboards with a 32-bit bus.

 # What's in a name?

The next logical CPU name should have been *586*, and that is what a lot of people call it. But Intel was unable to copyright and protect the 386 and 486 names. Several companies developed direct replacement clones of the 386 and 486. Intel was rather unhappy that the courts let the companies get away with this. It made Intel even more unhappy that the clone makers could call their products by the same name. So this time they came up with the name, *Pentium*, which they were able to copyright. They derived the word Pentium from the Greek word *pente*, meaning five. Several companies have developed compatible clones of the Pentium. Intel cannot prevent anyone from developing a clone of their Pentium, but they can prevent them from calling it a Pentium. Some of the companies that have developed clones of the Pentium are Cyrix with their M1, AMD

with their K5, and NexGen with their 586. I am using a NexGen 586 90-MHz system to write this page.

Intel has already introduced their next generation CPU, the P6. Ordinarily, they would have waited for a while so they could sell more Pentiums before introducing the next generation. But the P6 was probably introduced a bit early because of pressure from the competition. There has been some speculation as to what they might eventually call it. If they followed the Pentium strategy, the Greek word for six is *hex*. Of course that word today generally has to do with witchcraft, spells, and bad things in general. The Latin word for six is *sex*. It is not very likely that Intel will call the P6 CPU a *hexium* or a *sexium*.

For most people, it really doesn't matter too much what Intel names it. As Shakespeare wrote, in Romeo and Juliet, "What's in a name? That which we call a rose by any other name would smell as sweet."

 # Why the need for more power?

You know that computers work by using digital data in the form of 1s and 0s. To form a 1 or a 0 means that a transistor must turn on or off. Data usually has a very large amount of 1s and 0s. It takes 8 bits, or a single byte, of data to form a single character such as an A or a B. There are about 400,000 bytes of character data for this book. That is a small amount compared to some types of data. A single color photo might require up to 25 million bytes of data.

The original PC operated at 4.7 MHz. The Pentium operates up to 120 MHz or more. The Pentium speed of 120 MHz is only 25.5 times greater than the original 4.7 MHz. But because of design improvements, the Pentium operates at over 300 times faster than the original PC.

If you do nothing but simple word processing, then the original PC would be all that you would need. But if you are processing graphics, large spreadsheets, or large databases you need a lot more power and speed. Data that might require an hour or more for an XT to process might take less than a few seconds for a Pentium. There are many PC

applications such as desktop video conferencing, multimedia, 3-D design, scientific modeling, speech and handwriting recognition, and many others, where the Pentium is ideal. A company might be paying an engineer $60 an hour to design and process critical data. If the engineer has to sit and wait for the computer to process the data, the company is wasting money. They are also wasting the engineer's time, which could be better spent doing productive work. In a situation such as this, a Pentium would pay for itself in a short time.

The Pentium is almost as powerful as some mainframes, yet it costs just a fraction of what a mainframe would cost. The Pentium is ideal for use as a network server.

 # Early software compatibility

There have been thousands of software programs written since the first PC was introduced in the early 1980s. Despite all of its power and speed the Pentium is still able to run any of the software developed for the first PC. It can easily shift from the slowest to the fastest.

Though the early software runs on the Pentium, most of it does not take full advantage of the Pentium power. So many software companies are now recompiling and modifying the older software to make it run better and faster on the Pentium.

 # Future software compatibility

Software lags behind hardware developments. Not much software has been developed that takes full advantage of the 32-bit bus of the 386 and 486. So it will be a while before much software is available to take advantage of the Pentium's 64-bit bus. But several companies are working overtime to develop it.

For instance, the Pentium's floating point operations are several times faster than the fastest 486. But there are not many general business type applications that can take advantage of this fact. You can expect several new and improved packages very soon.

 # Ways that the speed is increased

Intel lists three ways to increase the speed of a CPU. Add more transistors along with a cache, increase the clock speed or frequency, and increase the number of instructions executed per clock cycle.

The 486DX CPU has an 8K cache built in among its 1.2 million transistors. The Pentium has two 8K caches. The Pentium also has a new superscalar technology. The term *superscalar* means that the CPU architecture consists of more than one execution unit or *pipeline*. The superscalar technology enables the Pentium to process data simultaneously through two different pipelines. A pipeline is an arrangement of registers within the CPU. They are also called *execution units*. Each register performs part of a task, then passes the results to the next register.

The early CPUs required several clock cycles to execute a single instruction. The 486 can execute many of its instructions in a single clock cycle. The Pentium has the ability to execute two instructions in each of its two pipelines simultaneously in a single clock cycle. So a Pentium could possibly process four times as much data as a 486 in the same amount of time.

 # Pentium OverDrive

Intel has designed an OverDrive chip for the Pentium that is similar in operation to the 486 OverDrive CPUs. The Pentium OverDrive CPU fits in those oversized empty sockets alongside the 486 CPU on many of the motherboards. The Pentium OverDrive can replace anything from a 486SX-25 MHz up to a 486DX2-66 MHz. If you are replacing a 25-MHz CPU, you can expect a performance increase up to 168%, depending on what software is being run. Increased performance for a 50-MHz system replacement is up to 60% greater. The present Pentium OverDrive operates at 63 MHz, but because of its superior processing capability, it can increase the performance of a 486DX2-66 MHz by more than 100%.

But not all 486 motherboards can accept the Pentium OverDrive. It must have a 237 or 238 pin socket. My 486DX2-66 has an empty socket, but it only has 150 pin sockets. If you don't know what your motherboard has, and you don't want to take the cover off your machine to check it out, you can call Intel at 800-538-3373. If your system was made by one of the larger vendors, you can give them the name of the vendor and your model number and they can tell you if your system is upgradable.

By the time you read this, Intel will probably have Pentium OverDrive CPUs that will be able to replace and upgrade the 486 DX4s and the Pentium 60-MHz and 66-MHz CPUs.

 # CISC vs. RISC

The original PC and all PCs up through the Pentium are complex instruction set computers (CISC). This means that the CPU has a set of instructions built into it. Whenever it is asked to perform a task, it might have to sort through several hundred instructions to find the ones needed to accomplish the task. Having to sort through the instructions takes a finite amount of time that slows the CPU.

A reduced instruction set computer (RISC) might have to sort through less than half the number of instructions in order to perform a task. The DEC Company has developed a RISC chip that only has 1.2 million transistors, but it is the fastest microchip in the world. Their Alpha AXP can perform 157 mips while the Pentium with 3.1 million transistors can only do 112 mips. Some of the newer DEC RISC CPUs operate at almost 300 MHz.

IBM teamed up with Apple and Motorola to develop the PowerPC RISC chip. It has 2.8 million transistors and can perform 100 mips.

So should you forget about the Pentium and buy a DEC Alpha or IBM-Apple-Motorola PowerPC RISC system? At this time, it might not be a good idea. There are well over 50,000 software programs available that run on the Pentium. Very few of these programs will run on the RISC systems unless they are translated or modified. If software has to be

translated into a form that the RISC machines can understand, it will slow them down considerably. It is possible that some programs can be recompiled. IBM and Apple are developing emulation systems that allow a RISC machine to use CISC software and vice versa. But again, such an emulation system would slow the system down. A few software companies are developing native programs for the RISC systems.

At this time, the Pentium is the fastest and most powerful system that can run all existing PC software.

Another big advantage of the Pentium is that there are well over 100 million PCs in use that are based on the Intel 80x86 architecture, the same as the Pentium. There are thousands and thousands of vendors competing for this PC market. The large number of vendors has made the market very competitive. This competition has made the computer industry about the only industry in the world where prices continually go downward. The intense competition also causes the manufacturers to continue to develop new and improved products.

At the present time, DEC has little or no competition for its Alpha system. The IBM-Apple-Motorola PowerPC also is a lone product with no competition. If a software developer has a choice of developing a program that can run on 100 million machines, or use time to develop a program that will only run on a very limited number, what system do you suppose he or she will choose? The same thing is true for the PC hardware designers and developers. They are all going to go with the greater opportunity for sales.

There is no doubt that the RISC systems have some advantages over the CISC systems. But it is highly doubtful that the RISC systems will ever become as prevalent as the CISC systems. At least, this will not happen for a while. In the meantime, I would suggest that you stay with the Pentium CISC systems.

Cost

When first introduced, the price of the Pentium CPU chip was about $950 each in quantities of 1000. The 486 CPUs were about this expensive when they were first introduced. Within two or three years,

the Pentium CPU will sell for about what the 486 CPU sells for at this time, $100 to $200 each.

The first Pentium systems were rather expensive at about $5000 for a basic system and up to $10,000 or more for one with lots of goodies. It cost me over $5000 to build my system. Less than one year later some systems are selling for less than $2000.

The lowered cost of the Pentium is causing some drastic cuts in the prices of the 486 machines. Almost everybody can now afford a 486 system. And for many, that might be all you need. But for just a few dollars more, you can have a Pentium.

Who needs a Pentium?

If you do any of the following you need a Pentium: multimedia applications, 3-D graphics, video applications, large number crunching, network server, or for many other tasks that were previously reserved for minicomputers and mainframes. There are hundreds of scientific, business, and personal applications that can be handled best by the Pentium. The Pentium system can perform very complex financial calculations quickly, so it could give a Wall Street broker an advantage over anyone who did not have a similar computer. Other applications are discussed in Chapter 13.

Several companies are building high-end Pentium servers. They have designed special motherboards for the system. Most motherboards will have 8 expansion slots and allow for a maximum of 128MB of RAM. The ALR Evolution VQ/60 has 11 expansion slots and allows one gigabyte of RAM. Most systems only have five to eight drive bays. Their system has 13. You probably won't need a system such as this for a small business or a home office.

I have had several computers. My first one was a Morrow with 64K of RAM and two single sided 140K floppy disk drives. I built my next computer, an XT with 256K of RAM, a double sided 360K floppy drive and a 20MB hard disk. Since that time, I have assembled several 286, 386, and 486 systems. I was always amazed and quite happy

with the differences and improvements in each newer system. But after I had used the systems for a while, I became rather indifferent to the system and took it for granted. I often found little faults here and there. It is somewhat like a new marriage after the honeymoon has worn off.

Before I built my Pentium, I used a 486DX2-66. It is fast, but there were times when I had to wait and twiddle my thumbs while it did its thing. I hate to wait. Even if it is only a few seconds, it seems like ages. If you are like me, you need a Pentium.

Another reason for owning a Pentium is for the status that it lends. If you go to a computer user group and listen to the members talk among themselves, many of them will be boasting about how big and powerful their system is.

Writer Sebastian Rupley, in an article about the Pentium for *PC Computing*, used the term *technolust* to describe how some people felt about the Pentium. I think I might be one of those people.

To a computerphile, owning a big powerful Pentium system is probably about the same feeling that the rich and famous have in owning a Rolls Royce. And it is a whole lot less expensive.

CHAPTER 2

Components needed to assemble a Pentium

THIS chapter briefly discusses some of the basic components needed to assemble a Pentium.

⇨ Anyone can assemble it

No special skills or expertise are needed to assemble a Pentium. You do not need to do any soldering or electronic testing. You won't need any special tools. Most components merely plug together. You need a few screws used to hold the disk drives in place, a couple of screws to secure and ground the motherboard, and one screw to hold each plug-in board in place. You need only a Phillips and a flat-blade screwdriver. A pair of long-nose pliers are helpful, but not essential.

It won't happen very often, but there may be a time when you need to remove and replace a plug-in chip, such a BIOS chip. There are metal fillers on the back panel that are used to cover any slot that doesn't have a plug-in board. The bent portion of these fillers makes an excellent tool for lifting chips out of their sockets. See Fig. 2-1.

Figure 2-1

Using a back panel blank filler as a chip removal tool

 # Basic components

There are several basic components needed to assemble a Pentium. You need a case in which to mount the motherboard, a power supply, one or two floppy disk drives, one or more hard disk drives, disk drive interface, and a monitor adapter. You need memory chips installed on the motherboard and you may have up to eight different boards plugged into the slots on the motherboard.

The basic peripheral components and devices that you need are a keyboard, mouse, monitor, and printer. There are several other optional components and devices that you may want such as a FAX-modem card, a scanner, a sound board and speakers, a microphone, a CD-ROM and its interface, and a backup tape drive.

 # Compatibility

The Pentium is vastly superior to the fastest and most powerful 486. But, except for the motherboard, it uses the same basic components as the 486. In fact, it uses the same basic components as those found on the old antique, obsolete XT.

Compatibility is not much of a problem today. I do a lot of my shopping at weekend computer swaps and through mail order. When I order by mail, I look through several computer magazines and decide which component is the better buy. I have few concerns about whether it will be compatible or not.

Later in the book, there are separate chapters in which each of the major components is discussed in detail. The detailed discussions of these major components will help you make a better and more informed choice when you purchase the components. If you are not an expert computer whiz, I suggest that you read those chapters before you buy your parts.

Barebones systems

You may see some very attractive advertised prices for "barebones systems." These systems are usually just a motherboard, case, and power supply. You should be aware that you would not be able to do any computing with a system like this. You would need all of the other components such as a monitor, disk drives, memory, keyboard, and other components listed below. If you are short of money, you could buy a barebones system and then add to it as you can afford it.

Motherboard

The motherboard is a large board that has the Pentium processor chip or central processor unit (CPU) and several other chips necessary for the operation of the computer. The motherboard may also have up to eight slots or connectors that accept plug-in boards. There are hundreds of different plug-in boards that can be used to configure the computer to do almost anything imaginable. The Pentium is downward compatible so that it can accept any board, even those developed for the original PC. At this time, not too many boards have been developed that can take full advantage of all of the Pentium power. New boards are being developed every day.

⇨ The CPUs

The type of CPU installed on the motherboard determines the type of computer. There are several different versions of Pentium and Pentium type of CPUs. When Intel develops a CPU, the first version usually operates rather conservatively. Then as they learn more about what they can do, they gradually increase the speed and make other improvements. Their first 386 operated at 16 MHz. It was then increased to 20 MHz, then 33 MHz. The AMD Company made a 386 clone and increased it all the way up to 40 MHz.

The speeds of the 486s were also gradually increased. But it can be rather difficult and expensive to design circuits that operate at high frequencies. Intel found that they could double the internal speed of their 486s and vastly increase the performance without adding too much cost to the external circuit design. So they developed the 486DX2-66, which doubled the internal speed of their 486DX-33. They then tripled the speed with their 486DX4 to have the 486DX-33 operate at 99 MHz. (They call it the 486DX4-100.)

They have done about the same thing with the Pentium CPUs. The first ones operated at 60 MHz and 66 MHz. They then increased the internal frequency of the 60 MHz by half to yield a 90 MHz. They have now doubled the 60 MHz to yield a 120-MHz chip. By the time you read this they will probably have Pentium CPUs that run at 150 MHz and soon up to 180 MHz.

I am not sure that some of these later improvements could not have been introduced immediately. But the computer industry has a lot in common with the soap industry in that they must continually improve and introduce new and better products.

One reason that Intel must come out with newer and improved CPUs is that they now finally have some competition. The Cyrix, AMD, and NexGen companies have developed clones of the Pentium that may outperform the Pentium in some areas. For years, Intel was the sole supplier of 80x86 type CPUs. They still have over 80% of the market, but they are being forced to look back once in a while to see who is gaining on them.

 # Motherboard types: ISA, EISA, VLB, PCI

There are several different types of motherboards based on whether they use the industry standard architecture (ISA) or the extended industry standard architecture (EISA). Some motherboards have a Video Electronics Standards Association (VESA) Local bus (VLB) and some have the Intel Peripheral Components Interconnect (PCI) bus. Some motherboards may have a combination of ISA and EISA. Some may be ISA with a VL bus, or ISA with a PCI bus, EISA with either the VL or CPI bus, or a combination of all of the above. As you can see, you may have a lot of options to choose from. Figure 1-1 in Chapter 1 shows an ISA VLB Pentium motherboard.

Motherboards are covered in greater detail in Chapter 4.

 # Memory

When a computer works on a file or processes data, the program or portions of it is loaded into random access memory (RAM) or dynamic RAM (DRAM). The CPU then accesses the RAM, pulls out a portion of the data, processes it, then sends it back to the RAM, and pulls out another portion to process. Data may be shifted back and forth between the CPU and RAM several times during the processing. After the processing is finished, the data is sent back to the hard disk, printer or to wherever it is directed.

Memory is a critical part of the computer. It can determine the speed and how much productive work that the computer can accomplish. Figure 2-2 shows some older SIMM memory modules with 30 contacts. These SIMMs were limited to about 4MB. Newer SIMM modules have 72 contacts and can have up to 32MB or more. See Fig. 5-1.

Memory is discussed in greater detail in Chapter 5.

Figure 2-2

Older SIMM memory chips with 30 contacts

 # Plug-in boards

The computer has made enormous contributions to business, science, and almost every aspect of our way of life. One reason that it was able to provide this contribution is because it is very versatile. Much of the versatility is due to the connector slots on the motherboard that allow different plug-in boards to be used. There are hundreds of different tasks that a computer can do with different plug-in boards.

There are a few basic type boards that are usually necessary in all computers such as the input/output (I/O) boards, the monitor adapter boards, and disk controller or interface boards. The I/O boards usually have connections for a printer cable, and parallel ports for a mouse or modem. Figure 2-3 shows an IDE I/O board that can control two floppies, two hard drives, has a LPT1 printer port, two serial COM ports, and a game port. The monitor needs an adapter to drive it and the disk drives must have a controller or interface adapter board.

Some motherboards may have many of the basic I/O and interface functions integrated onto the motherboard. You would not need a board for the functions that are integrated on the motherboard. This

Figure 2-3

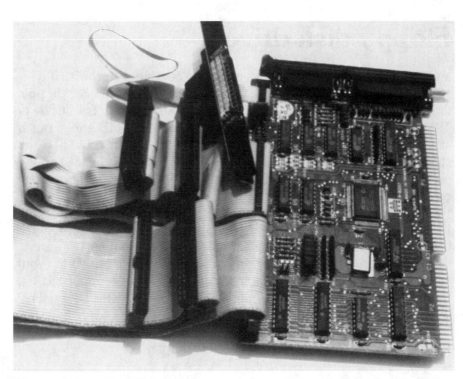

This multifunction I/O board can control two floppy disk drives, two IDE hard drives, a printer port, two serial COM ports, and a game port.

integration can save having to use one or more of the motherboard slots. Some motherboards may have less than eight slots if they offer built-in integration.

Besides the basic boards needed, there are many other boards that can be used to configure a computer to do hundreds of different tasks. Here are just a few of the many other boards that can be plugged into the slots: FAX-Modem boards, sound system boards, scanner adapters, network boards, special video boards. There are many different manufacturers and variations in most boards so you may have thousands of options when it comes to choosing a board. There are literally billions of dollars worth of boards available for your computer.

 # Floppy disk drives

You need at least one floppy drive in your computer. Almost all software comes on floppy disks. There are both 5¼" and 3½" floppy drives and disks. The most data that can be stored on a 5¼ floppy is 1.2 megabytes (MB). The 3½" floppy can store 1.44MB and is much smaller. Most companies are now adopting the 3½" size, but there are still thousands of software programs on 5¼" disks. You never know when you may need a 5¼" drive. Since the 5¼" and 3½" floppy drives costs less than $50 each, it is a good idea to install both.

One disadvantage of installing two floppies is that they require two bays in which to be mounted. There are some companies who are now manufacturing a combination 5¼" and 3½" floppy drive that only requires a single bay. This combination drive may cost about $10 more than two drives bought separately. The small extra charge is well worth it.

Floppy disks and drives are discussed in Chapter 6.

 # Hard disk drives

There are dozens of hard disk drive manufacturers and they make hundreds of different hard disks. Almost any hard disk will operate on a Pentium, but if you get one that does not have enough capacity or is too slow, you may be hampered in producing much work. Even if you don't need it at the moment, you should buy the fastest and highest capacity that you can afford. You can never have too much disk memory.

There are two main types of hard disks that are most used today, the IDE and the SCSI. It is always possible that a drive can fail or that data can be erased or damaged. It is very important that you have extra copies or backups of your critical data. I recommend that you install both an IDE and a SCSI drive. That way you can easily and very quickly back up one drive to the other. The prices of hard drives have reduced to less than 50 cents per megabyte.

Hard drives are revisited in Chapter 7.

Case and power supply

There are several different cases that can be used for the Pentium. Most cases also come with a power supply. There are desktop cases, mini-tower cases, medium tower cases, and large tower cases. You should pick a case that can hold all of the boards and drives that you may want to install. Some desktop and mini-tower cases may only have two or three externally accessible mounting bays for drives. You should look for a case that has at least three externally accessible bays. You need externally accessible bays to mount a 3½" floppy drive and a 5¼" floppy drive. CD-ROMs are an essential part of computers today, so you need an externally accessible bay to mount it. You may even want to install two CD-ROM drives. You may also want to mount a tape backup system, a Bernoulli, a magneto-optical (MO) drive, or some other removable hard drive. Most cases have two or more bays for mounting hard drives that don't need to be accessed from outside the case.

The desktop and mini-tower cases may not be big enough for your Pentium system. The Pentium motherboard would fit in almost any case, but you should look for a medium tower or large tower case. These cases may allow up to eight different drives and devices to be installed.

Most people set their monitors on the desktop cases. The tower cases could also be placed on the desktop and laid on their side. But most people place them on the floor so they don't take up desk space.

The desktop cases with a 200-watt power supply may cost less than $50. The medium tower with a 250-watt supply may cost about $75 and a full tower with a 300-watt supply may cost $100 or more. There are variations in all of these cases and some may have such things as a digital readout or extra fans. You should get nothing less than a 250-watt power supply, a 300-watt would be even better.

In most of the cases, the power supply has a four-wire power cord that is about 20 inches long for the front panel power switch. The switch has four plug-in terminals. Usually you have to unplug the wires from the switch in order to mount the switch on the front panel, then plug them back in. **It is important that the power**

switch be connected properly. The black wire carries the 110 volts coming in and the white wire is the ground for the black wire. The other two wires carry the 110 volts back to the power supply. There is usually a diagram on the power supply that shows how the switch should be connected.

 # Don't lose your cool

If you are in a hot environment, it might be a good idea to buy an extra fan for your case. Heat is an enemy of semiconductors. If a circuit is designed properly, the semiconductors should last indefinitely. There is nothing to wear out in a semiconductor. But overheating can destroy them. One very big problem with the Pentium is that it gets very hot. If it is not kept cool, it will burn out. Almost all Pentiums now come with a small fan mounted on it. This fan should come with a small Y power connector so it can share power from one of the four power cables from the power supply.

Ordinarily, the only cooling in a computer case is provided by the fan that is installed in the power supply. This fan is supposed to draw cool air in from the front of the case, pull it over the plug-in boards, then expel it out the back of the power supply. You should make sure that all openings in the case, such as the slots on the back panel, are covered so that the cooling system works properly. You should not place anything in the front of the computer that would prevent air from entering the case. There should also be space at the rear so the fan can expel the air.

 # Mounting hardware

The case should have all of the hardware, such as screws and plastic standoffs, for mounting the motherboard and drives. A small speaker should also be included with the case.

The case also has several wires that connect to switches and light emitting diodes (LEDs) on the front panel. An LED indicates power-on, the hard disk activity, and several other functions. A reset switch

reboots the computer when pressed. The wires from the LEDs and switches connect to pins on the front of the motherboard. Because the cases and motherboards are made by different manufacturers, they are all different. There are no standards so you may have trouble matching the wires to the proper pins. Most motherboards have some sort of markings near the pins. You should also get some sort of documentation with the motherboard that shows what each pin is for.

 # Power supply function

The computer uses low voltage direct current (dc). The power supply takes 110 volts of alternating current (ac) from the wall socket and steps it down to a low dc voltage. The electronics in the chrome plated enclosure convert the voltage to 5 volts dc (Vdc) and 12 Vdc. Most of the disk drives require 12 Vdc for operation. The electronics in the computer require +5 Vdc and −5 Vdc. Some of the newer CPUs and components only require 3 Vdc. This means that they use less power and create less heat.

 # Static electricity

Unless you open the cover of the power supply, the highest voltage in the computer is 12 Vdc. So there is no danger of getting a shock if you should happen to touch something inside the computer. But there is a danger to the components because you may have up to 4000 volts of static electricity on your body. It is very easy to walk across a carpet and build up this much electricity. If you should happen to touch a board with fragile electronic components, it could severely damage them. You should always touch the metal portion of the computer case that is plugged in or some other object to discharge yourself before handling any boards or electronic components.

 # Power strips

You will have several devices such as the monitor, the computer, a printer, and other peripherals, to plug in when you get your computer

assembled. If you set it up in your home, you may have trouble finding enough nearby outlets. Even in some offices and workplaces, there never seem to be enough outlets. It is much more convenient to purchase a power strip with about six outlets. Better yet is a power distribution panel with individual switches for each device. I use one that sits under the computer. It has a master switch and a separate switch for the computer, monitor, printer, and two auxiliary switches. It is very convenient. With the master switch I can turn on all of my equipment, or turn off any that I don't need at the moment, such as the printer. Most computer stores carry them at a cost of $12 to $20.

Surge protection

If you are in an area where there are large electric motors and other electrical equipment that is switched on and off, then you should get a power strip with a good surge protector. Each time an inductive device switches on and off, it throws a high voltage spike back into the electrical system. A large spike could possibly cause some damage to your system or to data that is being processed.

Some power strips claim to offer surge protection, but they may only have an inexpensive capacitor across the input line. This would help a little bit, but a good surge protector should have many more components such as metal oxide varistors and inductors. The better surge protectors can even protect against lightning strikes. When hit by lightning, a thermal fuse shuts your system down. You might have to replace the thermal fuse after a lightning strike.

Surge protectors might have from three to six or more power outlet connectors. It might also have telephone jacks for modem protection.

A surge protector might cost from $30 to over $100. The cost is very minimal compared to the cost of your Pentium.

UPS

No, this UPS does not mean the delivery service. For computers, UPS means *uninterruptible power supply*. If you live in an area

where there are a lot of electrical storms or where there are frequent blackouts and brownouts, then you need a good UPS. If you happen to be working at your computer and there is a power loss, even for a fraction of a second, you will lose all data that was in RAM. A good UPS will take over and supply power long enough for you to save your data to disk and shut down.

Many of the UPS systems also offer surge protection. There are several different types and sizes of UPS equipment. Some UPS systems are designed to power large networks.

There are several different companies who manufacture UPS systems and products. Of course, there are many different prices. The price depends primarily on the amount of wattage that the system must provide. A UPS for a Pentium system may cost from $150 up to $500. A UPS system for a large network may cost up to $5000 or more.

Here is just a brief list of companies that provide UPS systems, there are several others:

> American Power Conversion   (800) 800-4272
> Best Power Technology   (800) 356-5794
> Clary Corp.   (800) 442-5279
> Deltec Corp.   (619) 291-4211
> Minuteman UPS   (800) 238-7272
> Tripp-Lite Mfg.   (312) 329-1777

If you call these companies, they will forward brochures and offer advice concerning a system that would be best for you.

⇨ Peripherals

There are several peripherals that you need to have a complete computer system, such as a keyboard, a monitor, a mouse, and a printer.

 # Keyboard

The original IBM keyboard cost about $250. I recently went to a computer show where one vendor had keyboards on sale for as little as $10. I have no idea how they could be made for such a small cost. The keyboard is a small computer in itself. It has an integrated chip and several electronic components in addition to the keys.

The keyboard is a very important part of your computer. I would suggest that you pay a little more than $10 and get a fairly good one. If you get a chance, go to a computer swap or a dealer store and try out several. There are lots of differences among keyboards. Some have very soft keys, some have stiff and some have an audible click when depressed. There are also differences in the placement of the keys. Try to find one that suits your taste and style. Keyboards are further explored in Chapter 9.

 # Monitor and adapter

There are hundreds of different type monitors. There are several different types and sizes of monochrome monitors, but there are many more types of color monitors. There are different screen sizes, different resolutions, different scan rate frequencies, and many other differences. And of course, there are many different prices. Ordinarily, the higher the resolution and the larger the screen, the more the cost.

The screens on color monitors have three different color dots: red, blue, and green. Electron beams can strike these dots and cause them to form any color. One of the critical factors in the resolution of a monitor is the dot pitch or spacing between two dots of the same color. Some low cost monitors may have a dot pitch of 0.39 millimeter (mm). The better systems have a dot pitch of 0.28 mm or less.

The monitor must have a plug-in adapter board to drive it. There are some very low cost adapter boards, but they may not be able to drive the monitor to its fullest resolution. A good adapter may cost as much or more than a monitor. The monitors and adapters are usually made by different manufacturers. It wouldn't do you much good to buy a

high resolution monitor and a low cost adapter or vice versa. The capabilities of the two should be fairly well matched.

Monitors and adapters are revisited in Chapter 10.

 # Multimedia components

The Pentium is an ideal machine for multimedia applications. Many of the multimedia applications require a CD-ROM drive. They are almost as essential as a floppy disk drive. In some instances, the CD-ROM is taking over some of the traditional floppy disk chores. Many of the software programs are so large today that they may require 20 or more floppy disks. Many companies are now distributing some of the software on CD-ROM discs. (Note that floppy disks are usually spelled with a *k*, CD-ROM discs with a *c*.) The software on a CD-ROM disc can save a lot of disk swapping and time.

There are hundreds of multimedia and other very useful applications that use the CD-ROM technology. I would strongly suggest that you install a CD-ROM drive.

CD-ROMs and multimedia are discussed in greater detail in Chapter 13.

 # Coming up next

In Chapter 3, I show how each of the components is connected together. Photographs and clear instructions show how easy it is to assemble a Pentium PC.

System assembly

THIS chapter should probably come much later in the book, but I want to show you how easy it is to assemble a computer. Unless you are an expert, I suggest you read the rest of the book to find out more about the various components before you buy them.

How much you can save

I have been asked many times how much you can save by building your own. It is impossible to give a concrete figure because there are so many variables and options. I dislike quoting prices because they change daily, usually downward.

A very large factor in the cost of a system is where you buy it. If you shop wisely, buy the components, and assemble them yourself, you can save from $100 and up to $500. The vendor must pay his employees and overhead and make a certain amount of profit in order to stay in business. Of course, he makes a small amount of profit on each of the individual components that are sold. By doing it yourself, you can usually save the amount that the dealer would charge for his profit.

Not all dealers have the same prices or aim for the same profit margin. Some dealers have more overhead than others. Some advertisements from several different companies, for equivalent systems, may have prices that vary from $100 and up to $500.

Another big factor in cost is brand name. The large brand name products nearly always cost more than the no-name brands. In many cases the no-name product works just as well.

Still another factor is how long the product has been on the market. If it is new, it will probably cost more. If it has been on the market for a while, then there will likely be some competition and the price will often be lower.

Whether the item is popular and in high demand is a price factor. If the item is in high demand, there will be several different vendors, each one vying for your dollar.

Barebones systems

At one time several companies advertised very good prices for barebones systems. A barebones system may be just a case, power supply, keyboard, and motherboard. If you were short of money, you could buy a system such as this and add to it as you could afford it. Most companies now seem to want to sell complete systems. That is a shame because the price for a complete system might be more than a person could afford at one time.

You can still start off with a barebones system, but you have to do the minor assembly yourself. Believe me it is very simple. Go to a swap meet or local computer show and look the systems over. Or if that isn't possible, look through computer magazines and check out the ads. You should be subscribing to several magazines so you can learn about computers and what is available. The *Computer Shopper* is one of the better ones for ads. Decide which system you want, then order the case that has the power supply included, then order the motherboard. Sometimes the motherboard is sold without a CPU. If it is advertised for a very low price, you might need to buy a separate CPU. It is usually a bit less expensive if you buy the motherboard with the CPU included. But it is possible to find a bargain motherboard at one place and a good price for a CPU at another.

You should be aware that there are hundreds of vendors for computer components. A motherboard, or any component, from one vendor might not be the same as one from another vendor. For instance, a low priced motherboard from one vendor might not

have any built-in functions. There are many ways to cut corners in order to save a few pennies. That is why you need to learn as much as you can about hardware. If you are fairly new in computing, please read the chapters about the main components before buying them.

There is no question that you can save money by doing it yourself. How much depends on how wisely, how well, and where you shop.

 # Differences in assembly

You may think that because the Pentium is powerful it would be more difficult to assemble. But there is very little difference in the assembly of a powerful Pentium and the assembly of any other computer, even the early XT. In fact, the Pentium may be even easier to assemble than an XT because it uses fewer screws and even fewer components. Your motherboard may have several integrated and built-in goodies, such as the IDE and floppy drive interface and memory modules that were not available ten years ago.

Some motherboards may be slightly different than others because of the built-in utilities and functions. They may also have the components placed differently on the motherboard. But they are all assembled into the system in the same basic way. Note also that they are still assembled the same way no matter whether the CPU on the motherboard is made by Intel, AMD, Cyrix, or NexGen.

 # Benchtop assembly

Here is a list of the major components that are needed for a minimum system. Later you may also want to add several other components, such as a modem/fax board, mouse, network card, and several other goodies. But it is best to start out with a minimum system.

➤ Case and power supply

➤ Motherboard

> ➤ Floppy drives

> ➤ Hard drives

> ➤ Controllers for drives (if they are not built-in on motherboard)

> ➤ Keyboard

> ➤ Monitor and adapter board

Before you start, gather all of your components and tools. You need a Phillips and a flat-blade screwdriver and a pair of long-nose pliers.

WARNING I mentioned electrostatic voltage earlier. Remember that you can build up thousands of volts on your body, so try to touch something to discharge yourself before touching any of the sensitive electronic components.

When I assemble a computer, I usually gather all of the components and assemble them on a bench top or kitchen table before I install it in the case. If there is any problem or trouble, it is fairly easy to find it. Note that the backside of the motherboard and other plug-in boards have sharp projections from the cut and soldered component leads. I usually lay a couple of newspapers on the table or bench top to prevent scratching or marring the table or bench.

Detailed steps are listed below, but in a few words, here is a basic benchtop assembly. Plug the power supply into the motherboard, making sure that the four black ground wires are in the center, then connect the keyboard, the floppy drives, hard disk drives, and the monitor. Then I apply power, boot the computer up and see if it works.

⇨ Step 1: Set all switches and jumpers

Motherboards from different manufacturers may have several alternate options and different ways that they can be configured. The many different possible configurations is one of the things that makes the computer so versatile and valuable.

You should have received some sort of documentation with your motherboard and each of your components. Check the

documentation and determine if there are any switches and jumpers that should be set to configure the component.

If you are new to computers and electronics, a jumper is usually a small block or cap that is placed over a set of pins. The jumper creates a short or solid path between the two pins. The jumpers are very small. It is almost impossible for a man with large fingers to handle one. That is one of the reasons you need the long-nose pliers. If you don't have long-nose pliers, you should be able to use a pair of tweezers.

The jumpers and switches often are used on a plug-in board to set it for a specific interrupt request (IRQ) line or the system memory address. Jumpers may be used to set the COM ports for the mouse, modem, sound card, and other peripherals.

Step 2: Install memory

Your motherboard will probably come to you with the SRAM already installed, but it may not have the SIMM installed. If the SIMM and SRAM memory chips have not been installed, you should install them now. Again, they are very susceptible to damage from electrostatic electricity, so make sure you discharge yourself before handling them.

Check your documentation. There should be a diagram of the motherboard showing how the memory is to be installed.

The single in-line memory modules (SIMMs) are very easy to install. See Fig. 3-1. Just place them in the proper slot on a slant, then lift them to an upright position and they will lock in. There is a cutout on one end of the SIMM assembly so they can only be installed the proper way. But it is possible to have one end of the SIMM not inserted fully. If a SIMM is not completely seated, or if they are not in the proper bank, the computer may not boot up.

The memory must be installed in banks, starting with Bank 0, then Bank 1, 2, and 3. Because most systems use interleaving, SIMMs must be installed in multiples of two banks. For 8MB, you need two 4MB SIMMs, for 16MB, you need two 8MB SIMMs.

Figure 3-1

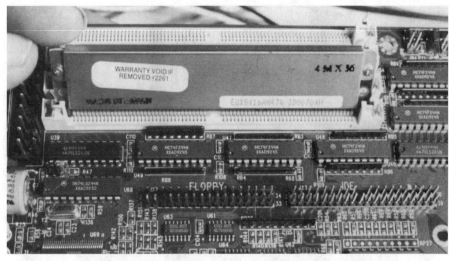

Installing a 4 × 36 16MB memory module on the motherboard

The SRAM for the motherboard cache is usually already installed. If it isn't, then you should consult your documentation. There are different types of SRAM. Your documentation should tell you which type you should use.

Step 3: Connect the power supply to the motherboard

The power supply has two six-wire cables that are plugged in side by side to the 12 pin motherboard connector. These cables are sometimes marked *P8* and *P9*.

WARNING It is possible to install these cables improperly. Each of the cables has two black wires for ground. When installed properly, the four black wires are in the center of the connector. If installed improperly, you could severely damage the motherboard components. You can see the four black wires in the center of the white connector in Fig. 3-2.

Figure 3-2

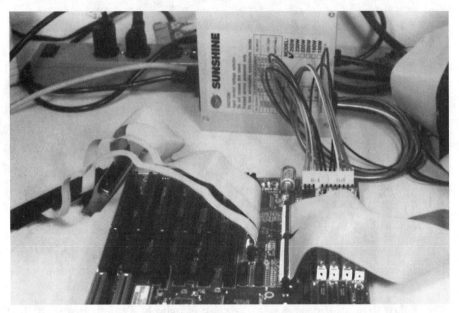

Power, floppy drive, and IDE hard drive cables and COM port cables connected to the motherboard

⇨ Step 4: Install floppy drives

There is a 34-wire ribbon cable with three connectors for your floppy drives. One end of the cable has several wires that were split and twisted. The connector on this end goes to the drive that you want to be your drive A:. See Fig. 3-3.

The connector in the middle of the cable goes to floppy drive B:. See Fig. 3-4. This connector can be plugged in incorrectly. The edge connector on the drive for the cable connector has a slit between contacts #2 and #3. The cable has a different-colored wire along one edge. This colored wire, red, black, or blue, goes to pin one in the connector. Make sure that the colored wire side is on the same side as the slit in the edge connector. When connecting drive B:, you should again look for the slit between the contact #2 and #3 and make sure that the colored wire side goes to that side.

Figure 3-3

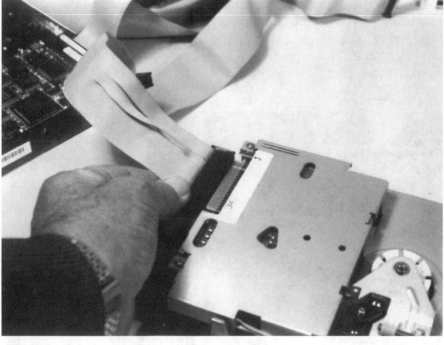

Connecting the floppy A: drive. Note the twisted wires.

Figure 3-4

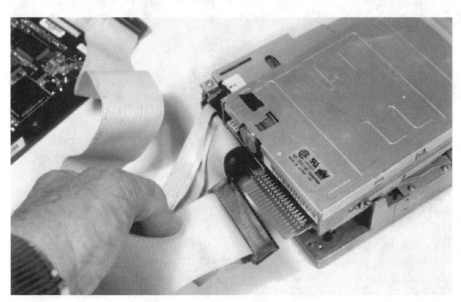

Connecting the middle connector to the B: drive

Figure 3-5 shows the power connector being attached to the A: drive. The white plastic shell of the power connectors are shaped so that they can only be plugged in properly. Note in Fig. 3-5 that the 3½" B: drive is on top. This drive uses a miniature power connector that plugs into the white connector at the left.

Figure 3-5

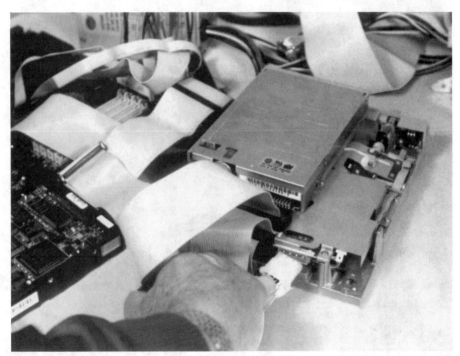

Connecting the power cable to a 5¼" floppy drive

It is possible to install a combination floppy drive that has both 1.2MB and 1.44MB. Figure 3-6 shows a combination drive on the left, a separate 1.44MB drive in the center and a 1.2MB drive on the right. The advantage of the combination drive is that it only requires one bay, one power cable, and one controller connection.

If you install one of the combination floppy drives, which I recommend, you only have one connector to plug in. The single connector goes to both drives. Again, make sure the colored wire of the cable goes to the side of the edge connector with the slit. In Fig. 3-7, I am preparing to connect the miniature power cable to the

Figure 3-6

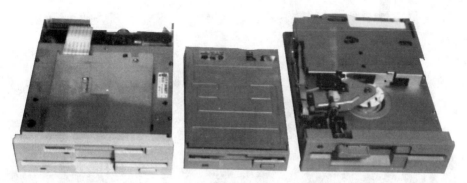

A combination floppy drive (left), a 3½" drive (center), and a 5¼" drive (right)

drives. Be careful when connecting the miniature power supply connector. On some combination drives, it is possible to plug the power connector in so it shorts out the power supply. If anything shorts out the power supply, it immediately shuts down and nothing operates. Since the power supply can shut down immediately, there is usually no damage done.

There should be a jumper or switch that allows you to configure the combination drives as either A: or B:. In Fig. 3-7, the configuration jumpers are four white jumpers between the controller connector and the miniature power connector. Check your documentation. Other drives may be different. The default factory configuration is usually for the 5¼" drive to be drive A:.

The other end of the ribbon cable plugs into your floppy disk controller board. See Fig.3-8. Make sure that the colored wire of the ribbon cable goes to pin one on the board. There should be some marking or indication on the board as to which is pin one. The floppy controller is probably integrated on the same board with the hard disk IDE interface. This board may also have connector LPT1, the connector for the printer and one or two port connectors for COM1 and COM2. The COM port connectors are for the mouse, a modem, or for other serial devices. The controller board may be plugged into any of the slots on the motherboard. I usually try to install the controller boards near the drives so the cables don't have to be draped over other boards.

Figure 3-7

Connecting the miniature power cable to a combo drive

Your motherboard may have the floppy and IDE interface integrated on the motherboard. This saves having to use a slot for a separate board. If the interface is integrated, there is a set of 34 pins to accept the floppy cable connector. There should be some indication on the motherboard as to which pin is number one. Make sure that the colored wire side of the connector goes to pin one. If the floppy drive cable is plugged in backwards, when you try to boot up from floppy drive A:, the disk will spin and it will erase the boot system from the floppy. (Never use your original software floppies except to make copies of them. Even then you should make sure that the originals are write protected.) Figure 4-2 in the next chapter shows a diagram of a Micronics Pentium PCI motherboard. Note that it has pins on the motherboard for COM1 and COM2, the printer, the floppy drives, and for IDE drives.

Figure 3-8

The other end of the floppy controller cable plugged into pins on the controller board. Make sure that colored wire side of the cable goes to pin one on the board.

⇨ Step 5: Install hard disk drives

If you install an IDE hard drive, you will have a 40-wire ribbon cable that is similar to the 34-wire floppy disk cable. The three connectors on the IDE cable are all the same. Like the floppy cable, it has a colored wire on one edge that indicates pin one. Most connectors on the drives have a plastic shell around them with a square notch on one side. The cable should have a connector with a square elevation that fits the notch on the drive connector plastic shell. This keys the connector so it can only be plugged in properly. See Fig. 3-9. If the connectors are not keyed, then look for some indication of pin one on the drive and connect the cable so the colored wire goes to that side. Figure 3-10 shows the power connection to the hard drive.

Figure 3-9

Connecting the 40-wire controller cable to an IDE hard disk drive. Note the square notch in the connector shell and the raised elevation on the connector. This keys the connector so it can only be plugged in properly.

Figure 3-10

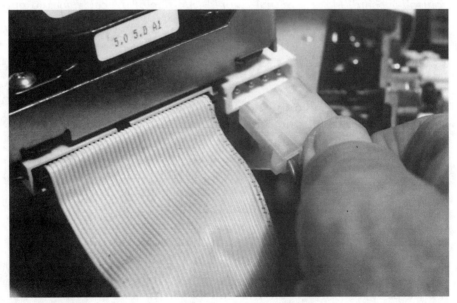

Connecting the power cable to the hard disk drive

If you are installing a second hard drive, it connects to the connector in the middle. The first IDE drive is called the *master* and the second one is the *slave*. Before connecting it you should check your documentation for any jumpers or switches that need to be set, such as those in Fig. 3-11, so they operate properly.

Figure 3-11

A ballpoint pen points to the small jumpers that must be set if you install a second IDE hard drive. Check your documentation.

The IDE system is supposed to be a standard, but many companies do not follow the standards exactly. If you are going to install two IDE drives, try to get two drives that are the same brand. They can have different capacities, but if they are made by different companies, there is a chance that some models may not work together properly.

Your panel has a small light emitting diode (LED) that flashes on and off to indicate hard disk activity. There is usually a small two-wire cable that plugs into the IDE controller board for this LED. Note that the LEDs are sensitive to plus and negative voltage. The IDE board

may be marked with a + sign near one of the pins. The two wires are different colors, usually red and black. The red wire go to the plus side, the black wires are usually ground wires.

Figure 3-12 shows the 40-wire IDE controller cable being connected to the controller board. Figure 3-13 shows the connection of a ten-wire cable for a COM port. This cable also has a different colored wire on one edge that indicates pin one.

If you are installing one or more SCSI drives, you need to check your documentation to set any switches or jumpers. Since the SCSI interface can handle up to seven devices, the drive probably needs to be set to a logical unit number (LUN) between 0 and 6.

The SCSI drives have a 50-wire ribbon cable that is similar to the 40-wire IDE cable. Figure 3-14 shows a SCSI cable being connected to my 1.05GB hard drive. Like other cables, it has a different color wire on one edge that indicates pin one. The connectors are probably keyed with notches and elevations so they can only be plugged in properly. If they are not keyed, then look for pin one and make sure

 Figure 3-12

Connecting the 40-wire IDE hard disk controller cable

Figure 3-13

Connecting a 10-wire cable for a COM port

Figure 3-14

Connecting the controller cable to a 1.05GB SCSI hard drive. The connectors are keyed so they can only be connected properly.

that the colored wire goes to that side. The connector on the other end of the 50-wire cable is connected to the SCSI card. Again, this connector is usually keyed so it can only be plugged in properly.

If you are installing more than one SCSI device, such as a second hard drive or a CD-ROM drive, check your documentation and set any necessary jumpers for the correct LUN. You may also have to remove or install termination resistors if you have more than one SCSI device.

Install the power cable to the SCSI devices. Most power supplies only have four cables. If you install more than four devices, you can get a small Y cable that allows two devices to be attached to one cable.

⇨ Step 6: Install the monitor

The next step is to plug your monitor adapter into any of the slots and connect the monitor cable to the adapter.

⇨ Step 7: Plug in keyboard

The keyboard cable is plugged into a connector on the back of the motherboard. It has a rounded connector that is keyed so it can only be connected properly. See Fig. 3-15.

⇨ Step 8: Turn on the power and boot up

Figure 3-16 shows the benchtop assembly completed. If everything was connected properly, the system should boot up. You need a floppy disk that can boot up your system. If you have DOS 6.0 or later, the disk that says *Disk 1-Setup* has the files necessary for booting up. Later you will want to boot from your hard drive C:. Once the computer starts to boot up, the CMOS system screen comes up. You can then enter the date, hour, the type of floppy and hard drives, and other information into your CMOS setup. You have to partition and format your hard drives before you can use them. The formatting procedures are discussed later in this chapter.

Figure 3-15

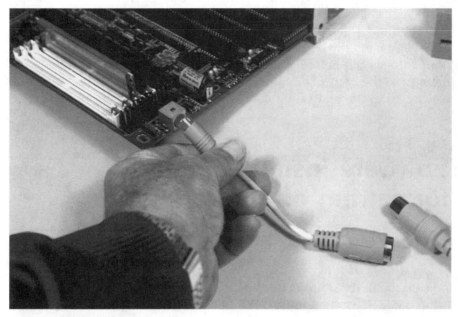

Connecting the keyboard cable

Figure 3-16

The benchtop assembly completed

I usually install both 1.2MB and 1.44MB floppy drives. If your boot disk is on a 3½" floppy, then you must make the 3½" drive the A: drive. You can only boot up from the A: drive with a floppy. Your floppy drives can be either A: or B:, depending on how you plug them in to the controller cable. The A: drive is the drive that is connected to the end of the cable that has several wires that are split and twisted.

 # Software installation and formatting of hard drives

Once the drives and plug-in boards are installed and connected, you can plug in the power cable. Put your boot disk in drive A: and turn on the power. Check your motherboard documentation and press the required keys on the keyboard to enter the setup mode. The keys to enter the setup mode depend on the BIOS that is installed on the motherboard. Often a message tells you which keys to press as the computer is booting up. Besides the system files needed for booting up, the boot floppy should have the FDISK and Format command on it.

 # Setup routine

When you install a hard disk, your BIOS must be told what type it is. The BIOS must also know the number and type of floppies you have, the time, the date, type of monitor, and other information. The setup routine asks several questions, then configures the BIOS for that combination. This part of the BIOS configuration is stored in low power CMOS semiconductors and is on all the time. Even when the computer is turned off a small lithium battery on the motherboard supplies power for the CMOS semiconductors.

In the early 1980s, IBM determined that there were only 15 different types of hard drives available. Information was made into a standard table that listed all of the characteristics of each drive. This table was included in the ROM BIOS of the IBM and all compatible clones. When you installed a hard disk, you just looked at the table to find which one of the 15 fit your hard disk and typed in the number. But soon more

and more different type drives were developed. The first 15 drive types remained standard, but as new types were introduced, each BIOS manufacturer produced different tables. When the number reached 46, it became apparent that there was no end in sight. There are now hundreds of different drives, each one a bit different than others. Most setup routines now allow you to enter type 46 or 47 and then type in data for any drive that does not fit any of the listed types.

The setup usually allows you to enter only two drives, C: and D:. But you may have two very large drives that are divided into several smaller partitions. So your D: drive may be a partition of the hard disk that is your C: drive. So ignore the designation for drive D:. You should enter the information for your first drive, the C: drive, then enter the information under the D: drive for your second drive. The CMOS setup would be less confusing if it asked for information about hard drive number 1, then number 2 instead of C: and D:. You probably have to use type 46 or 47. Check your documentation and type in the number of cylinders, heads, and sectors.

WARNING You should write your drive type down somewhere. (In fact, you should have a copy of all of your CMOS setup.) If you have data on your hard drive and for some reason you remove the drive, or your on-board CMOS battery goes completely dead, you cannot access your hard drive unless you tell the CMOS setup exactly what type it is or whatever data you used to format the drive.

Booting from a floppy

WARNING Never boot up with a floppy disk version that is different from the DOS version used to format the hard disk. There is a short boot record on the hard disk. If a different version is used to boot up, you might lose all of your data on the disk.

Disk partitions and formatting

The early versions of DOS would not allow a hard disk with a greater capacity than 32MB. DOS can now recognize and handle hard disks

that have a capacity of several gigabytes. In order to handle large capacity hard disks, DOS allows you to partition them into smaller logical units by using the FDISK command. Each partition then appears to DOS to be a separate hard drive.

FDISK options

When you type FDISK, if you are using MS-DOS 6.2 or a later version, this message will be displayed:

MS-DOS Version 6.2
Fixed Disk Setup Program
Copyright Microsoft Corp. 1983, 1993
FDISK Options
Current Fixed Disk Drive: 1
Choose one of the following:
1. Create DOS partition or Logical DOS Drive
2. Set active partition
3. Delete Partition or Logical DOS Drive
4. Display partition information
5. Change current fixed disk drive (Option 5 is only displayed if you have more than one drive).
Enter choice: [1]
Press ESC to exit FDISK

If you choose 1, and the disk has not been prepared, a screen like this comes up:

Create DOS Partition or Logical DOS Drive
Current Fixed Drive: 1
Choose one of the following:
1. Create Primary DOS partition
2. Create Extended DOS partition
3. Create logical DOS drive(s) in the Extended DOS partition
Enter choice: [1]
Press ESC to return to FDISK Options

If you want to boot from your hard drive (I can't think of any reason why you would not want to), then you must choose 1 to create a primary DOS partition and make it active.

Partition size

I would recommend making a partitions of not more than 200MB. If there are several partitions on a disk and one of them fails, you might be able to recover the data in the other partitions. If your disk is one large partition and it fails, you may not be able to recover any of the data, especially if the FAT is destroyed. Central Point PC Tools and late versions of DOS can be set up to make a mirror image of the FAT. If the primary FAT is destroyed, you can still use the mirror image to reconstruct the FAT.

Using FDISK can be a bit confusing. The manual that comes with MS-DOS 6.2 is no help at all. MS-DOS has on-disk help for all of its commands, just type help and the command name. But the Help FDISK help is not much help. The Microsoft Press is a division that primarily prints books about how to use Microsoft software. If their manuals were well written, you would not need to buy an extra book to learn how to use the software.

In order to make several partitions you must first choose the option number 2 to Create Extended DOS partition. It tells you how much space is available, which will be the entire drive. You cannot partition the drive at this point. Accept the figure given for the entire drive. If you try to partition the drive at this point, whatever you choose will be all that you can use. For instance, with option number 2, if you have a 500MB drive and you try to divide it into two 250MB partitions, it will figure that the entire drive is to be only 250MB. You will not be able to use the other 250MB. You must tell it to use the 500MB that is available. Then press ESC to return to the options, then choose option number 3, Create Logical DOS Drives in the Extended DOS partition. You can now divide this partition into as many drives as you want.

 # High-level format

After the FDISK partitioning, the disk must be formatted. Formatting organizes the disk so data can be stored and accessed easily and

quickly. If the data was not organized, it would be very difficult to find an item on a large hard disk. I have about 3000 files on my two hard disks. Those files are on tracks and sectors that are numbered. A file allocation table (FAT) is set up to record the location of each track and sector on the disk.

A brief analogy of a disk organization would be similar to that of a developer of a piece of land. He would lay out the streets and create blocks. He would then partition each block into lots and build a house on each lot. Each house would have a unique address. A map of these streets and house addresses would be filed with the city. A track would be analogous to a street, and a sector number would be similar to a house number.

The FAT is similar to an index in a street atlas or a book. When a request is sent to the heads to read or write to a file, it goes to the file allocation table, looks for the location of that file, and goes directly to it. The heads can find any file, or parts of any file, quickly and easily.

Formatting is not something that is done every day, and can be rather difficult in some cases. One reason the disks do not come from the manufacturer preformatted is that there are so many options. If you have a 540MB hard disk, you probably want to divide or partition it into two or three different logical disks.

After the FDISK options have been completed, return to drive A: and high-level format drive C:. Because you want to boot off this drive, you must also transfer the system and hidden files to the disk as it is being formatted so you must use a /S to transfer the files. Type FORMAT C: /S. DOS displays a message that says:

WARNING! ALL DATA ON NON-REMOVABLE DISK DRIVE C: WILL BE LOST!
Proceed with Format (Y/N)

If you press Y the disk light should come on, and you might hear the drive stepping through each track. After a few minutes, it displays:

Format complete
System transferred
Volume label (11 characters, ENTER for none)?

You can give each partition a unique name, or volume label if you wish to. You can test your drive by doing a warm boot by pressing Ctrl, Alt, and Del at the same time. The computer should reboot.

Now that drive C: is completed, if you have other partitions or a second disk, format each of them.

 # System test

Now that the disks are installed and formatted, try copying files to them. The first thing to do is to copy the DOS files onto drive C:. Try copying from one disk to another and then erase them. Exercise the system and look for any faults.

 # Step 9: Install the system in the case

If the system seems to work properly on the bench, then install it in the case. You should have received a small bag of hardware with your case. You should have some white plastic standoffs that have a round head and a narrow groove such as those in Fig. 3-17. In addition to the white standoffs, you should have a small brass standoff that screws into the metal case. See Fig. 3-18. The brass standoff is installed either in the front center or rear so it will ground the motherboard to the case.

Figure 3-17

The white plastic standoffs for the motherboard

Figure 3-18

A small brass standoff provides grounding for the motherboard to the case.

If you install your system in a desktop case, the bottom of the case has wide slots that become narrow to lock in the white standoffs. Install the white plastic standoffs on the motherboard, align the motherboard so the round heads of the standoffs fit in the slots, then slide it into place. Install a screw in the front and one in the back. One of the screws should go to the brass standoff so the motherboard is grounded to the case and is also made secure.

There are several wires from the front panel with small connectors that plug into pins on the front of the motherboard. The long nose pliers are handy for inserting these connectors on the pins. There are wires for the small speaker, for light emitting diodes (LEDs) on the front panel to indicate power on, hard disk activity, and several other functions. The motherboard might or might not have labels or markings as to where each wire connects. Since the cases and motherboards are made by different companies, there may be some wires that are not needed for your particular motherboard.

Install the floppy and hard drives in the bays. Reconnect the cables and install the boards in the slots on the motherboard.

CHAPTER 4

The motherboard

THE motherboard is the biggest and most important board in the computer system. The motherboard has the central processing unit (CPU) chip, such as a 386, 486, or Pentium. The type of CPU in the system determines the type of system. The primary difference in personal computers is the motherboard with its CPU. The Pentium motherboard looks very much like the 386 or 486 motherboards. Figure 4-1 shows a Pentium motherboard. Figure 4-2 shows the various chips and slots on the motherboard. Note that it has built-in connections for a printer, floppy drives, IDE hard drives, and COM1 and COM2. Some of the newer motherboards now have two sets of pins for Enhanced IDE drives and for IDE CD-ROM drives. Unfortunately, not all motherboards have all of these functions built in.

Figure 4-1

A PCI Pentium motherboard

Figure 4-2

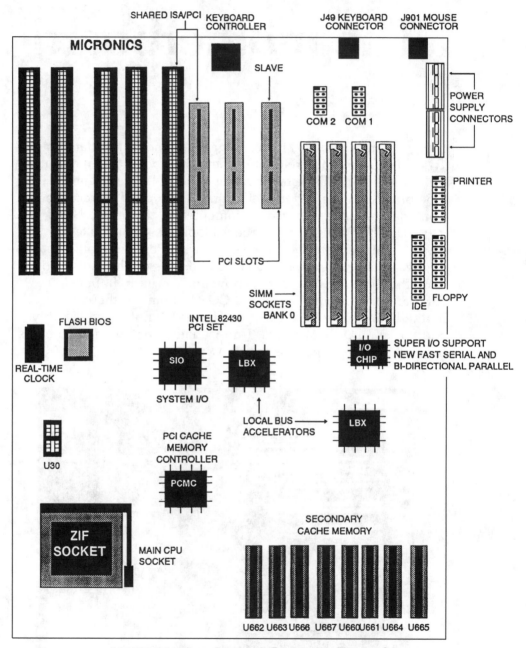

M5Pi Motherboard System Board

A diagram of a Pentium motherboard that shows chip, slot, and socket locations

Except for the motherboard, all the rest of the components in a computer may be the same. For instance, a 286 and the most powerful Pentium may both use the same type floppy drives, hard drives, keyboards, and plug-in boards. Even the RISC type motherboards use the same basic type components.

The motherboard has slot connectors, or an expansion bus, so different boards can be plugged in. It has a small battery, crystal oscillators, timing chips, memory chips, and several other chips that are necessary for the operation of the computer.

Table 4-1 shows some of the characteristics of a few of the CPUs.

Differences in Various CPU Chips					Table 4-1
	XT	**286**	**386**	**486**	**Pentium**
Transistors	29,000	134,000	275,000	1,200,000	3,100,000
Frequency	4.7–10	6–25	16–40	25–100	60–120
MIPS	0.75	2.66	11.4	54	112+
Bits	8	16	32	32	64
Memory	640K	16MB	4GB	4GB	4GB

Intel has recently introduced their next generation CPU, the P6. It has 5.5 million transistors. They are busy working on the next generations, the P7 and P8. The P6, P7, and P8 will probably have a more complete name eventually, but at the time of this writing, that is all we have.

In Table 4-1, mips is an acronym for millions of instructions per second. Note that the most the XT could do was 0.75, the 66-MHz Pentium can do 112 mips, which is almost 150 times faster than the XT. We have truly come a long way since 1981.

Note that the 386, 486, and Pentium can address up to 4 gigabytes (GB) or 4,000,000,000 bytes of memory. (The prefix *giga-* means billion.) If you used the 30-pin 4MB single inline memory module (SIMM), you would need 1000 of the 4MB SIMMs to make 4GB. Of course, you could also install 72-pin 16x32 modules, which have

64MB per SIMM and it would only require 62.5 SIMMs. At the present time, I don't know of any vendor who makes a motherboard that would accept that much memory. Most Pentium motherboards are designed to accept up to 128MB of RAM.

Four gigabytes of RAM is probably a bit more than you will ever need. But then at one time, they didn't think we would ever need more than 640K. I have no doubt that someday we will have motherboards with 1GB of memory installed. It would only require 16 of the 64Mb SIMMS to make up 1GB of RAM.

The Pentium vs. RISC

The Pentium has 3.1 million transistors in its CPU. The 66-MHz Pentium is capable of performing 112 million instructions per second (mips). Some of the reduced instruction set computers (RISC) type CPUs are capable of over 100 mips. The DEC Alpha RISC can do over 150 mips, but the Pentium is the first complex instruction set computer (CISC) system that can come close to the RISC. The DEC Alpha RISC CPU can run at up to 300 MHz.

To a great extent, the cost of a computer closely correlates to the cost of the CPU. The IBM and Apple RISC CPU costs about half as much as a Pentium CPU. However, the DEC and some of the other RISC CPUs are much more expensive than those made by Motorola for IBM and Apple.

The RISC machines require special software, so the overall cost to operate may be higher. All CPUs are different. Ordinarily, software is written for a specific type CPU. A computer works because the software gives instructions to the CPU. Software instructions, whether entered from disk or from a keyboard, causes a unique digital voltage to be produced. This voltage goes to the CPU and causes certain transistors to be turned on or off. Since the Intel and Motorola CPUs are different, an instruction written for the Intel 80x86 CPUs would turn on or off different transistors than those written for the Motorola 680xx CPUs. Software that is written for the 80x86 and that written for the 680xx are like two foreign languages. They cannot understand the instructions unless

they are written in their own language. That is why you can't take software that is written for the Macintosh and run it on a machine that has an Intel 80x86 CPU.

The RISC type CPUs can only recognize instructions that are written in their own language. If you want to run a DOS program or a Macintosh program on a RISC machine, the program has to be revised or compiled to recognize the software instructions. A compiler can convert a high-level programming language into a machine-level language of 0s and 1s that the CPU can recognize. What makes it even more complicated is that RISC CPUs made by different companies are all different and each needs its own special software. There is no standardization for the RISC machines. Even the IBM PowerPCs and the Apple PowerPCs are not compatible.

There are some programs that can interpret and emulate the DOS and Macintosh programs so they can be run on a RISC machine, but they will run a bit slower because it will take time to do this. Speed is the primary reason for RISC type machines so if you have to use software to emulate programs, the advantage of RISC may be lost.

At this time, there are a few software companies who are developing native software for the Apple PowerPCs. IBM is also developing some software for their PowerPCs, but it will be sometime before there is anywhere near the number of applications that are available for the ISA type machines. Also, at this time there are very few manufacturers of RISC type motherboards. A motherboard with a very high speed RISC CPU that is made by a company other than IBM, Apple, or Motorola may cost as much as $4000. There are many Pentium motherboard manufacturers. The competition will keep the prices fairly reasonable. The Pentium is able to run all present software. Lots of new software that will take full advantage of the 64-bit bus is still being developed at this time.

Intel, AMD, NexGen, Cyrix, and others have realized that RISC technology does have several benefits. In their latest designs, these companies have incorporated and mixed many features of RISC technology with CISC to provide the best of both worlds.

Architecture

The architecture of the computer refers to the overall design and the components it uses. The architecture is also concerned with the type of bus that is used. The bus is the internal pathways over which data is sent from one part of the computer to another. The 8-bit systems use 8-bit parallel paths, 16 bit uses 16, 32 bit uses 32, and 64 bit uses 64. The flow of data over a bus is often compared to the flow of traffic on a highway. If there are only two lanes, the flow of traffic may be limited. Adding more lanes can vastly improve the flow of traffic.

ISA

The industry standard architecture (ISA) is what was once known as the IBM compatible standard. IBM more or less abandoned the standard when they introduced their micro channel architecture (MCA) in 1987. There were far more IBM compatible clone computers in existence than computers manufactured by IBM. Since IBM was now directing most of its efforts toward the MCA, the clone makers took over the standard and changed the name.

An ISA computer can be anything from the oldest and slowest XT up to the newest and fastest Pentium. The old XT 8-bit bus had 8 parallel lines connected to the same pins on all of the slot connectors for plug-in boards. When the 286 was being developed by IBM, it became apparent that an 8-bit bus was too slow and was clearly inadequate. So they devised a 16-bit slot connector by adding a second 36 contact connector in front the original 62 contact connector. This was a brilliant innovation.

Compatibility

There were about five billion dollars worth of 8-bit hardware in existence at the time IBM introduced their 16-bit AT 286. The industry loved it because they could use either 8-bit or 16-bit plug-in boards.

This downward compatibility still exists even with the latest, fastest, and most powerful Pentium. However, there is a price to pay for the compatibility. The CPU operates over a special memory bus to communicate with RAM at the CPU's rated frequency. The 386 and 486 are 32-bit systems; 64 bits for the Pentium. But the systems can only communicate with their plug-in boards and peripherals over a 16-bit bus. Even though the Pentium can operate at 100 MHz, to be able to run all previous software and hardware, the ISA bus is limited to a speed of about 8 MHz and an I/O bus width of 16 parallel lines.

⇨ MCA

When IBM decided that the 16-bit ISA system was inadequate, they designed the micro channel architecture (MCA) system. This architecture was a 32-bit bus system for plug-in cards and memory. Figure 4-3 shows an 8-bit ISA board on top and an MCA board on the bottom. This wider bus was a much faster and more powerful system. But IBM also wanted to be downward compatible with the available software, even if they weren't compatible with the hardware. So the speed from the plug-in boards and peripherals was still limited to 8 to 10 MHz.

Figure 4-3

An 8-bit ISA board on the top and an MCA board on the bottom

Before they introduced their MCA systems, IBM had been losing a large share of their business to the low cost clones. They had let the design of the original PC slip away from them. This time they very carefully patented everything about the MCA and kept most of the critical specifications secret. They developed a machine that only they could manufacture and sell without any competition from the cloners.

The big problem was that the new MCA system could not use any of the billions of dollars worth of hardware that was available. The connector contacts of the MCA boards were much smaller than those on the ISA boards. There was no way they could be used in ISA systems. New boards had to be designed for the MCA slots.

IBM was confident that the added speed and power of their new system would more than make up for the added expense. In addition, IBM had a very large and loyal following, especially among the large corporate buyers. Many of the large corporations have pretty deep pockets. But most of the ordinary buyers usually have to watch their budget. IBM computers had always been expensive. The new MCA PS/2 systems were even more expensive than the original IBM PCs. The boards needed for the MCA systems were also very expensive. There were millions of clones in existence. Because of the large number of systems, and the competition of the many vendors, the cost of a board for a clone was much less than that for a PS/2.

IBM is now a changed company. At one time you had to go through authorized dealers to buy any IBM product or to have any repairs. They have now set up several companies for selling in the direct market. They will sell you any of their products through mail order.

 # EISA

A group of compatible or IBM clone makers realized that IBM was right about needing a wider bus and more room for expansion and improvement. They devised the extended industry standard architecture (EISA). This standard specified a new connector with almost double the number of contacts and added several new improvements to the ISA standard. Unlike the IBM MCA system, the

EISA system was downwardly compatible with all previous hardware. The billions of dollars worth of present boards could still be used with the EISA system, even the old 8-bit plug-in boards.

The standard contact on an ISA connector is 0.06" wide. There is a 0.04" space between each contact. The EISA board was designed with a second set of contacts immediately below the ISA contacts. A connecting trace is placed in the 0.04" space between the ISA contacts for the lower set of EISA contacts. The EISA plug-in slot on the motherboard has two sets of contacts to match ISA and EISA contacts on the plug-in boards. The EISA boards have cutouts on the boards to match bars across the lower EISA section of the slot connector. When an ISA board is plugged in, the bars prevent it from being inserted deep enough to contact the EISA contacts. Figure 4-4 shows an EISA board.

Like the MCA system, the EISA system provides a 32-bit bus. Also like the MCA, they wanted to remain downward compatible with earlier software and hardware. Therefore the communication between the plug-in boards was still limited to a speed of 8 MHz.

Most EISA systems are still rather expensive compared to the ISA systems. They are great for high end systems, but most people can get by with a relatively inexpensive ISA system.

Figure 4-4

An example of an EISA board

The VESA local bus

The PC bus has long been a bottleneck. The 8-bit bus at 4.77 MHz was okay for the XT. The 16-bit bus was a great leap forward when the 286 was introduced. The 286 CPU communicated with its RAM over a 16 memory bus at whatever speed the CPU operated at. But in order to remain compatible with previous hardware and software, the input/output (I/O) bus speed was locked in at 8 to 10 MHz.

When the 386 and 486 were introduced, they communicated with their RAM over a 32-bit memory bus at the speed of the CPU. But like the 286, the I/O bus still operated on a 16-bit bus at 8 to 10 MHz. Some peripherals such as fast hard disks and monitors were slowed down considerably.

The Video Electronics Standards Association (VESA) developed a set of specifications for a VESA local bus (VLB) that eliminated some of the bottlenecks.

The VLB specification added a second slot connector in line with the 16-bit slot connector. This solution is similar to that used to migrate from the 8-bit slot to the 16-bit, which added a second connector to the 8-bit slot so both 8-and 16-bit cards can be used. The VL bus is quite similar. It adds a second connector in line with the 16-bit connectors so both VL and 16-bit boards can be used in these slots. This connector uses 116 miniature contacts that are similar to the MCA connectors. The connector provides a 32-bit path from the plug-in boards and peripherals to the CPU. The VL bus is a direct extension of the CPU bus and runs at the same speed as the CPU. The VL bus increases the performance of a PC considerably, yet adds very little to the cost of the system. Figure 4-5 shows an Alaris motherboard with a NexGen 90-MHz CPU on the left and my Pentium 60-MHz motherboard on the right. On the left of each motherboard are two VLB slots. Figure 4-6 shows a VLB IDE interface and multi I/O board.

Thousands of vendors have adopted the VL bus configuration. There is a lot of competition so prices of the VL bus plug-in boards are quite reasonable.

Figure 4-5

A NexGen 586 90 MHz on the left and a Pentium 60 MHz on the right. On the left of each motherboard are two VLB slots.

Figure 4-6

A VESA local bus multifunction I/O board. This board is an IDE hard disk interface, a floppy controller, has a printer port, two COM ports, and a game port.

The VL bus is not a perfect solution. The VL system only allows three connectors. They are ordinarily used for fast IDE hard disks, video adapters, and network interface cards (NICs).

The VL bus allows communication over the 32-bit lines at the same speed as the CPU. But the other input/output (I/O) components in

63

the system are still relegated to the 16-bit bus at 8 to 10 MHz. Even the Pentium has this same standard bus speed for non-VLB I/O components and peripherals in order to remain backward compatible.

The Intel PCI bus

Intel introduced their Peripheral Component Interconnect (PCI) local bus in July 1992, a month before the VL bus was officially introduced. To integrate the PCI bus circuit on a motherboard involves special chips and is a bit more expensive than the VL bus. In addition, plug-in boards for the PCI bus are more expensive than VLB. So it took some time before PCI was widely accepted. But Intel has used their considerable clout to promote the bus, and it now appears that it will be the bus of choice for 486, Pentium, and other high-end systems.

The VL bus connects directly to the CPU. The PCI bus is a bit different than the VL bus in that it is a separate bus. It may be installed in line with a standard 16-bit connector or as a standalone connector. Many of the PCI bus connectors and boards are standalone. Boards designed for the VL bus system are not standalone since the boards use both the 16-bit and the VL bus pins. Figure 4-1 shows a Pentium motherboard with three white PCI slots. For comparison, refer back to Fig. 1-1 that shows a Pentium motherboard with two VLB slots on the upper part of the board.

It can sometimes be very frustrating when adding a plug-in board. Often you have to set several dip switches or jumpers so it does not conflict with the assigned interrupt request (IRQs), serial and parallel ports, and direct memory access (DMA) channels of other plug-in boards.

One of the advantages that the PCI bus has over the first version of the VL bus is that the PCI is a plug and play system. It has an auto-configuration capability that automatically configures a PCI add-in board if the board meets the plug and play specifications. The original version of the VL bus was a "plug and pray system." Version 2 of the VL bus is a plug and play system.

Eventually, all plug-in boards will conform to the plug and play specification. Of course you will still have to do it the old-fashioned way when installing those boards designed before the plug and play specifications were adopted.

Another advantage of the PCI is that it may allow up to ten connectors. But for most practical purposes, the same three used in the VL system, the hard disk, video, and network, are all that is needed at this time.

The VLB and PCI bus can be used with ISA, EISA, MCA and RISC type motherboards. Many of the less expensive Pentium systems still use the VL bus. Most manufacturers prefer the VL bus because it is less costly to integrate. But most experts agree that in the future, the PCI will be the bus of choice, especially on the high-end systems.

Figure 4-7 shows two monitor adapter graphics accelerator cards. At the top is a VLB card and a PCI card at the bottom.

Figure 4-7

Two monitor adapter graphics accelerator boards: a VLB board (top) and a PCI board (bottom)

 # ISA-EISA-VL-PCI combo

Several manufacturers have developed combination motherboards. They may have two or three ISA and EISA slots, with two or more VL connectors and two or more PCI connectors. This would seem to be the best of all worlds.

 # Built-in goodies

It is amazing how soon you can fill up all of the available slots on the motherboard. One way to get around having to use plug-in boards is to have many of the functions built-in on the motherboard. Most motherboards now have several built-in functions. See the diagram of Fig. 4-2. One of the arguments against built-in functions is that the functions may become obsolete, or they may become defective. But if necessary the on-board utilities can usually be disabled and replaced with a plug-in board. Here are some of the things that may be built in.

 # IDE and EIDE interface

Many motherboards now have the integrated disk electronics (IDE) or enhanced IDE (EIDE) interface for hard disks and a floppy disk controller built-in on the motherboard. They have rows of pins protruding from the motherboard that accept the ribbon cables from the drives. The EIDE is much faster than the older IDE and can control up to four devices, including some CD-ROM drives. The newer motherboards now usually have two sets of EIDE pins.

 # SCSI interface

Many of the Macintosh models have built-in SCSI interfaces. That is one of the reasons for their popularity. The PC industry has been lax in not following suit. SCSI is something that is essential, not only for multimedia, but for many PC applications. A few motherboard manufacturers are now including a built-in SCSI interface.

 # Serial ports

Many motherboards provide pins for two serial ports. Mice, modems, and many other devices need a serial port. Some multifunction boards provide them, but it is much simpler to have them built-in on the motherboard.

 # Printer port

There are very few computers that are not tied to a printer of some sort. There are still a few printers that use the serial port, but most printers today use one of the two parallel ports, LPT1 or LPT2. Many of the motherboards now have a set of pins for LPT1. Otherwise you need to buy a plug-in card such as a multifunction board.

Game ports

Many of the multifunction boards sold today have a game port for joysticks used with several of the games that are available. With the increased interest and popularity of multimedia, the game port has become almost mandatory. Some motherboards have a set of pins for a game port built-in.

Monitor adapter

Every computer needs a board or adapter to drive the monitor. Some motherboards have had built-in monitor adapters for some time. They are great for many applications. The main problem is that the developers keep making the adapters faster, with better resolution, true colors, and more complex. If your adapter is built-in, then you are stuck with whatever resolution or functions that it provides. Most of the motherboards with built-in functions have jumpers or switches that allow you to disable those functions so a board can be plugged in to take over the built-in functions.

 # Other motherboard chips

Besides the CPU and memory chips, there are several other chips and systems on the motherboard. The early PCs and the AT had a very large number of chips. I have an early 286 motherboard with 1MB of RAM in the dual in-line pin (DIP) chips that takes up about one fourth of the entire board. Altogether, it has over 150 separate chips on it.

The Chips and Technology Company, using very large scale integration (VLSI), combined several of motherboard chips into just a few chips. Other companies followed them so today we have only a small number of chips on the motherboard.

The smaller number of chips means fewer solder connections, more reliability, more speed, less board real estate required, and lower costs. Some motherboards are now as small as one third the size of the original XT and may have only five or six large VLSI chips on them.

 # ROM BIOS

You won't have to worry about read only memory (ROM). ROM is memory that cannot ordinarily be altered or changed. ROM comes with the motherboard. The principal use of ROM in PCs today is for the basic input/output system (BIOS).

The BIOS chip is second in importance only to the CPU. Every time you turn your computer on, the BIOS does a power on self test (POST). The BIOS checks all of the major components to make sure that they are operating properly. It also facilitates the transfer of data among peripherals. Many BIOS chips also have diagnostics and several utilities built-in. BIOS sounds a bit like BOSS and that is its principal job.

The BIOS performs its important functions under the control of firmware programs. These programs are similar to software programs except that the ROM is actually made up of hundreds of transistors that are programmed to perform certain functions.

Most newer BIOS chips now use flash memory. Until recently, the ROM BIOS programs were usually burned into electrically programmable read only memory (EPROM) chips. Special devices were used to input a software program into the ROM chip. As the program voltages pass through the chip, the transistors are turned on and off to match the input program. When a normal transistor has voltage applied to it, it turns on or off as long as the voltage is present. The EPROM transistors are different from ordinary transistors. When the EPROM transistors are turned on or off, they remain in that condition.

Fairly large programs and text can be stored on a ROM chip. The ROM BIOS for an early XT could be programmed onto a 64K ROM chip. The 486 ROM BIOS uses a 512K. All of the text of the book you are holding in your hand can be stored in less than 512K.

Figure 4-8 shows EPROM chips of 64K, 128K, 256K, and 512K. Note the glass covered window. Ordinarily, once the program is burned into the ROM, this window is covered with an opaque tape. If the tape is removed and the transistor circuit in the window is exposed to ultraviolet light, the ROM can be erased and can then be reprogrammed.

Figure 4-8

Some EPROM chips. Left to right: a 64K, 128K, 256K, and 512K.

Companies that manufacture the BIOS chips are constantly improving and adding new functionality to the BIOS. You can perform some useful upgrades to an older computer by just installing a new BIOS. For instance, some older BIOS chips may not be able to recognize some of the newer technologies that were developed after they were made. A new BIOS chip may cost from $50 up to $100.

Most newer Pentium motherboards now have a BIOS in a flash memory chip. (Refer to the Fig. 4-2 diagram.) Instead of having to open the computer case, and remove and replace the BIOS chip, the flash memory chips can be updated and upgraded by software from a floppy disk or even downloaded by modem through the telephone line.

 # Keyboard BIOS

The keyboard is a small computer in itself and has its own special BIOS chip on the motherboard. A scan code or signal is sent to the BIOS when a key is pressed and another signal is sent when the key is released. When two keys are pressed, it can detect which one was pressed first. It can also detect when a key is held down longer than normal and will start beeping at you. The last 20 keystrokes are stored in the keyboard memory and are continually flushed out and replaced by new keystrokes.

 # System configuration and CMOS

When you install a hard drive, you have to tell the system configuration setup what kind it is, the number of heads, sectors, and other information. The configuration system also needs to be informed as to what kind of floppy drives you have. If you want to reset the time or date, you do it with the system setup.

The system configuration or setup is stored in complementary metal oxide semiconductors (CMOS). These CMOS transistors use very little power. So there is a small battery mounted on the motherboard that can keep the transistors turned on so they retain the date and time and setup information even when the computer is turned off. These batteries may last from three to five years. The batteries were soldered to the older motherboards which made it very difficult to replace them. Most of the newer motherboards have a plug-in type battery. The 90-MHz NexGen motherboard from Alaris has a large round flat lithium battery, similar to camera batteries, that is easy to replace. This battery can be seen in Fig. 4-5 in the bottom left corner. The Pentium motherboard has a round tubular battery that is soldered on the rear of the motherboard.

The early PCs did not have the CMOS setup with the on-board battery. You had to input the time and date each time you turned on the computer. It is helpful if the time and date is correct because every time a file is created, DOS stamps the file with the time and date. This makes it very easy to determine which of two files is the later one.

Timing

A computer depends on precise timing. Several of the chips on a motherboard control the frequency and timing circuits. The timing is so critical that there are usually one or more crystals on the motherboard that oscillate at a precise frequency to control the timing circuits.

Memory

The older PCs reserved about one fourth of the motherboard area for memory chips. The early boards used 64K chips. (64K is 64,000 bytes.) It took nine chips to make 64K and that is all that some of the motherboards had. Later they developed 256K chips and up to 640K was installed on some motherboards. Still later they developed single in-line memory modules (SIMMs) with 30 contacts with up to 4MB in a single module. Today we have 72 contact SIMMs with up to 64MB that allow us to install up to 128MB on a motherboard in less space than it took for the original 64K. You can see the white slots for SIMMs in Fig. 4-5.

DMA

The direct memory access (DMA) system allows some processing to take place without having to bother the CPU. For instance, the disk drives can exchange data directly with the RAM without having to go through the CPU.

IRQ

The interrupt request (IRQ) system is a very important part of the computer. It can cause the system to interrupt whatever it is doing

and take care of the request. Without the interrupts, nothing would get done. Even if the computer is doing nothing, it must be interrupted and told to perform a task.

There are 16 IRQs, numbered from 0 to 15. Each input/output (I/O) device on the bus is given a unique IRQ number. Software can also perform interrupt requests. There is a priority system and some interrupts take precedence over others.

Sixteen IRQs may seem like a large number, but it isn't nearly enough. Several of the interrupts are reserved or used by the system so they are not available. It would have been wonderful if the Pentium had provided about twice as many, but no such luck.

If you want to see how your system is using IRQs, if you have DOS 6.0 or later, just type MSD (for Microsoft Diagnostics). This command will not only let you look at your IRQs, it will tell you about most of the other important elements in your computer.

 # Expansion slots

Most motherboards have 8 connector slots for plug-in boards. Some may have less if they have several built-in functions. The Alaris NexGen motherboard shown in Fig. 4-5 has seven slots while the Pentium on the right has only six, but this Pentium has built-in functions for floppy and IDE drives, serial, and printer ports. There are several billion dollars worth of boards that have been developed for the PC. You can plug one or more of these boards into a slot and expand the utility and function of your computer.

There are some motherboards with a single slot for the low profile type computers. A board is plugged into the single slot. This board has three slots on one side and two on the other for accepting horizontally mounted plug-in boards. The major problem with this board is that it is very difficult to plug in five boards in one of these systems, especially the long boards. There just isn't enough room for the cables and drives and boards. I would not recommend this type of motherboard.

The Pentium OverDrive

Many of the 486s have a large empty 238 pin socket on the motherboard. Some of the older 486s have smaller sockets that may have from 150 pins. If your motherboard has this type of socket, it can probably accept the 486 OverDrive, but it cannot be upgraded with a Pentium OverDrive.

If your motherboard has the 238 pin socket, and it conforms to the Intel specifications, it lets you install a Pentium OverDrive chip. The Pentium OverDrive can transform a 20-MHz 486 system into a 50-MHz Pentium system. A 25-MHz or 50-MHz 486 system can be transformed into a 63-MHz Pentium system.

If you wonder about the advantage of buying a Pentium OverDrive, Intel claims that it will give a 50% boost in performance over the 486DX2. But there are some disadvantages. The 486 motherboard was designed for a 32-bit 486 system. The OverDrive cannot give you the full 64-bit bus of a Pentium. The initial list price of the Pentium OverDrive was $449. That price will be less by the time you read this.

Another disadvantage is that you have already paid three or four hundred dollars for the 486 CPU in your system. It would be nice if Intel would take your old CPU in on trade. After all, the transistors in a CPU do not wear out. The CPU that is removed is every bit as good as a brand new one. You might be able to take it to a swap meet and sell it to a dealer. But don't expect to get much for it, especially if it is an older 486 25-MHz or 33-MHz chip. Depending on your situation, I am not sure that a Pentium OverDrive is worth the extra money. You might be better off buying a 100-MHz DX4, which would give you about the same computing power as the Pentium OverDrive operating at 63 MHz. At this time, the DX4-100 costs about $100 less than the Pentium OverDrive.

Intel FaxBack

If you have a FAX machine or a modem/fax board, you can call Intel's FaxBack line and have them fax you all the information you need about the various CPUs. Call their voice line at (800) 525-3019 and just follow the instructions. You will probably need to have them send you their FaxBack catalog, item number 9010, which gives a brief listing of what is available. Item 9000 gives the list price of several of the products. You might find some vendors who sell for less than the list price. You can check the ads in computer magazines for vendors who sell the OverDrive chips.

Intel has detailed instructions for the OverDrive upgrade that they will fax to you. The detailed instructions cover most of the hundreds of 486 machines made by various manufacturers that can be upgraded. Page 6 of the item number 9306 has a list of the manufacturers according to the first letter of their name. For instance, if you have a Dell system, you would ask for document number 3232. In many cases, you merely remove the old CPU and plug in the OverDrive, but some motherboards require that jumpers be changed. The instruction set for each machine is about 16 pages, so be sure that you have plenty of paper in your fax machine.

Most vendors who sell motherboards also sell the OverDrive CPUs, though they may not advertise this fact. Ads are very expensive, so not everything is listed in ads. If you can't find a vendor, you can call Intel at (800) 538-3373 and they can send you an Upgrade Guide and give you a list of vendors in your area.

Upgrading an older computer

If you have an older computer, you can easily upgrade it by installing a new Pentium, a NexGen 586, a Cyrix M1, or an AMD K5 motherboard. A new motherboard gives you all of the advantages of a new Pentium, but is much less expensive than buying a complete new system. You should be able to use most of your old components since all PCs use the same basic components other than the motherboard.

Except for the case, there probably isn't much you could use from an old XT. The XT keyboard looks just like the 286 and all later keyboards, and even has the same connector, but it is electronically different. Keyboards are relatively inexpensive and may cost from $10 to $50.

Instructions for upgrading to a Pentium motherboard

Step 1: Know your CMOS setup

Important! You must be able to tell the CMOS setup on your new system what type of hard disk drive you have. If you do not furnish all of the proper information as to the type, the number of cylinders, heads, and sectors, you may not be able to access the data on your hard disk.

If you don't have your system configuration written down somewhere, run your system CMOS setup to determine the data. Many of the older machines used several different methods to access the CMOS setup. If you have documentation, it should tell you how to access the setup mode. On most systems, you are given the opportunity to press something such as the Escape key and Del key while the system is booting up. On some systems, if you hold down a key of the keyboard while it is booting up, it gives you an error and tells you to press F1. This usually puts you into the setup mode. Run it and write down the type of drives, the number of cylinders, heads, sectors, landing zone, and any other information given. You may not be able to install your drives with your new motherboard unless you tell the new CMOS memory exactly what kind they are. If you cannot install your hard disk drives, you cannot access any of your data on them. You might not need it, but you should stop and make a complete backup of your hard disk before you remove the old motherboard.

The next thing to do is to shut off the power and disconnect the power cord and the keyboard cable. You probably have several other cables on the back of the PC. It is very easy to forget how and where

things were plugged in. It might be a good idea to use a felt marking pen and put a distinctive mark on the cable connector and the board connector. When you get ready to plug the cables back into the new boards, all you have to do is line up the various marks on the cables and board connectors. This assures that every cable is plugged back into the new system.

 # Step 2: Remove case cover

Locate and remove the screws that hold the case or cover on. For most early systems, there were five screws on the back panel, one in each corner and one in the top center. The four screws that hold the power supply in place should not be removed. Once the cover screws are removed, you can slide the cover off toward the front.

 # Step 3: Make a diagram before disassembly

Once the cover is removed, before doing anything else, take a piece of paper and make a rough drawing of where each board is plugged in and any cable that might be plugged into it. Then, use a felt marking pen to mark each cable and connector in a way that you can be sure to match the cable and connectors back up to the same board. For instance, if you mark a slash on the cable connector and board near one end, it is easy to match the two when you plug them back together. Some cables can be plugged in backwards or upside down. You can prevent this if the connectors are marked. Note in particular how the two connectors from the power supply are plugged into the motherboard. Note that the four black wires are in the center. These two connectors must be connected to the new motherboard in the same way.

Most of the cables are ribbon cables from the floppy and hard drives to the controller. If at all possible, leave the cables connected to the boards and just pull the boards out of the motherboard slot. You shouldn't have to remove any of the disk drives. Leave the cables plugged into the drives if possible.

There are cables from the power supply plugged into the motherboard, usually near the right rear corner of the motherboard. At the front there may also be several small wires for the front panel light emitting diodes (LEDs) and for the speaker. If these small wires and connectors are not marked, you might take some masking tape and put labels on them. Your new Pentium motherboard has similar pins for the connectors, but they may be in a different location.

Once all of the boards are removed and all of the cables are disconnected, look for a screw near the front and in the center of the motherboard and another in the rear of the motherboard.

When these screws are removed, pull the motherboard to the left then lift it out. You may have to jiggle it a bit. The motherboard has grooved plastic standoffs that slide into raised slots.

 ## Step 4: Set switches and jumpers and install new motherboard

You should have received some documentation with your new motherboard. Set any switches or jumpers that are needed to configure the system. Install any extra memory chips. You may have to use the memory from your old motherboard. The SIMMs are very easy to remove and install, just press the lever at the ends. To install, just drop in the slot at an angle and pull forward until the catches at the ends engage. The SIMMs have a notch on one end so they can only be inserted properly. Make sure they are completely seated, otherwise the computer will not boot up.

You may have to remove the white plastic standoffs from your old motherboard and use them on your new one. To remove the standoffs, use a pair of pliers and compress the portion of the standoff on the topside of the motherboard.

There may be extra mounting holes in the motherboard. Make sure that you have installed the plastic standoffs in the proper holes, then drop the motherboard into the slots and push it to the right until it locks in place. Replace the screws in the front and back of motherboard.

Connect all the front panel LED wires and the speaker wires. The motherboard should have some markings to indicate where each small connector should be plugged in. You may have to refer to your documentation for some wires. Your new motherboard may not use all of the front panel LED wires.

Next, connect the power supply cables to the motherboard.

NOTE This connector can be plugged in wrong. When connected properly, the four black wires will be in the center adjacent to each other.

The power supply connector is usually in two separate cables with six wires in each cable. They are sometimes marked *P8* and *P9*.

Step 5: Reinstall boards

Reinstall all of your plug-in boards and reconnect any cables that were disconnected. Connect the monitor and keyboard. Plug in the power cord. Recheck all of your connections to make sure that everything is plugged in properly then turn on the power. You should try the system before you put the cover back on. This way if it doesn't work, it is fairly easy to check all of the boards and cables to make sure they are installed correctly.

Step 6: Turn on and boot up

If you have reconnected everything right, the system should work. Run the setup routine to tell the CMOS and the BIOS the time, the date, and other information. You must input the exact numbers for cylinders, heads, and sectors for the type of hard disks that you have. Otherwise you cannot access your hard drive.

Step 7: Reinstall cover

Turn on the power and try it out. If everything works okay, put the cover back on and congratulate yourself for saving a bundle.

Upgrading to a 90-MHz NexGen

In December 1993, I paid $1350 for a motherboard with an Intel 60-MHz Pentium. I can buy the same motherboard today for about $450. For an Intel 90-MHz motherboard, it would cost about $725, for an Intel 100-MHz, about $870. At the time of this writing, it is impossible to find an Intel 120-MHz motherboard. If you could find one, it would cost about $1150.

I recently bought a motherboard with a 90-MHz NexGen 586 CPU from the Alaris Company at (510) 770-5700 for $459 and used it to replace my Pentium 60 MHz. I checked some ads in current computer magazines and found that an equivalent motherboard with an Intel 90-MHz CPU would have cost about $725 or $266 more. Prices listed are for comparison only at this time and will probably be less by the time you read this. The NexGen CPU will run all of the software that the Intel CPU runs. In some cases, NexGen will run the software even a bit faster.

Figure 4-5 shows the Pentium 60-MHz motherboard and the Alaris NexGen 90-MHz. I ran the Norton Utilities Sysinfo on both units. This utility does a test of the CPU speed and an overall throughput performance test of the system. It is not as sophisticated as some tests, but it is easy and does give a fairly good comparison of two different systems (Table 4-2). Peter Norton used the old original IBM XT as 1 for the base from which to compare later models. The old XT operated at 4.77 MHz, but the 90-MHz NexGen is 190.4 times faster than the XT. We have come a long way in a very short time.

Norton Utilities Sysinfo Comparison of CPU Speeds					Table 4-2
	XT	**386-33**	**486-33**	**60 MHz**	**90 MHz**
CPU speed	1	35.9	71.2	190.4	248.7
Overall perf.		24.9	50.5	130.7	169.4

 # Some minor problems

It seems that there always have to be a few problems. The Pentium motherboards have a small fan that must be connected to a power supply cable. Without the fan the Pentium CPUs will overheat and burn out. Most power supplies only have four power cables. If you have two hard disks, and two floppies, you may not have an extra power cable. Most companies supply a small Y cable that allows you to share one of the four cables. The Alaris motherboard did not have a Y cable so I had to go out and buy one.

Another problem was that my 60-MHz motherboard had several built-in functions, such as the serial ports, printer port, floppy drive, and IDE controllers. The Alaris board had none of these built-in functions. So I had to buy a multifunction I/O board for these devices. The board is not that expensive, but it does require the use of one of your precious slots. I called the company and they said that their next revisions, especially their PCI version, would have the built-in goodies.

Except for these small problems, the system works great.

 # Upgrading to DX4

If you are a bit short of money, you can upgrade an older computer to a DX4 and get about the same performance of a Pentium 60-MHz system. I am looking at a current ad in the *Computer Reseller News* (a free magazine to qualified subscribers, see address in Chapter 17). The price of a VESA local bus motherboard with an AMD 486DX4-100 is $245. For a combination ISA, VESA, and PCI local bus motherboard with an AMD 486DX4-100, the price is $265.

Replacing the motherboard is the same for all systems. You would use the same steps to upgrade to a DX4 as listed above for the Pentium upgrades.

Which Pentium motherboard should you buy?

There are several motherboard vendors. By the time you read this, the Cyrix M1 and the AMD K5 Pentium CPU clones should be on the market. Intel is trying to stay a step ahead and has introduced a 120-MHz version of the Pentium. NexGen, Cyrix, and AMD will soon have equivalent CPUs. Intel has introduced their next generation P6, and NexGen's 686 should be on the market by the time you read this. The clone CPU systems may cost $100 less than the equivalent Intel CPU. The competition helps to drive the prices down and also causes newer and better designs.

Each company tries to differentiate their product from the others. So you will have several choices. Some companies may claim that their system runs certain tests a few microseconds faster than another. Because of this, they may charge a lot more money than one that is a fraction of a second slower. Which system you choose should depend on what you want to use your computer for and how much money you want to spend.

The VESA local bus systems are still very popular, but the PCI is used more on the high end systems. They are both good systems, but the PCI may be a bit faster for high end applications.

The motherboard may or may not have several on-board built-in options, such as serial and parallel ports, EIDE and floppy drive interfaces, and a SCSI interface. A few companies are also now integrating sound chips onto the motherboard so all you have to do is plug in a couple of speakers.

Some ads list motherboards for a very low price. Usually in small print, it may say without CPU. Several companies are now selling CPUs, so you may be able to shop around, buy a motherboard at one place and the CPU that you want from another.

 # Sources for Pentium motherboards

I do a lot of my buying and shopping by mail order. I look through computer magazines such as the *Computer Shopper*, *Byte*, *PC World*, *PC Magazine,* and about 50 others and compare prices and products. Several of the computer magazines have a section near the back where they list the products advertised for that month. The items are categorized and grouped by product type. The page number for each ad is listed so it is easy to find what you are looking for. This is a great help when you consider that the *Computer Shopper* may have 1000 large tabloid-sized pages.

If you live near a large city, there are probably several computer dealers in your city. You can ask them about components. The local dealers may be a bit more expensive than mail order, but the local dealer may be able to help you if you have any problems. So the extra cost may be worth it.

Again, if you live in a large city, there are probably computer swap meets every so often. Most of your local dealers meet at a large auditorium, or fairgrounds, and set up booths to sell their wares. Most dealers usually offer very good prices and discounts. You can go from booth to booth and compare prices and products.

I often go to swap meets even if I don't need anything. There is usually a large crowd and lots of excitement in the air. It's almost like a circus.

CHAPTER 5

Memory

MEMORY is one of the most critical elements of the computer. Computing as we know it would not be possible without memory. The PC uses two primary types of memory, ROM and RAM.

ROM

Read only memory (ROM) is memory that cannot be altered or changed. The principal use of ROM in PCs is for the basic input/output system (BIOS). The BIOS contains routines that set up the computer when we first turn it on. It facilitates the transfer of data among peripherals.

RAM

If we open a file from a hard disk or a floppy, the files and data are read from the disk and placed in random access memory (RAM). When we load in a program, be it word processing, a spreadsheet, database, or whatever, we are working in the system RAM. If we are writing, programming, or creating another program, we are working in RAM.

Actually it is dynamic RAM or DRAM. Random access means that we can find, address, change, or erase any single byte among several million bytes.

We can also randomly access any particular byte on a floppy or hard disk. We cannot randomly access data on a magnetic tape system. The data on the tape is stored sequentially. In order to find a

particular byte, we would have to run the tape forward or backwards to the proper area.

Being able to randomly access the memory allows us to read and write to it immediately. It is somewhat like an electronic blackboard. Here we can manipulate the data, do calculations, enter more data, edit, search databases, or do any of the thousands of things that software programs allow us to do. We can access and change the data in RAM very quickly.

RAM memory is an essential element of the computer. Of course, if you are working on a large file you need a lot of RAM. If you are using Windows and you don't have enough RAM, some portions of the file may be loaded onto a special area of the hard disk and used as a swap file.

 # RAM volatility

An important difference in ROM and RAM is that RAM is volatile. That is, it disappears if the machine is rebooted or if you exit a program without saving it. If there is a power interruption to the computer, even for a brief instant, any data in RAM is gone forever.

You should get in the habit of saving your files to disk frequently, especially if you live in an area where there are power failures due to storms or other reasons. One of the excellent features of WordStar and most other word processors is that it can be set up to automatically save open files to disk at frequent intervals.

 # How RAM is addressed

Each byte of memory has a separate address. The cells in the memory bank could be analogous to the "pigeon holes" for the room keys of a large hotel. They would be arranged in rows and columns so the pigeon holes would correspond to each room on each floor. If the hotel had 100 rooms, you could have ten rows across and ten down. It would be very simple to find any one of the 100 keys by counting across and then down to the particular room number. Memory addressing is a bit more complicated than the hotel pigeon holes, but with just 20 address lines (2^{20}) any individual byte out of one million bytes (1MB) can be quickly accessed. Actually 1MB, or 2 to the 20th power, would equal 1,048,576 bytes.

One byte is also called a *word* so the old 8-bit XTs can only address one word at a time. The 16-bit 286 can address two words, 32-bit 386 and 486 systems can address four words, and the 64-bit Pentium can address 8 words at a time.

The CPU and the RAM bus

The CPU is the brains of the computer. Almost everything that happens in a computer must travel over a bus path and go through the CPU.

You have a very fast and powerful Pentium. You probably have several plug-in boards and peripheral components. These components communicate with the CPU over a 16-bit bus at about 8 MHz. But data that moves between the RAM and the CPU has its own special memory bus. Data moves back and forth on the bus between the RAM and CPU at the CPU speed or frequency. If you have a 100-MHz Pentium, then the CPU can pull 8 words or 8 bytes of data out of RAM, process it and send it back at a rate of 100 million times per second. Just a few years ago, we thought the XT was fast when it could pull one byte out of memory, process it and send it back at a rate of 4.75 million times per second. You might also have several plug-in boards installed on a VL bus or a PCI bus that communicates with the CPU at the CPU frequency.

The amount of work that a computer accomplishes depends on how fast it can process data. There may be billions of bits in a software program. It may take a lot of shifting and adding and moving around to process the program. The faster the computer can handle these billions of iterations, the better.

The original PC had an eight-bit memory bus connected to the CPU. The bus was doubled to 16 bits for the 286 CPU. It was doubled

again to 32 bits for the 386 and 486 CPUs. For the Pentium the bus width is whatever the motherboard is designed for. It could be 32 bit, 64 bit, or even 128 bits. For a 128-bit bus, some designers have developed a 64-bit bus going in one direction to the CPU and another 64-bit bus returning from the CPU. The computer technology has come a long way in just a few short years.

The bus has been likened to a highway. If there are only eight lanes, it may be rather slow. Twice as many cars can get through on a 16-lane highway, and four times as many if there are 32 lanes. If there are 64 lanes, the traffic can really whiz along.

 # A brief explanation of memory

Computers operate on binary systems of 0s and 1s or off and on. A transistor can act like a switch that can be turned off or on to represent the 0s and 1s. Two transistors can represent four different combinations: 1) both off; 2) both on; 3) #1 on, #2 off; 4) #1 off, #2 on. A bank of four transistors can represent 16 different combinations. With eight transistors, we can have 256 different combinations. It takes 8 transistors to make one byte. With them you can represent each letter of the alphabet, each number, and each symbol of the extended American Standard Code for Information Interchange (ASCII). With eight lines, plus a ground, the eight transistors can be turned on or off to represent any single one of the 256 characters of the ASCII code. With 20 lines and 20 transistors, plus a ground line, you can address 1MB, with 24 bus lines, you can address 16MB. If one more bus line is added to make it 25, you can address 32MB. For each line added, the potential addressable memory doubles.

 # Programs that stay in RAM (TSR)

Besides the application programs that must be loaded into the 640K of RAM, there are certain DOS system programs that must be in RAM at all times. These are programs such as Command.com and the internal commands. There are over 20 internal commands such as COPY, CD, CLS, DATE, DEL, MD, PATH, TIME, TYPE, and

others. These commands are always in RAM and are available immediately. The Config.Sys file and any drivers that you may have for your system are also loaded into RAM.

Terminate and stay resident (TSR) files are normally loaded into the 640K of RAM. There are memory resident programs such as SideKick Plus (SideKick has now been revised and updated for Windows), and others that can pop up any time you press a key. Portions of RAM can also be used for a very fast RAM disk and for buffers and print spooling.

All of these things contribute to the utility and functionality of the computer and make it easier to use. But unfortunately, they take big bites out of our precious 640K bytes of RAM. There may be less than 400K left for running applications after loading all these memory resident programs.

Many application programs cannot run if you have less than 600K of free RAM. Some are now so large that they need up to 4MB in order to run properly. These programs are designed to run in extended memory.

Late versions of DR DOS from Novell, MS-DOS, and IBM's PC DOS can now load much of the operating system and TSRs in upper memory. Upper memory is that 384K of memory above 640K. Several other memory management programs have been developed to help alleviate this problem. One excellent program is DESQview from Quarterdeck Office Systems, (310) 392-9851.

Motherboard memory

The old XT motherboard could only accept 640K of memory on the motherboard. There were large dual-inline pins (DIPs) that took up about one fourth of the entire motherboard. Most memory today is in the form of single inline memory modules (SIMMs). They take up very little space and can store enormous amounts of memory.

The 32-bit 386 and 486 CPUs communicate with their RAM over a 32-line bus. The Pentium is a 64-bit CPU. All of these CPUs can

address 4 gigabytes or 2^{32} = 4,294,967,296 bytes. A gigabyte is a billion bytes.

Although the CPUs can address 4 gigabytes of RAM, without special software DOS will not let you access more than 640K. (Incidentally, 4 gigabytes of DRAM, in 1MB SIMM packages, would require 4096 modules. You would need a fairly large board to install that much memory. It would also be rather expensive. At $35 per megabyte, 4096 modules would cost $143,360.)

Windows, OS/2, and several other software programs let you break the 640K barrier and use all of the extended memory available.

In its virtual memory mode, the Pentium can address 64 terabytes, or 64 trillion bytes, that is 64,000,000,000,000 bytes. If you used 200MB hard disks, you would need 320,000 of them to store this much data.

Virtual memory is a method of using part of a hard disk as RAM. Many large programs cannot run unless the entire program resides in RAM. So the program can be partially loaded in the available RAM and the rest of it in a virtual RAM section of the hard disk. Of course, having to access the disk for data can slow the processing down considerably. But it is one solution. The virtual disk system must be implemented by the operating system.

 # Single inline memory module (SIMM)

Your computer motherboard has sockets for single inline memory modules (SIMMs). Older motherboards had sockets with 30 contacts that would accept SIMM assemblies of 256K, 500K, 1MB, or 4MB SIMMs. Most of the newer motherboards have sockets with 72 contacts for the n × 36 SIMMs. A few motherboards have both the 30 contact and 72 contact slots. NexGen and some of the other CPUs supports 256MB SIMMs, even though they are not available at this time.

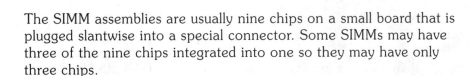

The SIMM assemblies are usually nine chips on a small board that is plugged slantwise into a special connector. Some SIMMs may have three of the nine chips integrated into one so they may have only three chips.

The early PCs used dual inline pin (DIP) chips with two rows of 8 pins, or 16 pins total. It required nine chips of whatever type memory designated. For instance, for 64K, it took 8 64K $\times$ 1 bit chips plus 1 64K $\times$ 1 bit chip for parity checking. If 256K chips were used, it took 8 256K $\times$ 1 bit chips, plus 1 256 $\times$ 1 bit chip for parity checking. Even with the high capacity SIMMs, it still takes nine chips to make up the designated memory. For a 4-megabyte SIMM, it takes 8 4096 $\times$ 1 bit plus 1 4096 $\times$ 1 bit for parity checking. The same system is used even for the n $\times$ 36 SIMM chips.

The Macintosh systems do not use the parity checking chip, so they have only the 8 x whatever the SIMM designation. Memory is one of the few areas where the components for Macintosh may be less expensive than those for ISA machines. I am looking at a memory ad in a current magazine. For an 8-chip Macintosh SIMM of 4 $\times$ 8, 70 ns, the price is \$120. For a 9-chip ISA SIMM of 4 $\times$ 9, 70 ns, the price is \$137. Some have said that the 9th chip for parity checking is not necessary. Of all the years that I have been using computers, I have never had a memory parity error.

Memory must be configured in banks. Most motherboards are designed for four banks: 0, 1, 2, and 3. Check your documentation that came with the motherboard. You must fill the lowest numbered bank before filling other banks.

Because memory is interleaved on most systems, you must install the SIMMs in multiples of two. You cannot intermix SIMMs of different values. For instance, for 16MB, you would have to install two 8MB modules. If you install a single module instead of the required two, the computer may not boot up. The screen may be completely blank. Interleaved memory is discussed in more detail below.

WARNING It is possible to have a module that is not seated properly. If this happens, the computer may not boot up. The screen may be

completely blank with no error messages or any indication of the problem.

You probably should not even consider installing 1MB SIMMs. Before buying memory, check your documentation for the type that you need. Many motherboards only provide four slots for memory. If you installed 1MB SIMMs you could only install 4MB of memory. You could probably get by with 4MB of RAM, but you would be much better off if you installed a minimum of 8MB. The 1×36 SIMM can give you 4MB in one 72 contact slot. The 2×36 gives you 8MB in each slot. There are also 4×36 for 16MB and 8×36 for 32MB. You can install 128MB in just four slots by using 8×36 SIMMs. Figure 5-1 shows a 4×36 16MB SIMM on the bottom and an older 30 contact 4MB SIMM at the top.

Figure 5-1

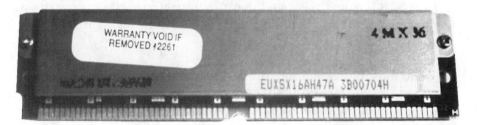

A 4×36 16MB SIMM memory module (bottom) and an older 4MB SIMM (top).

The SIMMs have speeds of 70 and 60 nanoseconds (ns). The smaller the number of ns, the faster. You should buy the speed recommended by your documentation. It is possible to mix SIMMs with different speeds, but the system is limited to the speed of the slowest SIMM.

I would suggest that you buy as much memory as you can afford. Memory is somewhat like money in that you can never have too much of it.

Since the memory comes in modules and is socketed, you can add as much as your motherboard allows. It is possible that a memory chip can fail. The BIOS does a power on self test (POST) every time the computer is booted. During this test, all of the memory chips are tested. MS-DOS 6.2 also does a more comprehensive memory test each time the computer is booted. If an assembly becomes defective, it is easy enough to replace it. One disadvantage of having large capacity SIMMs is that if a chip fails, you have to replace the whole SIMM. The price in a current magazine for an 8 × 36 or 32MB SIMM is $955. Another company advertises a 16 × 36 or 64MB for $2525. Fortunately, memory chips don't fail very often. Most dealers give you a lifetime replacement guarantee if one of their modules fail. Be sure to ask for this guarantee if you are buying high-capacity SIMMs.

You may have to set some switches or install some jumpers to configure your motherboard to the amount of memory that you have installed. Check the documentation that you got with your motherboard.

 # Prices

Almost all of the computer components have dropped except for memory. Software and systems are being designed to use more and more memory so there is a big demand for it. Eventually the prices should start coming down. At the present time, memory costs about $35 per megabyte. Hopefully, it will be less by the time you read this, but don't count on it. I have checked prices in some back issues of computer magazines and they are higher at the present time than they were a couple of months ago.

 # Installing the chips

One of the first things that you should do before touching your expensive memory chips, or any sensitive electronic device, is to discharge any static electric charge that you may have on you. To discharge yourself, touch some metal object such as an unpainted metal case of a computer, a metal lamp, or some other object that is

plugged into an outlet. The object that you touch does not have to be turned on.

A SIMM chip is very easy to install. It has a cutout on one end so it can only be inserted one way. Just lay the assembly slantwise in the socket, then push it to an upright position. There is a small hole in each end of the SIMM board. There is a projection on the socket that fits in this hole when the SIMMs are inserted in the socket. Spring loaded clamps on each end lock the assembly in place. To remove the assembly, press the clamps on each end.

 # The need for more memory

If you bought a new motherboard through mail order, you may have received it with 0K memory. You probably know that *0K* does not mean *okay*, it means *zero K*, or no memory. The price of memory fluctuates quite a lot. Ads are sometimes made up and placed two or three months before the magazine comes out. Because of the fluctuating prices some vendors do not advertise a firm price for memory. Besides, if they included the price of the memory, it might frighten you away. They usually invite you to call them for the latest price.

For some applications, you may need to buy several megabytes of memory. In the old days, we got by fine with just 64K of memory. Many of the new software programs such as the spreadsheets, databases, and accounting programs now require at least 4 to 8MB or more memory.

 # Some memory basics

Dynamic RAM or DRAM is the most common type of memory used today. Each memory cell has a small etched transistor that is kept in its memory state, either on or off, by an electrical charge on a very small capacitor. Capacitors are similar to small rechargeable batteries. Units can be charged up with a voltage to represent 1s or left uncharged to represent 0s. But those that are charged up immediately start to lose their charge. So they must be constantly "refreshed" with a new charge.

Steve Gibson, the developer of SpinRite, compared the memory cell capacitors to a small bucket that has a hole in the bottom. Those buckets, or cells, that represent 1s are filled with water, but they immediately start leaking out through the hole in the bottom. So they have to be constantly refilled. You don't have to worry about filling those buckets, or cells, that represent 0s. A computer may spend 7 percent or more of its time just refreshing the DRAM chips. Also each time a cell is accessed, that small voltage in the capacitor flows through a transistor to turn it on. This drains the charge from the capacitor, so it must be refreshed before it can be accessed again. In our bucket of water comparison, when the cell is accessed, the bucket is turned upside down and emptied. So if it represents a 1, it must be refilled immediately. Of course, it takes a finite amount of time to fill a bucket or to place a charge on a capacitor. If the memory cell has a speed of 70 nanosecond (ns), it may take 70 ns, plus the time it takes to recycle, which may be 105 ns or more, before that cell can again be accessed.

 # Refreshment and wait states

The speed of the DRAM chips in your system should match your system CPU. You might be able to install slower chips, but your system would have to work with wait states. If the DRAM is too slow, a wait state has to be inserted. A wait state causes the CPU and the rest of the system to sit and wait while the RAM is being accessed and then refreshed. Wait states could deprive your system of one of its greatest benefits, speed. A terrible waste of time.

If the CPU is operating at a very high frequency, it may have to sit and wait one cycle, or *one wait state* for the refresh cycle. The wait state might be only a millionth of a second or less. That may not seem like much time. But if the computer is doing several million operations per second, it can add up.

It takes a finite amount of time to charge up the DRAM. Some DRAM chips can be charged up much faster than others. For instance, the DRAM chips needed for an XT at 4.77 MHz may take as much as 200 nanoseconds (ns) or billionths of a second to be refreshed. A 486 running at 25 MHz would need chips that could be refreshed in 70 ns or less time. Of course, the faster chips cost more.

 # Interleaved memory

Most of the newer faster systems use interleaved memory to prevent having to insert wait states. The memory is always installed in multiples of two. You may install two banks of 2MB, 4MB, 8MB, 16MB, 32MB, or 64MB of memory.

One half of the memory would be refreshed on one cycle, then the other half. If the CPU needed to access an address that was in the half already refreshed, it would be available immediately. If the needed address happened to be in the side being refreshed, it would have to wait. Interleaving does reduce the access time somewhat, but it isn't a perfect solution.

 # Extended data out and synchronous DRAM

As the CPUs keep getting faster and faster, it is increasingly difficult to develop DRAM chips that can keep up. A new type of DRAM being manufactured by Micron Technology at (208) 368-4000, is called *Extended Data Out (EDO)*. It operates about 10 percent faster than ordinary DRAM and is still fairly reasonable in cost. It uses a wider bandwidth during the address select so there are few cache misses. The motherboard must be designed to accept the EDO DRAM. Several companies, such as Dell and Micronics, are using the EDO memory on their new 120-MHz Pentium systems.

Another type of memory that is still not generally available is *Synchronous DRAM (SDRAM)*. It will be rather expensive and will be used primarily on high-end type of systems.

Several other types of memory are being developed such as *Burst EDO, Rambus DRAM, fast Page Mode DRAM, hyperpage DRAM,* and *synchronous graphics RAM (SGRAM)*.

⇨ SRAM

Static RAM is made up of actual transistors. They can be turned on to represent 1s or left off to represent 0s and will stay in that condition until they receive a change signal. They do not need to be refreshed but they revert back to 0 when the computer is turned off or if the power is interrupted. They are very fast and can operate at speeds of 15 ns or less.

A DRAM memory cell needs only one transistor and a small capacitor. It takes a very small amount of space for a DRAM cell. Each SRAM cell requires four to six transistors and other components. So SRAM is much more expensive than DRAM. The SRAM chips are assembled in the DIP type package so they are physically larger and require much more space than the DRAM chips. Because of the physical and electronic differences, SRAM and DRAM chips are not interchangeable.

Your motherboard has sockets for SRAM chips. Many of the early 486 motherboards only had sockets for up to 256K. The newer motherboards may have sockets for up to 1MB or more. Though most motherboards are sold without DRAM memory, quite often, the motherboards come with the SRAM already installed.

If your motherboard does not already have the SRAM, or you want to add more, check your documentation to make sure you get the proper kind. There are both 32K and 64K SRAM chips. The 32K chips have 28 pins, the newer 64K chips have 32 pins. Some of the newer motherboards may have sockets that can accept either 28- or 32-pin SRAM. So you may have a choice of installing 256K, 512K, or 1MB of SRAM. Using 32K SRAM chips, you would need 16 chips for 512K. Check your motherboard documentation for instructions on how they should be installed. Be careful because it is possible to plug them in backwards. Look for some indication on the motherboard concerning which is pin one. There should be a slight U-shaped indentation on the end of the chip that has pin one. You may also have to set some switches or install some jumpers to configure your motherboard for the amount of SRAM that you install. Check your documentation. If you refer

to Fig. 5-2, you can see eight SRAM chips installed in the upper right corner of the motherboard.

Figure 5-2

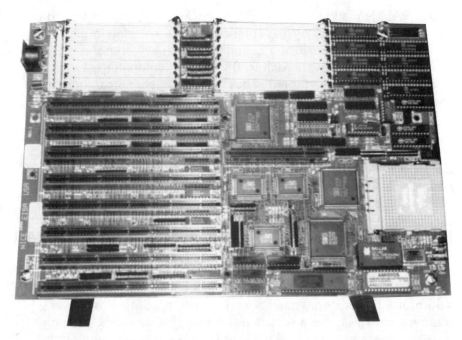

Some SRAM chips installed on an EISA VLB Pentium motherboard. The SRAM chips are the 8 long chips in the upper right corner.

Cache memory

A cache system can speed up computer operations quite a lot. When running an application program, the CPU often loops in and out of certain areas and uses portions of the same memory over and over. A cache system is usually made up of very fast memory chips such as SRAM that can store the often used data so it is quickly accessible to the CPU.

The data that is moved back and forth between the CPU and RAM are electrical on and off voltages. The electrons move at almost the speed of light. Still it takes a finite amount of time to move a large amount of data. It takes even more time to access the RAM, find the data that is needed, then move it back to the CPU.

The computer may be slowed down considerably if it has to search the entire memory each time it has to fetch some data. If data that is often used is stored in a cache, it can be accessed by the CPU very quickly. A good cache can greatly increase the processing speed.

Level 1 and level 2 caches

The 486 CPU has an 8K built-in cache among its 1.2 million transistors. This built-in cache is called a *level 1 cache* or *L1*. Since it does not have to travel outside the CPU, it operates at the same internal speed as the CPU. Many of the CPUs operate externally two to three times slower than the internal speed.

The Pentium uses two separate 8K L1 caches. This doubles the number of cache ports and the overall speed of the processing.

The 486 and Pentium CPUs can also use a *level 2 (L2)* or *external cache* made up of fast SRAM. The speed and static characteristics of SRAM make it an excellent device for memory cache systems. But an external L2 cache cannot match an L1 cache.

The next generation P6 CPU has 5.5 million transistors. It retains the two 8K built-in L1 caches, but they also added a 256K L2 cache. The L2 cache is a separate die that is enclosed in the same housing of the CPU. The L2 cache communicates with the CPU over a very short 64-bit interface or special bus. The P6 initially will operate at 133 MHz. But in a very short time it will no doubt exceed 200 MHz.

The fastest Pentium at this time operates at 120 MHz, but it will be revved up to 180 MHz or more in a short time.

Disk cache

Cache memory should not be confused with disk caching. Often a program may need to access a hard disk while running. If a small disk cache is set up in RAM, the CPU can import the data from a RAM

cache much quicker than reading it from even the fastest hard disk. So a disk cache set up in RAM can help a program to run much faster.

There are several commercial disk caching programs, but if you have MS-DOS 6.0 or later, it has a SmartDrive command that lets you set up a disk cache in RAM.

Some SCSI and IDE hard disk interface controllers may have a disk cache.

 # Hit rate

A well designed cache system may have a *hit rate* of over 90%. This means that each time the CPU needs a block of data, it finds it in the nearby, fast cache. A good cache system may increase the speed and performance considerably.

 # CMOS

The complementary metal oxide semiconductors (CMOS) use very little power to keep them alive. They are actually SRAM transistors that store your system setup. Several of the computer features that are configurable, such as the time, date, type of disk drives, and other features that can be changed by the user are stored in CMOS.

You should take a pad and write down all of the features stored in your CMOS setup. For instance, if you lose the data in your CMOS, and you don't know what type of hard drive is in the setup, you cannot access your data on the hard drive.

A lithium or a rechargeable battery keeps the data current when the computer is turned off. If your computer is not used for a long period of time, you may have to reset the time. If you have to reset the time quite often, you may need a new battery. The early IBM AT used batteries that only lasted a couple of years. Most motherboards today have lithium batteries that should last four to five years. Many of these batteries are soldered to the motherboard and may be difficult

to replace. The Alaris NexGen motherboard uses a flat round lithium battery such as those used in cameras and watches. It is held in place with a clip and is very easy to replace. Some other motherboards have a small square battery with pins that plug into a socket.

Once a battery goes dead or is disconnected to be replaced, all information in the CMOS is lost and must be reinput.

Clock rate

Computers operate at very precise clock rates. The Central Processing Unit (CPU) is controlled by timing circuits and crystals. The original PCs and XTs operated at 4.77 MHz; the DX4s operate as high as 100 MHz and the Pentium as high as 120 MHz at this time.

Many systems are just too fast for some of the other components. Some of the newer BIOS chips allow you to insert wait states.

Why the 640K limit?

When DOS was first introduced in 1981, one megabyte of memory was an enormous amount. It was believed that this amount would be more than satisfactory. After all, many of the CP/M machines were getting by fine with just 64K of memory. So DOS was designed to operate with a maximum of one megabyte. Of this one megabyte, 640K would be used for running programs and applications. The other 384K was reserved for purposes such as the BIOS, the video control, and other special hardware control. This 384K is called the *upper memory area* and is divided up into blocks called *upper memory blocks* or *UMBs*.

Sometimes when I try to load and run a program, I get an error message "Not enough memory," or "Insufficient memory." But I have 32MB of DRAM in my computer. I know that the program that I am trying to run is less than 500K. So why shouldn't I be able to run it if I have 32MB?

The reason is simple. The program that I am trying to run is a DOS program that cannot handle extended memory. It is limited to the 640K of conventional memory. But if the program is only 500K, why can't it run in the 640K?

When I booted up my computer, the Command.Com and several other internal DOS commands were loaded into that 640K. In addition, any terminate and stay resident (TSR) programs were also loaded into the 640K. Any drivers for special devices such as a fax-modem, a CD-ROM, or other device drivers listed in my Config.sys and Autoexec.bat are also loaded into the conventional memory. After all of this stuff is loaded, there may be less than 400K left. So if the program is larger than 400K, it will not run. Many programs and applications today are so large that they may need 600K or more of RAM. You can easily see how much of the 640K is free by using the CHKDSK command.

Tremendous improvements have been made in computer technology since the original PC. But in spite of all of the improvements in the technology, we are still limited to the original 640K unless we have programs such as Windows that can take advantage of any extra extended memory that we may have. One reason for this limitation was to make sure that the computers remained compatible with, and could still run, the billions of dollars worth of software that was already created. We still occasionally hear someone complain about the 640K barrier. But this backward compatibility is one of the foremost factors that made the computer what it is today.

The 640K barrier is not really much of a problem today. Much of the reserved 384K upper memory space is never needed by the system. MS-DOS and several other programs such as DESQview can load the internal commands, drivers, and TSRs into the unused 384 of upper memory. In most cases, you can have over 600K left for running programs.

The MS-DOS version 5.0 and later, has a MEMMAKER command that can search the 384K of upper memory and find all of the unused cracks and crannies. After this, every time you boot your computer, it automatically loads most of the internal commands, drivers, and TSRs into these upper memory blocks (UMBs).

Windows, Windows NT, and IBM's OS/2 are not limited to the 640K barrier. These systems let you use all of the RAM that is available if it is needed. You will not need DOS to run Windows 95. It will allow you to seamlessly use all of any extended memory.

⇨ Conventional memory

Conventional memory is the one megabyte of memory that includes the 640K. DOS type applications are loaded into this area and processed here.

Figure 5-3 is a diagram of how conventional memory is arranged.

Figure 5-3

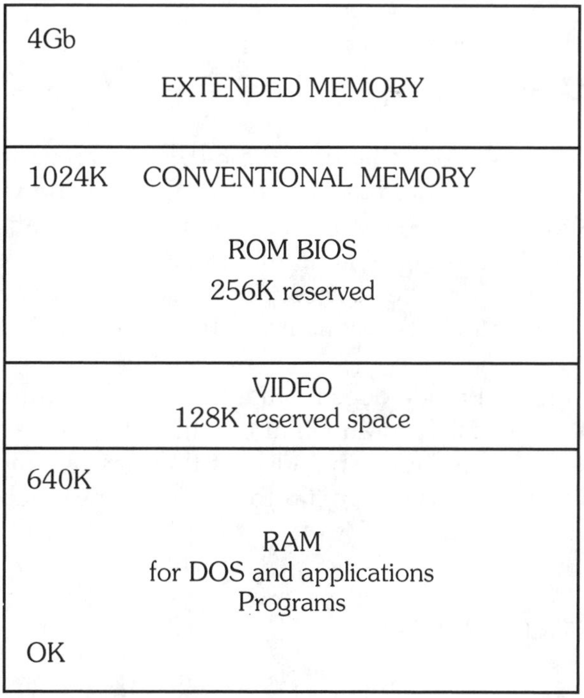

```
┌─────────────────────────────────────┐
│ 4Gb                                  │
│                                      │
│         EXTENDED MEMORY              │
│                                      │
├─────────────────────────────────────┤
│ 1024K    CONVENTIONAL MEMORY         │
│                                      │
│             ROM BIOS                 │
│           256K reserved              │
│                                      │
├─────────────────────────────────────┤
│             VIDEO                    │
│         128K reserved space          │
├─────────────────────────────────────┤
│ 640K                                 │
│                                      │
│              RAM                     │
│       for DOS and applications       │
│             Programs                 │
│                                      │
│ OK                                   │
└─────────────────────────────────────┘
```

Memory arrangement

 # Extended memory

Extended memory is memory that can be installed above one megabyte. Software programs designed for Windows, Windows NT, and OS/2 can use extended memory.

Windows, Windows NT, and OS/2 can also use extended memory to run two or more programs at the same time, or do multitasking.

 # Memory modes

There are two different memory modes, the real and standard or protected.

 ## Real mode

The real mode is the mode that uses the 640K. When an application is being processed, the program is loaded into RAM memory. The CPU uses the RAM to process any data that is input. Computations, changes, or calculations are done in memory, then sent back to the disk, screen, printer, or other device. For most single user applications this processing is done in the standard 640K or less of RAM.

Operating in the real mode doesn't cause much of a problem if you are running fairly small programs that can fit in the available RAM. But if you are trying update a spreadsheet that has two megabytes in it, you are in trouble. It is like trying to put a gallon of gelatin into a quart bowl.

 ## Protected mode

In the protected mode, the AT type machines can run several programs at the same time. Each program runs in a 640K area of memory. In effect, this memory has a wall around it so it does not interfere with any other memory area.

Flash memory

You might want a laptop or notebook computer for the times when you are on the road. If you do buy one, make sure that it has the PCMCIA connectors for flash memory.

Intel developed flash memory, which is similar to Erasable Programmable Read Only Memory (EPROM). Flash memory is fairly slow compared to DRAM and SRAM so it can't replace them. But it can be equivalent to hard disk memory. The hard disk is a mechanical device that will eventually wear out or fail. The flash memory is strictly electronic and should last several lifetimes. A disadvantage is that flash memory is still rather expensive and limited in the amount of memory that can be installed on a card.

 # Video RAM

Video RAM (VRAM) chips are a bit different than DRAM chips. They are special memory chips that are used on the better (and more expensive) monitor adapter cards. The VRAM chips are unusual in that they have double ports so they can be accessed and refreshed at the same time.

 # Printer memory

Your laser printer probably came with a minimum amount of memory or about 512K. A laser printer determines where each dot on a printed page should be, then prints the whole page. Most printers require memory that is installed on special proprietary boards. You may need to add more memory for better printing speed. Most lasers perform much better if they have a minimum of 2MB.

 # Buying chips

Buying chips that are faster than what your system can use only costs you extra money. It doesn't hurt to use faster chips, or even to

intermix faster ones with slower ones. Just make sure that you buy only the type that fits in your system.

 # How much memory do you need?

The amount of memory you need depends primarily on your uses of your computer. For word processing or small applications, you can get by with 640K. You should have at least 4MB, 8MB is even better, if you expect to use Windows, large databases, or spreadsheets.

Having lots of memory is like having a car with a large engine. You may not need that extra power very often, but it sure feels great being able to call on it when you do need it.

CHAPTER 6

Floppy
drives and disks

I N the early days, it was possible to run PC programs with only floppy disk drives. Floppy disks were all that we had. Some PCs had a single floppy drive. Almost all of the early drives used single-sided floppy disks that were from 140K to 180K. It was a great leap forward when IBM introduced a PC with two floppy drives that could handle double-sided floppy disks. Even if you were fortunate enough to have a PC with two floppy drives, doing any kind of computing involved an endless amount of disk swapping and took forever to get anything done.

 ## The floppy evolution

The 140K systems were soon replaced with 320K double-sided systems, then 360K, then 1.2MB and then 3½" 1.44MB. The 2.88MB 3½" drive is available, but the drive and the disks are still rather expensive. It is not used by many people.

Most software programs today are very user friendly. The more user friendly they are, the larger they are. Today most programs are shipped on several 1.44MB disks in a compressed form. They must be uncompressed before they can be used. Many of the programs require from 25MB up to 60MB or more to be installed and to be able to run. It would be impossible to run programs such as these with a floppy disk system.

At the present time, the majority of all software programs come to us on floppy disks. But many companies are beginning to use CD-ROMs. One small CD-ROM disc can store over 600MB. This can

hold all of the software program and include a very large instruction manual on disc. Eventually all software will be distributed on the high capacity CD-ROMs. No matter how you receive it, the software is usually copied to a hard disk.

 # How floppy drives operate

Computers rely to a very large extent on magnetism and voltage. Magnetism and voltage are closely interrelated. Magnetic lines of force can be produced when voltage is passed through a coil of wire that is wrapped around a piece of iron. The process can be reversed to produce voltage by passing a coil of wire through a magnetic field.

The amount of magnetism or voltage produced in these processes varies enormously depending on such factors as the voltage level, the number of turns of wire, the properties of the iron core, the frequency of the voltage, and many other factors.

The floppy drive spins a disk much like a record player. The disk is made from a type of plastic material called *polyethylene terephthalate*, which is coated with a magnetic material made primarily of iron oxide. It is similar to the tape that is used in cassette tape recorders. The drive has a head that is basically a piece of iron with a coil of wire around it. The iron core for the head is shaped somewhat like a C. When voltage is passed through the coil of wire, a magnetic field is produced between the ends of the C. When a pulse of voltage passes through the head, the spot on the disk beneath the head is magnetized. When it is played back, the magnetized spot on the disk causes a small voltage to be produced in the head.

Of course, the voltage produced by the magnetism on the disk is very small, so it must be amplified. Placing this small voltage on the base of a transistor can cause it to act like a switch to turn on a larger voltage. Most of the voltages used in computers is direct current, usually 3 to 5 volts dc. Transistors can be used to turn the direct current on and off. When the current is on, it can represent a 1, when it is off it can represent a 0. A transistor can be switched on and off millions of times per second. Computer software programs control the various transistors causing them to turn on or off.

A pulse of electricity that represents a 1 causes the head to magnetize that portion of track beneath the head. If the next spot of the same track is not magnetized, it can represent a 0. When the tracks are read, the head detects whether each portion of the track is magnetized or not. If the spot is magnetized, it creates a small voltage signal to represent a 1, or a 0 if it is not magnetized.

Computers operate with a very precise clock rate based on internal crystal oscillators. If a voltage remains high for a certain length of time, it can represent two or more 1s, or if it is off for a certain length of time, it can represent two or more 0s.

The floppy disks are divided into several concentric tracks. Each track is then divided into sectors. It is amazing that the head can find any one byte on a floppy disk that may have over a million bytes. It is even more amazing that the same system can find any one byte on a hard disk that may have over 2 billion bytes or 2 gigabytes. More about disk organization later.

High-density drives and disks

The 360K floppy drive is as obsolete as the horse-drawn buggy. (Of course, the horse and buggy is still used by the Amish people in Pennsylvania, and there are some people who still use the 360K floppy drives.) The 1.2MB floppy drive can read and write to either format. The main difference between a 360K and a 1.2MB floppy disk is the resistance to being magnetized, or the *Oersted (Oe)*. The 1.2MB disk has an Oe of 600, the 360K has an Oe of 300. The higher Oe means that the material requires a higher head current for magnetization.

In order to store 1.2MB on a floppy disk, 80 tracks on each side of the disk are laid down. These 80 tracks are just half as wide as the 40 tracks of a 360K disk. The 1.2MB drives switch to a lower head current when writing to the 360K format.

There is not as much difference between the 3½" 720K and 1.44MB floppy disks. The 720K usual has an Oe of about 600 and the 1.44MB may be about 700. The 1.44MB floppies have a square hole in the right rear corner of the disk. The drive has a small microswitch

that checks for the square hole in the right rear corner of the 1.44MB disks. If it finds a square hole there it lets you read and write to the 1.44MB format. If it does not find the hole it automatically reads and writes to the 720K format. There have been times when I needed to make a diskcopy of a 720K disk, but did not have a blank 720K. I just put a piece of tape over the square hole of a 1.44MB disk and it works fine as a 720K.

 # The all-media or combination floppy drive

The 5¼" floppy drives will eventually be phased out, but it will be sometime before it happens. I recommend that you install both a 5¼" drive and a 3½". Ordinarily, this would mean that you have to have two available bays. Many of the desktop computers provide only three or four bays to mount drives. You might not have space to mount two floppies, two hard drives, a tape backup drive, and a CD-ROM.

The CMS Enhancements Company, (714) 222-6316, noted this problem. They created an all-media floppy drive by combining a 1.2MB and a 1.44MB floppy drive into a single unit. The 5¼" part of the drive can handle 5¼" 360K and 1.2MB floppies; the 3½ part handles 720K and 1.44MB floppy disks. The combination drive requires only a single drive bay. The two drives are never both used at the same time, so there is no problem. They can even share most of the drive electronics.

Teac, Canon, and several other companies are now manufacturing the combination drives. At the present time, the combination drives cost less than $100. Figure 3-6 shows a combination floppy drive.

 # Disk drive motors

Disk drives have two motors. One motor drives the spindle that rotates the disk. Then, a stepping motor, or actuator, moves the heads back and forth to the various tracks.

Spindle motor

Some of the old 5¼" floppy drives used an "O" ring belt to drive the spindle. Modern floppy drives use a direct drive where the spindle is just an extension of the motor shaft. When a disk is inserted a plastic cone is lowered onto the disk that centers and locks it to the spindle.

The motors are regulated so the speed is usually fairly constant. The speed of the old 5¼" 360K floppy drive is 300 rpm. The 5¼" 1.2MB drive rotates at 360 rpm, even when reading and writing to a 360K disk. The 3½" floppy drives rotate at 300 rpm. If the speed is not regulated and constant, you may not be able to read the disk.

 # Head actuator motor

The head actuator motor is electronically linked to the File Allocation Table. If a request is received to read data from a particular track, say track 20, the actuator motor moves the heads to that track. Floppy drives have two heads, one on top and bottom. They are connected and move as a single unit.

Several large companies such as Sony, Toshiba, Fuji, Teac, and others manufacture the floppy drives. Each company's prices are within a few dollars of the others. Most of them are fairly close in quality, but there may be minor differences.

On some of the older drives, a fairly large actuator stepping motor is used to position the heads. It is very quiet and works smoothly as it moves the heads from track to track. It has a steel band around the motor shaft that moves the heads in and out.

The actuator stepping motors on most of the newer drives are small cylindrical motors with a worm screw. The motors groan and grunt as they move the heads from track to track. Other than being a bit noisy, they have worked perfectly.

 # Head misalignment

If the software tells the actuator motor to move the heads to track 20, it knows exactly how far to move the heads. If for some reason, the steel band or the worm screw that is attached to the actuator motor shaft becomes loose or out of adjustment, the drive may not be able to find the proper tracks. If the hub of the disk you are trying to read has become worn or not centered exactly on the spindle by the cone, the heads may not be able to find a track that was previously written, or one that was written on another drive.

If your heads are out of alignment, you can write and read on your own machine, since you are using the same misalignment to write and read. But another drive may have trouble reading a disk recorded with misaligned heads. And you may not be able to read disks recorded on another drive. You could take such a drive to a repair shop and they could align the heads, but it would probably cost more for the repair than for a new floppy drive. Many shops charge from $75 to $100 an hour for service. You can buy a new floppy drive for about $40.

 # Floppy controllers

A floppy drive must have a controller to direct it to specific tracks and sectors. In the early days, the controller was a large board full of chips. Later, manufacturers integrated the floppy disk controller (FDC) onto the same board as the hard disk controller (HDC). These were large full-length boards that were rather expensive at about $250. Now the floppy drive controllers (FDCs) are usually built into a single VLSI chip and integrated with a hard disk controller or IDE interface. The controllers that cost as much as $250 a few years ago now cost less than $10. Many of the motherboards now have the FDC and the IDE hard disk interface built-in. These motherboards usually have a set of upright pins for the flat ribbon cable connectors.

 # Drive select jumpers

It is possible to have four different floppy drives connected to one controller. The floppy drives have a set of pins with a jumper so each

drive can be set for a unique number. The pins may be labeled DS0, DS1, DS2, and DS3 or some manufacturers label them DS1, DS2, DS3, DS4. The vast majority of systems use only two drives so two of the sets of pins are hardly ever used.

These jumpers also let you determine which drive is A: or B:. In most cases, you use them as they come from the factory and never have to worry about these jumpers. Most drives are received with the second set of pins jumpered, which means they are set for drive A:. If you install a second floppy drive, it will also have a set of pins jumpered just like the A: drive. Don't change it. Since the floppy cable has some twisted wires in it, the controller automatically recognizes it as drive B:. This can be confusing and you may or may not get any documentation at all with your drive. Fortunately, they usually work fine as received from the factory.

The combination drives usually have small jumper pins near the miniature power cable connector. The combos have two columns of pins, one for each drive. There are six pins in each column and four pins in each column are jumpered. Again, you should never have to reset or bother with these pins. The two drives share a single controller cable connector. If you want to use the 5¼" drive as drive A:, then plug the end of the cable with the twisted wires into the cable connector. If you want the 3½" 1.44MB drive to be drive A:, then plug in the middle connector that has no twists. Again, fortunately, there is usually no need to move the jumpers.

Extended density drives

The 3½" extended density (ED) 2.8MB floppy drives have been available for a couple of years, but not too many people are using them. The 2.8MB disks have a barium ferrite media and use perpendicular recording to achieve the extended density. In standard recording, the particles are magnetized so they lay horizontally in the media. In perpendicular recording, the particles are stood vertically on end for greater density.

The ED drives require a controller that operates at 1 MHz. The other floppy controllers operate at 500 kHz. Several companies are now integrating the ED controller with the other floppy controllers.

The ED drives are downward compatible and can read and write to the 720K and 1.44MB disks. At the present time, the ED drives and disks are still rather expensive. They will come down eventually.

The virtual drive

DOS reserves the letters A and B for floppy drives. If you only have one drive, you can call it both. For instance, you can say, copy A: to B: The drive copies whatever is in the drive, then prompt you to insert a disk in drive B:. Of course, you could have said copy A: to A: and gotten the same results.

Very high-density drives

The floppy technology continues to advance. Several new higher capacity drives and disks are now available.

Bernoulli drives

The Iomega Corporation, at (801) 778-1000, has a high capacity Bernoulli floppy disk system. Their system allows the recording of up to 150 megabytes on special 5¼" floppy disks. Using the Stacker compression software, the 150MB floppy holds 300MB. With a Bernoulli drive, you need never run out of hard disk space. The Bernoulli can be used instead of a hard disk or in conjunction with a hard disk.

The Bernoulli disks spin much faster than a standard floppy, which forces the flexible disk to bend around the heads without actually touching them. This is in accordance with the aerodynamics principle discovered by the Swiss scientist, Daniel Bernoulli (1700–1782).

The Bernoulli floppy disks spin at 2368 rpm. The ordinary floppy spins at 300 rpm. In order to keep the Bernoulli from flexing too much at the high speed, the floppy is placed within two steel plates.

The Bernoulli system stores data on one side of the floppy only. For the lower capacity systems, a single floppy is used; for the higher capacity disks, two floppy disks are sandwiched together and each is recorded on the outer side.

The average seek time for the Bernoulli systems is 32 ms. The better hard drives have about 10 ms.

Since the floppies can be removed and locked up, they are an excellent tool for security. They are also an excellent tool for making backups of your hard disks. You can back up 300MB in just seconds with Bernoulli. It would take hours using floppy disks and a lot of intensive swapping of disks.

Look in the computer magazines such as the *Computer Shopper* or *PC World* for ads and current prices. Or call Bernoulli for brochures and nearest dealer.

 # The Zip drive

Iomega has also developed a small, low-cost drive, called the Zip drive. It uses a 3½" disk that is similar to the 3½" floppy disk. The big difference is that this disk can store 100MB. The drive is very inexpensive at less than $200 and the 100MB disks cost less than $20 each. The drive can be mounted internally or externally. This drive is ideal for making backups or can even replace hard drives.

 # Data compression

Data compression can double your disk capacity. One of the most popular compression programs is Stacker from Stac Electronics, (800) 522-7822. MS-DOS versions 6.0 and up come with a compression utility. DR DOS 7.0 and IBM PC DOS also have compression utilities.

At one time, data compression wasn't completely trusted. But bulletin boards have been using it for years with very few problems. Many of

the backup programs use compression so fewer disks are needed. Compression has matured and it is now trustworthy and reliable. Compression programs are now fast and transparent to the user.

The compression programs can be used with floppy and hard disks to double their capacity. Compression can be the least expensive way to increase disk capacity.

 # Differences among floppy disks

The 5¼" 360K and the 3½" 720K disks are called *double-sided double-density (DS/DD)*. The 5¼" 1.2MB and the 3½" 1.44MB are called *high-density (HD)*. The 3½" 720K double-density disks are usually marked DD, the high-density disks are usually marked HD. But the 5¼" 360K and the 1.2MB disks usually have no markings. They look exactly alike, except that the 360K usually has a reinforcing ring or collar around the large center hole. The high density 1.2MB disks do not have the ring.

One of the major differences between the 720K and the 1.44MB is that the high density 1.44MB has two small square holes at the rear of the plastic shell, while the 720K has only one. The 3½" drive has a small media sensor microswitch that protrudes upwards. If it finds a hole on that side of the disk, it knows that it is a 1.44MB disk. If there is no hole, it is treated as a 720K.

When looking at the back side of a 3½" disks, the square hole on the right rear of the shell has a small black slide that can be moved to cover the hole. A small microswitch on the drive protrudes upward and checks this hole when the disk is inserted. If the hole is covered, the switch is pressed downward, allowing the disk to be written on. If the hole is open, the switch protects the disk so it cannot be written on or erased. The 3½" write protect system is just the opposite of the system used by the 5¼" disks. They have a square notch that must be covered with opaque tape to prevent writing or unintentionally erasing the disk. (Incidentally, you must use opaque tape. The 5¼" system uses a light to shine through the square notch. If the detector in the system can see the light through the notch, then it can write on

the disk. Some people have used clear plastic tape to cover the notch with disastrous results.)

There might be a time when you would want to make a diskcopy of a 720K and all you have are 1.44MB disks. Or for some reason you might want to use a 1.44MB as a 720K. You can cover the hole with any kind of tape and it will format as a 720K.

Another difference between the 5¼ and the 3½" disks is that the 5¼" floppy has a small hole near the center. A light shines through this hole to indicate where track one begins. The 3½" disks don't need this hole.

360K and 1.2MB

Although the 360K and 1.2MB disks look exactly alike except for the hub ring on the 360K, there is a large difference in their magnetic media formulation. Several materials such as cobalt or barium can be added to the iron oxide to alter the magnetic properties. Cobalt is added to increase the Oersted (Oe) of high density floppy disks. Barium is used for the 2.88MB extra high density (ED) disks. Oe is a measure of the resistance of a material to being magnetized. The lower the Oe, the easier it is to be magnetized. The 360K has an Oe of 300, the 1.2MB is 600 Oe. The 360K disks are fairly easy to magnetize or write to, so they require a fairly low head current. The 1.2MB is more difficult to magnetize so a much higher head current is required. The 1.2MB system can switch the current to match whatever type of disk you tell the system you are using.

If you place a 360K floppy in a 1.2MB drive and just type format, it will try to format it as a 1.2MB. But it will find several bad sectors, especially near the center where the sectors are shorter. These sectors will be marked and locked out. The system may report that you have over a megabyte of space on a 360K disk. This disk could be used in an emergency, for instance to move data from one machine to another. But I would not recommend that you use such a disk for any data that is important. The data is packed much closer together when it is recorded as 1.2MB. Since the 300 Oe of the 360K disks are so easy to magnetize, it is possible that nearby data may migrate and eventually deteriorate and become unusable.

 # 720K and 1.44MB

The 3½" disks have several benefits and characteristics that make them superior to the 5¼" disks. The 720K disk can store twice as much data as a 360K in a much smaller space. The 1.44MB can store four times as much as a 360K disk in the same small space.

The 720K 3½" disks may have an Oe of 600 to 700. The 1.44MB may have an Oe of 700 to 720. The Oe of the extra high density 2.88MB disks may be about 750.

The 3½" floppy disks have a hard plastic protective shell, so they are not easily damaged. They also have a spring loaded shutter that automatically covers and protects the head opening when they are not in use.

The 3½" systems are much more accurate than the 5¼" systems in reading and writing. The 5¼" drive systems have a cone shaped hub for the large center hole in the disks. If the disks are used for any length of time, it is possible for the hole to become stretched or enlarged. If the disk is not centered exactly on the hub, the heads will not be able to find and read the data.

The 3½" floppies have a metal hub on the back side. This gives them much greater accuracy in reading and writing, even though the tracks on the 3½" systems are much closer together.

 # One-way insertion

It is possible to insert a 5¼" floppy upside down, backwards, or sideways. When I first started using computers, I inserted a floppy that had some original expensive software on it into a drive. I waited for a while and nothing happened. Then I got an error message, Not ready reading drive A. Abort, Retry, Fail? I almost panicked. I thought for sure that I had destroyed the software. I finally discovered that I had inserted the floppy upside down. I was still scared that I had damaged the disk. So I did what I should have done when I first got the program. I put a piece of tape over the square notch to write protect it, then I made a diskcopy backup of the disk. I found that the software was still okay.

You can't actually damage a disk by inserting it upside down. You can't read it because the small hole that tells DOS where track one begins is on the wrong side when inserted upside down. And of course, you can't write to it or format because of the small hole and also because the write protect notch is on the other side.

The 3½" disks are designed so they can only be inserted properly. They have arrows at the left top portion of the disks that indicate how they should be inserted into the drive. They have notches on the backside that prevent them from being completely inserted upside down.

Disk format structure

Before a disk can be used, it must be formatted into tracks and sectors.

Tracks

Formatting consists of laying out individual concentric tracks on each side of the disk. If it is a 360K disk, each side is marked or configured with 40 tracks, numbered from 0 to 39.

If it is a 1.2MB, 720K, or 1.44MB, each side is configured with 80 tracks, numbered from 0 to 79 on the top and bottom of the disk. The top is side 0 and the bottom is side 1. When the head is over track 1 on the top, it is also over track 1 on the bottom. The heads move as a single unit to the various tracks by a head actuator motor or positioner. When data is written to a track, as much as possible is written on the top track, then the head is electronically switched and it continues to write to the same track on the bottom side. It is much faster and easier to electronically switch between the heads than to move them to another track.

 # Cylinders

If you could strip away all of the other tracks on each side of track 1 on side 0 and track 1 on side 1, it would be very flat, but it might look like a cylinder. So if a disk has 40 tracks, such as the 360K, it has 40 cylinders; the 1.2MB and 1.44MB each have 80 cylinders.

 # Sectors

Each of the tracks are divided up into sectors. Each track of the 360K is divided into 9 sectors, each of the 1.2MB tracks are divided into 15 sectors, each of the 720K tracks are divided into 9 sectors, each of the 1.44MB tracks into 18 sectors, and the 2.88MB tracks into 36 sectors. Each sector can contain 512 bytes. Multiplying the number of sectors times number of bytes per sector times the number of tracks times two sides gives the amount of data that can be stored on a disk. For instance, the 1.2MB has 15 sectors times 512 bytes times 80 tracks times two sides would be $15 \times 512 \times 80 \times 2 = 1,228,800$ bytes. The system uses 14,898 bytes to mark the tracks and sectors during formatting so there is actually 1,213,952 bytes available on a 1.2MB floppy.

Figure 6-1 is a diagrammatic representation of how the tracks and sectors are laid out on a disk.

 # Clusters or allocation units

DOS allocates one or more sectors on a disk and calls it a *cluster* or *allocation unit*. On the 360K and 720K disks, a cluster or allocation unit is two sectors. On the 1.2MB and 1.44MB each allocation unit is one sector. Only single files or parts of single files can be written into an allocation unit. If two different files were written into a single allocation unit, the data would become mixed and corrupted.

 # File allocation table (FAT)

During formatting, a file allocation table (FAT) is created on the first track of the disk. This FAT acts like a table of contents for a book.

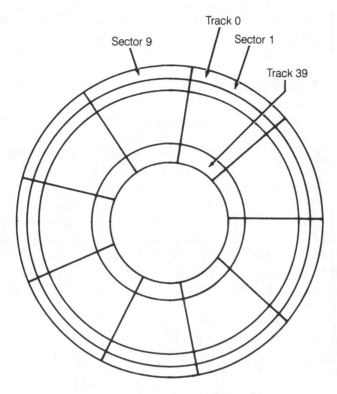

Figure 6-1

A diagram showing how the tracks and sectors are laid out on a disk

Whenever a file is recorded on a disk, the file is broken up into allocation units. The head looks in the FAT to find empty units, then records the parts of the file in any empty units it can find. Part of the file may be recorded in sector 5 of track 10, part in sector 8 of track 15, and any other place it can find empty sectors. It records the location of all the various parts of the file in the FAT. With this method, parts of a file can be erased, changed, or added to without changing the entire disk.

 # TPI

The 40 tracks of a 360K are laid down at a rate of 48 tracks per inch (TPI) so each of the 40 tracks is 1/48 of an inch wide. The 80 tracks of the high density 1.2MB are laid down at a rate of 96 TPI, so each

track is ¹⁄₉₆ of an inch. The 80 tracks of the 3½" disks are laid down at a density of 135 per inch or 0.0074 inch per track.

 # Read accuracy

The 5¼" disks have a 1⅛-inch center hole. The drives have a flexible plastic cone that presses down through the center hole of the disk when the drive latch is closed. This centers the disk so the heads will be able to find each track. The plastic material that the disk is made from is subject to environmental changes and wear and tear. The flexible cone may not center each disk exactly so head to track accuracy is difficult with more than 80 tracks. (If you have trouble reading a disk, it might be off center. It might help if you remove the disk and re-insert it.) Most of the 360K disks use a reinforcement hub ring, but it probably doesn't help much. The 1.2MB floppies do not use a hub ring. Except for the hub ring, the 360K and 1.2MB disk look exactly the same.

If your drive consistently has trouble reading your disks, or especially reading disks recorded on another machine, the heads may be out of alignment.

The 3½" disks have a metal hub on the back that is used to center the disks. The tracks of the 3½" floppies are narrower and greater in density per inch. But because of the metal hub, the head tracking accuracy is much better than that of the 5¼" systems.

 # Some differences between floppies and hard disks

Hard disks have very accurate and precise head tracking systems. Some hard disks have a density up to 3000 or more tracks per inch so much more data can be stored on a hard disk.

The floppy disks have a very a smooth lubricated surface. They rotate at a fairly slow 300 rpm. Magnetic lines of force deteriorate very fast with distance. So the closer the heads, the better they can read and write. The floppy heads are in direct contact with the floppy disks. Hard disks rotate at speeds from 3600 up to 7200 rpm. The heads and surface would be severely damaged if they came in contact at this speed. So heads "fly" over the surface of each disk, just a few millionths of an inch above it.

 Comparison of floppy disks

Table 6-1 shows some of the differences in the various types of floppy disks. Notice that the maximum number of root directories is the same for the 720K, the 1.2MB, and the 1.44MB. The 2.88MB has four times the capacity of the 720K, yet allows only 16 more root entries. This means that you can enter 224 different files on a 1.2MB disk, but if you try to enter one more, it will not accept it, even though you may have hundreds of unused bytes.

Capacities of Various Disk Types

Table 6-1

Disk type	Tracks per side	Sectors/ track	Unformatted capacity	System use	Available to user	Maximum directories
360K	40	9	368640	6144	362496	112
1.2M	80	15	1228800	14898	1213952	224
3½"	80	9	737280	12800	724480	224
3½"	80	18	1474560	16896	1457664	224
3½"	80	36	2949120	33792	2915328	240

The reason is that the DOS file allocation table was designed for this limited number of files. There is an easy way around this problem. Just create sub directories like those created on a hard disk. Just type MD for make directory. If necessary, you can even make sub directories of the sub directories.

Formatting

To format a 360K disk with the 1.2MB drive, type FORMAT A /4. To format a 1.2MB disk, you only have to type FORMAT A:. If you

insert a 360K disk without the /4, it will try to format it to 1.2MB. It will probably find several bad sectors.

To format a 720K disk on a 1.44MB B: drive, type FORMAT B: /f:720. To format a 1.44MB disk, just type FORMAT B:.

The format command in newer versions can take a very long time before it starts. It searches the floppy disk then saves any information it finds on the disk. If you decide later that you want to unformat the disk, just type unformat. But for most cases, you don't want to unformat a disk. Especially if it is one that has never been formatted before. You can speed up the formatting process by typing format a:/u. This performs an unconditional format. If the disk has been formatted and used previously, you can type format a:/q. This gives you a quick format by just erasing the first letter of the files in the file allocation table of the disk.

The MS-DOS manual is not too much help for many commands, including help for formatting. The on-disk help is much better for most commands. If you have trouble with the format command, just type help format. For any command that you need help with, just type help then the command.

 # Format batch files

Here are some batch files that save me a lot of time in formatting disks. Here is how I made my batch files:

```
COPY CON FM36.BAT
C: FORMAT A: /4/U
^Z

COPY CON FM12.BAT
C: FORMAT A:/U
^Z

COPY CON FM72.BAT
C: FORMAT B: /F:720/U
^Z

COPY CON FM14.BAT
C: FORMAT B:/U
^Z
```

The ^Z indicates the end of the file. It is made by pressing F6, or the ^ over the numeral 6 and Z. With these batch files I only have to type FM36 for a 360K, FM12 for a 1.2MB, FM72 for a 720K or FM14 to format a 1.44MB.

⇨ Cost of disks

All floppy disks are now quite reasonable. The 1.2MB HD disks are selling at discount houses for as little as 21 cents apiece, or 25 cents each if preformatted. The 1.44MB are selling for 35 cents each or 39 cents each if preformatted. There are several discount mail order floppy disk stores. Check the computer magazines for ads.

These are real bargains. At one time, I paid as much as $2.50 each for 360K floppy disks.

CHAPTER 7

Choosing and installing a hard disk

LARGE books have been written about hard disks. But even a whole book cannot cover all of the questions that you may have about hard disks. This chapter covers some hard drive basics, some of the different types of hard drives, and how to install them in the computer. This chapter also explains how to format and configure hard disks once they are installed.

The IBM term for hard disk drives is *Direct Access Storage Devices* (*DASD*, pronounced *dazdee*). The hard drives are also called *Winchester* drives. The IBM plant that developed the first hard drives is located near the Winchester House in San Jose, California. The house was built by the widow of the famous inventor of the Winchester .30-.30 repeating rifle. The first IBM hard disk had 30 tracks and 30 sectors per track. Since the IBM system was a 30/30 someone hung the name Winchester on it. You don't hear it too often nowadays, but for several years all hard drives were called Winchester drives.

A hard disk is a precise piece of machinery. The tracks may be only a few millionths of an inch apart. The head actuator must move the heads quickly and accurately to the specified track. In the early 1980s a 20MB hard disk cost over $2500. You can buy a 2-gigabyte hard disk today for about $800 or less. That is 100 times greater capacity for one third of the cost.

Floppy and hard drive similarities

A hard disk drive is similar to a floppy disk drive in some respects. Floppy drives have a single disk; the hard drives may have an assembly of one or more rigid disk. The hard disks platters are coated with a magnetic plating, similar to that of the floppy disks. Depending on the capacity, there may be several disks on a common spindle. A motor turns the floppy spindle at 300 rpm; the hard disk spindle may turn from 3600 rpm up to 7200 rpm.

Just like the floppy, there is a read/write head on the top and one on the bottom of each disk. On floppy disk systems, the head actually contacts the disk; on a hard disk system, the head *flies* just a few millionths of an inch from the disk on a cushion of purified air. If the head contacts the disk at the high speed that it turns, it would cause a *head crash*. A crash can destroy the disk, the head, and all the data that might be on the disk.

 ## Tracks and sectors

Like the floppy disk, the hard disk is formatted into several individual concentric tracks. A 360 floppy has 40 tracks on each side; a high capacity hard disk may have 3000 or more tracks per side. Also like the floppy, each hard disk track is divided into sectors, usually of 512 bytes. But the 360K floppy system divides each track into 9 sectors; a hard disk system may divide each track into as many as 84 sectors.

 ## Clusters and allocation units

A sector is only 512 bytes, but most files are much longer than that, so DOS lumps two or more sectors together and calls it a *cluster* or *allocation unit*. If an empty cluster is on track 5, the system records as much of the file as it can there, then move to the next empty cluster, which could be on track 20. DOS combines sectors into allocation units depending on the capacity of the hard disk. For a 100MB disk DOS combines four sectors, or 2048 bytes, into each allocation unit; for 200MB each allocation unit is composed of 8

sectors or 4096 bytes. The higher the capacity of the disk, the more sectors each allocation unit has.

One slight disadvantage to this is that if you have a lot of short files, it may use up a lot of disk space. No two files can be written in the same allocation unit. So if a file is only 96 bytes long, depending on the cluster configuration, you may have space for 4000 or more unused bytes in an allocation unit.

 # File allocation table

The location of each part of the file and which cluster it is in, is recorded in the file allocation table (FAT) so the computer has no trouble finding it. Usually the larger the hard disk partition, the more sectors are assigned to each cluster or allocation unit.

A 500MB hard disk would actually have 524,288,000 bytes. Dividing this number by 512 bytes to find the number of actual sectors gives 1,024,000 sectors. If each allocation unit is made up of four sectors, there would only be 256,000 of them; if eight sectors are used, then DOS would only have to worry about the location of 128,000 allocation units. If DOS had to search through 1,024,000 entries in the FAT each time it accessed the hard disk, it would slow things down considerably. The FAT is updated and rewritten each time the disk is accessed. A large FAT would take a lot of time and disk space.

The FAT is very important. If it is damaged or erased, you will not be able to access any of the data on the disk. The heads just wouldn't know where to look for the data. The FAT is usually written on track 0 of the hard disk. Because it is so important, a second copy is also made near the center of the disk so if the original is damaged, it is possible to use the copy.

 # Cylinders

Just like the floppy, each same numbered track on the top and bottom of a disk platter is called a *cylinder*. Since a hard disk may

have up to ten or more platters, the concept of cylinders is a bit more realistic than that of a single floppy disk. Incidentally, the BIOS chips in some of the older computers may not allow you to install a hard disk that has more than 1024 cylinders and 63 sectors, which is about 504MB. It is possible to install a disk larger than 500MB by using special driver software. One of the reasons for developing the Enhanced Integrated Disk Electronics (EIDE) specification was to overcome this limitation. EIDE is discussed in more detail later in this chapter.

Head actuators or positioners

Like the floppy, a head motor or head actuator moves the heads from track to track. The head actuator must move the heads quickly and accurately to a specified track then detect the small variations in the magnetic fields in the specified sectors. Some of the older hard disks used a stepper motor similar to those used on floppy disk drives to move the head from track to track. Most all hard disks now use a voice coil type of motor that is much smoother, quieter, and faster than the stepper motors.

The voice coil of a loudspeaker is made up of a coil of wire that is wound on a hollow tube that is attached to the material of the speaker cone. Permanent magnets are then placed inside and around the outside of the coil. Whenever a voltage is passed through the coil of wire, it causes magnetic lines of force to be built up around the coil. Depending on the polarity of the input voltage, these lines of magnetic flux will be either the same or opposite the lines of force of the permanent magnets. In magnetism, like poles repel each other, opposites attract. The polarity of the voltage then causes the magnetic lines to move the voice coil in or out.

Figure 7-1 shows a hard drive with the cover removed to show the heads and disks. The voice coil actuator is the section in the rear left corner of the assembly. It can quickly and accurately swing the arm and head to any track on the disk.

Figure 7-1

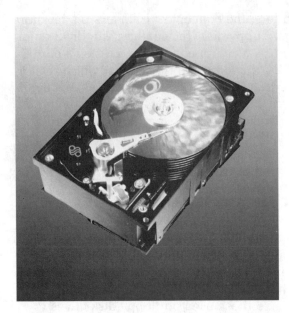

A Seagate hard disk with the cover removed. The voice coil actuator that moves the heads is in the rear left corner.

 # Speed of rotation and density

Just like the floppy system, as the disk spins beneath the head, a pulse of voltage through the head coil causes the area of the track that is beneath the head at that time to become magnetized. If this pulse of voltage is turned on for a certain amount of time, then turned off for some amount of time, it can represent the writing or recording of 1s and 0s. The hard disk spins much faster than a floppy so the duration of the magnetizing pulses can be much shorter at a higher frequency.

The recording density depends to a great extent on the changes in magnetic flux. The faster the disk spins, the greater the number of changes. This allows much more data to be recorded in the same amount of space.

Head spacing

The amount of magnetism that is placed on a disk when it is recorded is very small. It must be small so it does not affect other recorded bits or tracks near it. Magnetic lines of force decrease as you move away from a magnet by the square of the distance. So it is desirable to have the heads as close to the disk as possible, within millionths of an inch.

 Disk platters

The surface of the hard disk platters must be very smooth. Because the heads are only a few millionths of an inch away from the surface, any unevenness could cause a head crash. The hard disk platters are usually made from aluminum, which is nonmagnetic, and lapped to a mirror finish. They are then coated or plated with a magnetic material. Some companies also use tempered glass as a substrate for the platters. A few companies are also experimenting with plastic such as that used for CD-ROM discs.

The platters must be very rigid so the close distance between the head and the platter surface is maintained. The early 5¼" hard disks were fairly thick in order to achieve the necessary rigidity. Being thick, they were heavy and required a fairly large spindle motor and lots of wattage to move the large amount of mass.

If the platter is made smaller, it can be thinner and still have the necessary rigidity. If the disks are thinner, then more platters can be stacked in the same area. The smaller disks also need less power and smaller motors. With smaller diameter disks, the heads don't have to travel as far between the outer and inner tracks. This improves the access time tremendously. Most drives today are 3½" or less in size.

You should avoid any sudden movement of the computer or any jarring while the disk is spinning because it could cause the head to crash onto the disk and damage it. Most of the newer hard disk systems automatically move the heads away from the read/write surface to a parking area when the power is turned off.

I worked for Ampex Corporation during the early 1970s. They developed one of the first hard disks for military use. It was 16¼ inches in diameter and was ¼ inch thick. It could store 1.5MB on each side for a total of 3MB, which was a tremendous amount at that time. See Fig. 7-2. Figure 7-3 shows a small drive made for a Personal Computer Memory Card International Association (PCMCIA) slot. This small drive can store about 100 times more data than the original large Ampex disk.

Figure 7-2

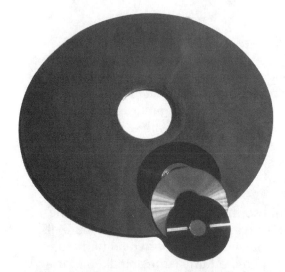

The large disk is an early hard disk that could store 1.5Mb on each side. The newer, smaller disks can store hundreds of times more data. Top to bottom: The 5¼" disk can store 200MB on each side; the CD-ROM disc can store 650MB; and the 3½" disk can store 200MB.

Figure 7-2

A small hard disk in the PCMCIA format

How they can make smaller drives

Some of the reasons they can make the hard disks smaller now are because better plating materials, thinner disks, better motors, and better electronics have been developed.

Zone bit recording

The old MFM drives divided each track into 17 sectors. A track on the outer edge of a 5¼" platter would be over 15 inches long if it were stretched out. You can determine this by using the simple math formula for π times the diameter. So π or 3.14159×5.25 is 16.493 inches in length. A track on the inner portion of the disk may only be 1.5 inches times π or 4.712 inches in length.

It is obvious that you should be able to store more data in the outer longer tracks than in the short inner tracks. That is exactly what the newer drives do by using zone bit recording (ZBR). The platters on the Maxtor 540MB drive is divided up into 8 different zones. Zone 1 has the inner tracks that are shorter. This zone has 48 sectors per track; the outer zone 8 has 87 sectors per track.

Rotational speed and recording density

The Recording Density or bits per inch (bpi) for each Zone also changes from the inner tracks to the outer tracks. The reason for this is that the speed at which the inner tracks pass beneath the heads is faster than that of the outer tracks.

The overall drive speed is still another way of increasing the amount of storage. The old MFM drives spun at 3600 rpm. The newer drives have a rotational speed of 6300 and up to 7200 rpm or more. The higher the speed of the disk, the higher the recording frequency and the higher the data density.

Of course, the rotational speed of the disk is also one of the factors that determines the seek, access, and transferal time. If you want to access data on a certain track, the faster the disk rotates, the sooner that sector is available for reading.

The hard disk technology has improved tremendously over the last ten years.

Partial response, maximum likelihood (PRML)

Another reason they can make the drives smaller is because of PRML system. This system was first developed by IBM several years ago. This system involves electronics that allows them to store up to 25% more data on a disk. The PRML system is being used by Quantum, Western Digital, and several companies.

Factors to consider in choosing a hard drive

You have the option of a very large number of different types and capacities of disks from which to choose. Of course, what you choose depends on what you need to do with your computer and how much you want to spend.

Capacity

When you consider capacity, buy the biggest you can afford.

You may have heard of Mr. C. Northcote Parkinson. After observing business organizations for some time, he formulated several laws. One law says, "Work expands to fill up available employee time." A parallel law that paraphrases Mr. Parkinson's immutable law might say, "Data expands to fill up available hard disk space."

Don't even think of buying anything less than 200MB. Better yet would be 500MB minimum. New software programs have become more friendly and offer more options. Most of the basic application programs that you need, such as spreadsheets, databases, CAD programs, word processors, and many others, each require 10 to 30 megabytes of disk storage space. Windows NT requires about 80MB.

Most of the major hard disk drives are fairly close in quality and price. My recommendation is to buy the highest capacity drive that you can possibly afford. Hard disk drives are now selling for less than 50 cents per megabyte.

 # Speed or access time

Speed or access time is the time it takes a hard disk to locate and retrieve a sector of data. This includes the time that it takes to move the head to the track, settle down, and read the data. For a high end, very fast disk, this might be as little as 9 milliseconds (ms). Some of the older drives and systems required as much as 100 ms.

 # IDE or AT type drives

The most popular drives today are those with Integrated Drive Electronics (IDE). They are sometimes called *ATA* (for *Advanced Technology Attachment*) drives because they were first developed for use on the 286 AT. The drives are similar to the SCSI drives in that all of their controller electronics are integrated on the drive. You do not need a controller card such as those required by the older MFM, RLL, and ESDI drives, but you do need an interface. The interface may be a plug-in card or it may be a set of upright pins on the motherboard.

 # Enhanced IDE

The BIOS in some older systems cannot recognize a hard disk with more than 1024 cylinders, so until recently many IDE drives had a

maximum capacity of 540MB. The Enhanced IDE (EIDE) specification handles drives up to 1.6GB. With a special BIOS, it is possible to go as high as 8.4GB.

The EIDE specification is somewhat similar to SCSI. It supports up to four IDE devices, including CD-ROM and tape drives. Many companies are now manufacturing CD-ROM drive for the EIDE interface. These CD-ROM drives are usually much less expensive than SCSI CD-ROM drives.

The old IDE specification has a transfer rate of 4.3 megabytes per second. The EIDE specification allows data transfer up to 13.3 megabytes per second. Of course, to achieve this transfer rate, you must have a hard disk that can meet the specification.

Installation configuration

The following configuration instructions are similar whether you are installing IDE or EIDE drives. You should receive some instructions with your drive documentation. If you are only installing a single IDE drive, the installation may be very simple. The drive probably has jumpers set at the factory that makes it drive #1 or master drive. Check your documentation and the jumpers, then just plug the 40 pin cable into the drive connector and the other end into a board interface or into a set of pins on the motherboard. You must make sure that the colored side of the ribbon cable goes to pin one on the drive and on the interface.

If you are installing a second IDE drive, you need to set some jumpers so the system knows which drive to access. When two IDE drives are installed, the IDE system uses the term *Master* to designate the C: or boot drive and the term *Slave* to designate the second drive. You have to place small jumpers on the drives to configure them. If the drives are not configured properly, you will get an error message that may tell you that you have a hard disk or controller failure. You will not be able to access the drives.

Some drives have pins that can be jumpered so they will be read-only. This is a type of write protection that is similar to write protecting a

Figure 7-1

The pen points to small jumpers that are used to configure IDE drives.

floppy. This could be used on a hard disk that had data that should never be changed or written over.

In Fig. 7-4 the pen points to some small configuration jumpers. Your drive will probably be different. You should have received some documentation with your drive. If you don't have the configuration information, call the company or dealer. Here are technical support numbers for some of the more popular companies:

➢ Conner Peripherals has technical support at (408) 456-3388. They have a BBS at (408) 456-4415 and FaxBack information at (800) 426-6637.

➢ The Maxtor Corp. has technical support at (800) 262-9867. They have a BBS at (303) 678-2222 for 2400 baud or (303) 678-2020 for 9600 baud. The modem should be set for 8 data bits, one stop bit, and no parity.

➢ Quantum Corp. offers free technical support at (800) 826-8022. Quantum also has a Fax on Demand System. If you call

(800) 434-7532 from your fax machine, they can send you documentation and configuration specifications for all of their products. When you call you should ask for their Product Catalog that lists all available documents by number. You can review the catalog and order whatever document you may need. Quantum also has a BBS at (408) 894-3214.

➤ You may call the Seagate Technology Corp. at (800) 468-3472 for technical support. Seagate also has a bulletin board that has a Technical Desk Reference file that lists most of their hard disk configurations. Their BBS is at (408) 438-8771. Set communications software for 8 bits, no parity, and one stop bit (8-N-1). The Seagate BBS also has some free software that can be downloaded. Their FINDTYPE and FINDINIT can help make installation of AT drives easier.

➤ You may call Western Digital at (800) 832-4778. They have a BBS for 2400 baud at (714) 753-1234, for 9600 baud and up, they have a BBS at (714) 753-1068.

⇨ IDE interface board

One reason that the IDE and EIDE drives cost less than SCSI drives is because of the very inexpensive interface. Figure 4-6 shows a VLB IDE interface card. It is also a multi input/out (I/O) card with an interface for IDE drives, a floppy disk controller, parallel printer ports, and two serial ports. An IDE or EIDE interface/multi I/O card can be plugged into any of the eight slots.

Since the IDE and EIDE interface is so simple and inexpensive many vendors have built it onto the motherboard by providing a set of upright pins on the motherboard. A single cable can be plugged into these pins to control two IDE drives. For EIDE systems there are two sets of pins. This saves the cost of a controller and also saves one of your slots. These motherboards usually also have a built-in controller for floppy drives, pins for the LPT1 printer port, and pins for serial ports.

When plugging the connectors into the pins be very careful that you locate pin one on the board and plug the cable in so the colored wire

goes to the pin one side. If you plug the cable in backwards, you could possibly damage some of the fragile transistors and electronics.

There are more expensive IDE and EIDE interfaces such as the VESA Local bus (VLB) or the Intel Peripheral Component Interconnect (PCI) bus. Some of these interfaces may have up to 2MB or more of RAM cache that can vastly accelerate the hard disk operations. Of course, the extra memory adds to the cost of the interface.

The older IDE systems are still good for most purposes. But for faster, larger capacity, high-end systems, you should look for EIDE drives and interfaces.

SCSI

Most companies who manufacture IDE and EIDE drives also make identical small computer system interface (SCSI, pronounced *scuzzy*) drive models. The built-in electronics on IDE and SCSI drives are very similar.

A SCSI board can interface up to seven different intelligent devices to a computer. SCSI devices are called *logical units*. Each device is assigned a logical unit number (LUN). The devices have switches or jumpers that must be set to the proper LUN. Sometimes you may see a reference that says SCSI can handle up to eight units. That is because the interface board is actually counted as a logical unit.

It is possible to install up to four different interface boards in a PC with seven different SCSI units on each of the four interface boards. So you should be able to run 28 different SCSI devices from a PC. But you can only have one device per letter of the alphabet. DOS reserves A and B for floppy drives and C for the boot drive so you could only have a maximum of 24 SCSI devices.

The different devices may be two or more hard SCSI type hard disk drives, one or more CD-ROM drives, a scanner, a tape backup unit, and other scuzzy products.

Besides handling up to seven SCSI products, many of the interface boards also have a built-in controller for two floppy drives.

You should be aware that not all SCSI interfaces are equivalent. There are some that are made for special purpose devices, so they may not have all of the functionality of other SCSI interfaces.

 # SCSI drivers

Most hard drives require that you enter the drive type into the CMOS setup. The setup lists several drive types that describe the hard disk characteristics. The setup allows only two drives and they must be the same particular type such as two IDE, two ESDI, two RLL, or two MFM drives. The SCSI interface has its own drivers so it does not have to be entered into the CMOS setup.

 # Advanced SCSI Programming Interface

Advanced SCSI Programming Interface (ASPI) is a set of standards that was first developed by the Adaptec Company. Adaptec has been one of the foremost companies in the design of SCSI products. The ASPI standard has been widely accepted by most other manufacturers. You still need a separate driver from each manufacturer for individual devices. These drivers are set up in your Config.Sys file, then the ASPI driver is installed in the Config.Sys. If the device drivers are software compatible to the ASPI specification, the ASPI driver then controls the other drivers. It is much easier to install SCSI devices that comply with the ASPI standard.

The Corel Company has one of the best drawing and graphics software programs available. Corel, at (800) 836-7274, has also developed one of the better programs for installing SCSI devices. CorelSCSI is ASPI software that supports hundreds of SCSI devices. It makes it very easy to daisy chain up to seven devices and install the device software drivers. CorelSCSI supports hard drives, removable hard drives, CD-ROM drives, CD-ROM Juke Boxes, DAT tape drives, QIC tape drives, WORM and Magneto-Optical hard drives, and other SCSI devices.

An industry committee designed another SCSI specification they called *Common Access Method (CAM)*.

Host adapters or interfaces

There are SCSI adapters for ISA, EISA, VLB, PCI, and MCA systems. Adapters may have one or more megabytes of cache memory. Some adapters may have a built-in floppy controller on the board. There are also 8-bit, 16-bit, and 32-bit SCSI adapters. Many of the newer adapters are plug and play and very easy to install.

Of course, the price of the adapters can vary considerably. The price depends on factors such as brand name, amount of cache, built-in goodies, and whether 8-, 16-, or 32-bit bus. SCSI adapters are usually more expensive than IDE interfaces.

Both Adaptec, at (408) 945-8600, and Future Domain, at (714) 253-0400, manufacture almost any type of adapter interface you could want.

 # Fast SCSI-2 and wide SCSI-2

SCSI-1 as defined in 1986 is an 8-bit bus with a transfer rate of 5 MHz. In 1992, ANSI added the SCSI-2, which can allow data transfer rates up to 10 MHz. It is backward compatible so it can also support SCSI-1 devices.

Wide SCSI-2 is a 16-bit bus that allows twice as much data to be transferred. The transfer rate can be as high as 20 MHz. This specification also allows as many as 16 devices, counting the host adapter. The wide SCSI-2 has a 68-pin connector.

 # Cables and connectors

The standard SCSI cable is a 50-wire flat ribbon cable. The standard connectors are Centronics types, but some devices may have a small miniature connector. Most devices have two connectors in parallel for attaching and daisy-chaining other devices.

Not all of the 50 wires in a flat ribbon cable are needed for data. Many of the wires are ground wires placed between the data wires to help

keep the data from being corrupted. The better, and more expensive, cables are round cables with twisted and shielded wires. This type of cable may be necessary for distances greater than six feet.

You should be aware that the advertised price of a SCSI device usually does not include an interface or cables. It may not even include any software drivers. Be sure to ask about these items whenever you order a SCSI device.

Removable disk drives

There are several companies that manufacture removable disk drives. There are several different models and types. There are some advantages and disadvantages in removable drives.

Bernoulli drives

The Iomega Company, (801) 778-1000, is no doubt the best known company for removable disk drives. They first began with a 20MB floppy cartridge, then 40MB, 90MB, and now they have a 150MB.

They can be used instead of, or with, a hard drive system. Iomega provides drives that operate with three different types of interfaces, the SCSI, IDE, and a proprietary interface.

The Bernoulli drives are the same size as the old standard half-height drives, so they can be mounted in a standard size bay. But Iomega also manufactures drives for external use. Since you need a power supply and cables, the external units are more expensive.

One disadvantage of the Bernoulli system is that it is a bit slower than the newer hard disks. Another is that it is somewhat limited in storage capacity compared to the newer hard disks. But one big advantage is that you do not have to worry about the Bernoulli drive crashing. If the head does come into contact with the soft floppy disk, it causes little or no damage.

The Bernoulli disk cartridges are very sturdy. They have a 1000 G rating, which means you could drop them about 8 feet with no damage. The cartridges are ideal for shipping data through the mails. Unless the mailman runs over the cartridge with a truck, the data should arrive intact.

The Zip drive

Iomega has developed the Zip, a drive which uses a 3½" disk that is similar to the 3½" floppy disk. The big difference is that this disk can store 100MB. The drive is very inexpensive at less than $200 and the 100MB disks cost less than $20 each. The drive can be mounted internally or externally. This drive is ideal for making backups or can even replace hard drives.

SyQuest drives

SyQuest, at (800) 437-9367, has several models of removable hard disk cartridges. Each cartridge is actually a single hard disk platter. SyQuest uses zone bit recording (ZBR) on some of their disks. At the present time, the maximum SyQuest cartridge capacity is 270MB. Data compression can be used to double the capacity.

For the increased capacity, they use ZBR to divide the disks into zones. The 105MB disk is divided into two zones. The outer, longer tracks are divided into 52 sectors per track, with 512 bytes per sector. The inner zone tracks are divided into 72 sectors per track, but each sector is only 256 bytes. This is unusual because almost all systems use 512 bytes per sector.

SyQuest also has 60MB and 80MB 1.8" removable drives that can be used in the PCMCIA type III slots.

They have both external and internal drives that operate off a SCSI adapter. Read the ads carefully; some vendors have advertised the drives at a very low price, then in very small letters at the end of the ad it says "Controller card optional."

 # PCMCIA hard drives

Several companies have developed 60MB to 340MB 1.8" drives that fit in the type III PCMCIA slots. These drives are ideal for lap top and notebook computers that have the PCMCIA slots. Many desktop computers are now installing PCMCIA slots. The small plug-in PCMCIA hard disks are much smaller than floppies, can store an enormous amount of data, and are very fast. Of course, they are ideal for security, for backup, or for transfer of data from one computer to another.

The PCMCIA specification allows a card or hard disk to be inserted or removed without having to shut off the power to the main system.

 # Magneto-optical drives

The magneto-optical (MO) drives are a combination of the magnetic and optical technologies. Magnetic disks, especially floppies, can be easily erased. Over a period of time, the data on a magnetic disk, hard or floppy, will gradually deteriorate. Some critical data must be renewed about every two years.

If a magnetic material has a high coercivity, or a high resistance to being magnetized, it will also resist being de-magnetized. (Coercivity is measured in Oersteds [Oe].) But the higher the Oe, the more current that is needed to magnetize the area. A large amount of current may magnetize a large area of the disk. In order to pack more density, the magnetized area must be very small.

The Oe of a material decreases as it is heated. Most materials have a Curie temperature whereby the Oe may become zero. By heating the magnetic medium with a laser beam, a very small current can be used to write data to a disk. The heated spots cool very quickly and regain their high coercivity. The disks can be easily written over or changed by heating up the area again with the laser beam.

The most popular MO drives at this time have a capacity of 128MB and 256MB. The MO disks have a minimum lifetime of more than 10 years without degradation of data.

Parallel port hard drives

SyQuest and other companies have parallel port models that can be used with lap tops, PS/2s, or any computer with a parallel port. These drives are great for backup, for removal and security, and for data transport.

Since these drives plug into the computer's only parallel port, the hard drives usually provide a parallel port connector for the printer.

 # Recordable CD-ROMs

There are several companies who now offer drives that can record CD-ROM discs. When first introduced, the recordable drives cost up to $10,000. Some are available today for less than $2000.

The CD-ROM blank disc can hold up to 650MB of data. This is a great way to back up or archive data and records that should never change. However, the blank CD-ROM discs cost less than $20 each, so if you wanted to change some of the data, just change the data and record it onto another disc.

Unlike magnetic media that deteriorates or can be erased, data on a CD-ROM should last for many, many years.

 # WORM drives

Write once, read many (WORM) drives use the optical technology similar to the CD-ROM. One of the differences is that there are no standards for the WORM drives. There are different sizes from 5¼ inches to 12 inches in diameter. Much more data can be stored on one of these drives.

Unlike the CD-ROM system that uses a single winding track from the center outward, the WORM drives use the same system used by hard drives, that is, separate concentric tracks and sectors.

The WORM drive systems are usually more expensive than the recordable CD-ROM systems.

Advantages of removable disk drives

Here are some of the advantages of removable disks or cartridges:

Security

There may be data on a hard disk that is accessible to other people. If the data is sensitive data, such as company design secrets or personal employee data, the removable disks can be locked up for security.

Unlimited capacity

With enough cartridges you never have to worry about running out of disk space. If you fill one cartridge, just pop in another and continue.

Fast backup

One reason people don't like to back up their data is that it is usually a lot of trouble and takes a lot of time. It may take several hours to back up a large hard drive onto tape; it may take only seconds or minutes to back up the same data onto a removable drive. A big advantage of the removable cartridge backup is that the data can be randomly accessed; a tape backup can only be accessed sequentially. If you want a file that is in the middle of the tape, you must run through the tape to find it.

Moving data to another computer

If you have two or more computer systems with the same type removable drives, you can easily transfer large amounts of data from one machine to another. It is possible to send the data on a cartridge through the mails to other locations that have the same type system.

Multiple users of one software copy

Most people don't bother to read the license agreements that come with software. And who can blame them. The agreements may be one or more pages long, in small type, and filled with lawyer-type jargon. Essentially, most of them simply say:

> You are granted the right to use one copy of the enclosed software on a single computer.

But supposing that you have several computers in an office. Some of the people may be doing nothing but word processing most of the time. Others may be running databases or spreadsheets. Occasionally, these users may have need to use one of the other programs for a short time. If these users all have standard hard disks, then legally, you need a separate copy of all of the software used on the computers. Some software programs may cost from $500 to $1000 or more. If you have several computers in an office, providing individual packages for each machine can be quite expensive.

If these computers had removable disks, then a copy of a software program could be installed on the cartridge and the cartridge could be used on the different machines when needed.

Some disadvantages of removable drives

Limited cartridge capacity

Many of the removable cartridges have a small capacity that may not be enough to store all of the data that you need to operate some of today's large programs. You could have the program on two separate cartridges, but in accordance with Murphy's law, there will always be times when you need to access a file that is on the other cartridge.

 # Cost of cartridges

Another disadvantage is that the removable drives may cost a bit more than a standard hard drive. Except for the ZIP drive disks, which cost less than $20, the cost for other cartridges may be from $70 to over $100 each. But if you consider that, with enough cartridges, the capacity is unlimited, the cost may be quite reasonable.

The MO disks are about the least expensive of all the cartridges, but the initial cost of the drive itself is much higher than other drives.

 # Access speed

Still another disadvantage is that some of the removable drives are a bit slower than most standard hard drives. The MO drives are especially slow because it takes time to heat the area with the laser. But if you don't mind waiting a few milliseconds, it shouldn't be too much of a problem.

 # Data compression

The capacity of all of the hard drives mentioned above can be doubled by using data compression with them. MS-DOS, IBM PC DOS, and DR DOS all have a disk compression utility. Stacker, from Stac Electronics, at (619) 431-7474, has one of the most popular stand-alone compression utilities. Some people worry about data compression, but I have never had any problems with Stacker.

Using data compression is certainly less expensive and easier than installing a second, or larger, hard disk.

 # Mean time between failures (MTBF)

Disk drives are mechanical devices. If used long enough, every disk drive will fail sooner or later. Manufacturers test their drives and assign them

an average life time that ranges from 40,000 to 150,000 hours. Of course, the larger the figure, the longer they should last (and the more they cost). These are average figures, much like the figures quoted for a human lifespan. The average person should live to be about 73 years old. But some babies die very young, and some people live to be over 100. Likewise, some hard disks die very young, some older ones become obsolete before they wear out. At one time, I thought that MTBF meant *Mean Time Before Failure*. But since it means *Mean Time Between Failures*, there is no guarantee that a new disk won't be defective the first time it is turned on.

 # Partition and formatting procedure

Before you can use an IDE or EIDE hard drive, its type must be entered into the CMOS setup. Then it must be partitioned and formatted. SCSI hard drives are not entered into the CMOS setup, but they must be partitioned and formatted. See Chapter 3 for these instructions.

 # Sources

Local computer stores and computer swap meets are a good place to find a disk. You can at least look them over and get some idea of the prices and what you want. Mail order is a very good way to buy a hard disk. There are hundreds of ads in the many computer magazines.

CHAPTER 8

Backup: disaster prevention

M AKING backups is a chore that most people dislike, but if your data is worth anything at all, you should be making backups of it. You may be one of the lucky ones and never need it. But there are thousands of ways to lose data. Data may be lost due to a power failure or a component failure in the computer system. In a fraction of a second, data that may be worth thousands of dollars could be lost forever. It may have taken hundreds of hours to accumulate and it may be impossible to duplicate it. Yet, many people do not back up their precious data. Most of these people are those who have been fortunate enough not to have had a major catastrophe. Just as sure as we have earthquakes in California, if you use a computer long enough, you can look forward to at least one unfortunate disaster. But if your data is backed up, it doesn't have to be a catastrophe.

By far, most losses are the result of just plain dumb mistakes. I have made lots of mistakes in the past. No matter how careful I am, I will make mistakes in the future. When the poet said, "To err is human," he could have been talking about me. And, possibly, thee.

Write protect your software

When you buy a software program you should make a diskcopy of the program and store the original away. If you should ruin the copy, you can always make a new copy from the original. But the very first thing you should do before you make a diskcopy is write protect the original floppies. It is very easy to become distracted and write on a program disk in error. This would ruin the program. The vendor might give you a new copy, but it would probably entail weeks of waiting and much paperwork.

If you are using 5¼" floppies, you should cover the square write protect notch with a piece of opaque tape. Don't use clear tape. The drive focuses a light through the square notch. If the light detector can sense the light, it allows the disk to be written on, read, or erased. If the notch is covered with opaque tape, the disk can be read, but cannot be written on or erased. Some vendors now distribute their programs on disks without the square notch.

If you are using 3½" disks, you should move the small slide on the left rear side so the square hole is open. The 3½" write protect system is just the opposite of the 5¼" system. The 3½" system uses a small microswitch. If the square hole is open, the switch allows the disk to be read, but not written on or erased. If the slide is moved to cover the square hole, the disk can be written on, read, or erased.

It takes less than a minute to write protect a disk. It might save months of valuable time. If a program disk is ruined because it was not protected it may take weeks to get a replacement for the original. You may even have to buy a complete new program.

Protect your original floppies

Your valuable original program floppy disks should be protected from dirt and dust, especially the 5¼" floppies. There is a simple, easy way to protect them. Just seal them in clear plastic sandwich bags.

Of course, you know that the originals should not be placed near any magnet or magnetic source. They also should not be exposed to heat or left in a closed car on a hot summer day. I ruined a half dozen disks one day by leaving them in a closed car where the sun could hit them.

.BAK files

There are functions in many of the word processors and some other programs that create a .BAK file each time you alter or change a file.

The .BAK file is usually just a copy of the original file before you changed it. You can call a .BAK file up, but you may not be able to edit it or use it unless you rename it. Usually, just changing the .BAK extension is all that is necessary. WordStar and several other word processors can be set up to automatically save any file that you are working on at certain times when there is no activity from the keyboard. If there is a power outage, or you shut the machine off without saving a file, chances are that there is a backup of it saved to disk.

Unerase software

One of the best protections against errors is to have a backup. The second best protection is to have a good utility program such as Norton's Utilities or PC Tools. These programs can Unerase a file or even Unformat a disk. When a file is erased, DOS goes to the FAT table and deletes the first letter of each file name. All of the data remains on the disk *unless a new file is written over it*. If you have erased a file in error, or formatted a disk in error, **DO NOT DO ANYTHING TO IT UNTIL YOU HAVE TRIED** using a recover utility. There are several unerase and undelete utilities such as Norton's Utilities from Symantec Corporation, at (408) 253-9600, PC Tools from Central Point Software, at (503) 690-8090, DOSUTILS from Ontrack Computer Systems, at (800) 752-1333, or any of several other recovery utilities. To restore the files, most of the utilities ask you to supply the missing first letter of the file name.

MS-DOS delete protection

Erasing or deleting files by mistake is so common that Microsoft licensed the undelete technology from one of the major utility companies and includes an Undelete command in late versions of MS-DOS. There are three levels of protection with Delete, Sentry, Delete Tracker, and the standard Undelete. PC DOS 7.0 from IBM also has similar undelete utilities.

The undelete command is available immediately from any DOS prompt and any directory. To find out more about the undelete command, type help undelete at any DOS prompt and any directory.

The early versions of MS-DOS made it very easy to format your hard disk in error. If you happened to be on your hard disk and typed FORMAT, it would immediately begin to format your hard disk and wipe out everything. Later versions will not format unless you specify a drive letter.

The early versions of DOS would also let you copy over another file. If two files were different, but you told DOS to copy one to a directory that had the file with the same name, the original file would be gone forever. MS-DOS 6.2 and IBM PC DOS 7.0 now ask if you want to overwrite the file.

Jumbled FAT

The all important file allocation table (FAT) was discussed in the previous chapter about disks. The FAT keeps a record of the location of all the files on the disk. Parts of a file may be located in several sectors, but the FAT knows exactly where they are. If for some reason track 0, where the FAT is located, is damaged, erased, or becomes defective, you will not be able to read or write to any of the files on the disk.

Because the FAT is so important, a program such as PC TOOLS and Norton Utilities can make a copy of the FAT and store it in another location on the disk. Every time you add a file or edit one, the FAT changes. So these programs make a new copy every time the FAT is altered. If the original FAT is damaged, you can still get your data by using the alternate FAT.

Norton Utilities from Symantec, at (408) 253-9600, is an excellent utility software package. If you accept the defaults when installing Norton Utilities 8.0, it adds a line to your autoexec.bat file that causes Norton to scan your disk and analyze the boot record, file allocation tables (FAT), analyze directory structure, analyze file structure, and check for lost clusters or cross linked files. It then reads the FAT and stores a copy in a different place on the hard disk.

 # Reason for smaller logical hard disks

Early versions of DOS would not recognize a hard disk larger than 32MB. DOS can now handle hard drive capacities up to several gigabytes. Most programs seem to be designed to be installed on drive C:. You could have a very large drive C:, but if this large hard disk crashed, you might not be able to recover any of its data. DOS allows you to use the FDISK command when formatting your disk to divide it up into as many as 24 logical drives. If the same disk was divided into several smaller logical drives, and one of the logical sections failed, it might be possible to recover data in the unaffected logical drives.

A very fast way to back up is to copy the data from one logical drive to another. This type of backup is very fast and very easy. But it doesn't offer the amount of protection that a separate hard drive would offer. Still it is much better than no backup at all.

 # Head crash

The heads of a hard disk *fly* over the disk just a few microinches from the surface. They have to be close in order to detect the small magnetic changes in the tracks. The disk spins at 3600 rpm on some older drives and up to 7200 rpm on some of the newer drives. If the heads contact the surface of the fast spinning disk, they can scratch it and ruin the disk.

A sudden jar or bump to the computer while the hard disk is spinning can cause the heads to crash. Of course, a mechanical failure or some other factor could also cause a crash. You should never move or bump your computer while the hard disk is running.

Most of the newer disks have a built-in safe park utility. When the power is removed, the head is automatically moved to the center of the disk where there are no tracks.

The technology of the hard disk systems has improved tremendously over the last few years. But hard disks are still mechanical devices. And as such, you can be sure that eventually they will wear out, fail, or crash.

I worked in electronics for over 30 years and am still amazed that a hard disk works at all. It is a most remarkable mechanical device. It is made up of several precision components. The mechanical tolerances must be held to millionths of an inch in some devices such as the flying head and the distances between the tracks. The magnetic flux changes are minute, yet the heads detect them easily and output reliable data.

Despite all of the things that could go wrong with a hard disk, most hard disks are quite reliable. Manufacturers quote figures of several thousand hours *mean time between failure (MTBF)*. However these figures are only an average, so there is no guarantee that a disk won't fail in the next few minutes. If a disk should fail and you get it repaired, it should last as long as their guarantee says before it fails again. A hard disk is made up of several mechanical parts. If the disk is used long enough, eventually it will wear out or fail.

Crash recovery

Despite the MTBF claims, hard drives do fail. There are lots of businesses that do nothing but repair hard disks that have crashed or failed. A failure can be frustrating, time-consuming, and make you feel utterly helpless. In the unhappy event of a crash, depending on its severity, it is possible that some of your data can be recovered, one way or another.

There are some companies that specialize in recovering data and rebuilding hard disks. Many of them have sophisticated tools and software that can recover some data if the disk is not completely ruined. If it is possible to recover any of the data, Ontrack Computer Systems, at (800) 752-1333, can probably do it. There are several others. Look in the computer magazine ads.

The cost for recovery services can be rather expensive. But if you have data that is critical and irreplaceable, it is well worth it. It is a whole lot cheaper to have a backup copy.

 # Preventing hard disk failures

During manufacturing, the hard disk platters are coated or plated with a precise layer of magnetic material. It is almost impossible to manufacture a perfect platter. Most all hard disks end up with a few defective areas after being manufactured. When the vendor does the low-level format, these areas are detected and marked as bad. They are locked out so that they cannot be used. But there may be areas that are borderline bad that won't be detected. Over time some of the areas may change and lose some of their magnetic characteristics. They may lose some of the data that is written to them.

There are several companies that manufacture hard disk utilities that can perform rigorous tests on the hard disk. These software programs can exercise the disk and detect any borderline areas. If there happens to be data in an area that is questionable, the programs can usually move the data to another safe area.

The ScanDisk command in MS-DOS 6.2 basically does what some of the standalone utilities do. It does a surface test of the hard disk and reports on any areas that are questionable. It can move any data from those areas to safer areas. It then marks the questionable areas as bad. The bad areas are listed in the FAT just as if they were protected files that cannot be written to or erased.

Disk Technician from Prime Solutions, at (619) 274-5000, is a much more sophisticated and comprehensive software program than ScanDisk. It can be set up to automatically check your hard disk every time you boot up. It can detect errors, recover data, and relocate data that is in danger.

SpinRite from Gibson Research, at (714) 362-8800, was developed by Steve Gibson, who writes a very interesting column for *InfoWorld*. Version 3.1 is a complete data recovery and disk repair system. It can

read and recover most data from both hard and floppy disks that DOS may tell you is unreadable. It analyzes and tests the disks for surface defects and moves endangered data to safe areas. SpinRite can work with most types of hard disks and disk compression systems.

The SpinRite user manual is about the briefest of any that I have ever seen. It only has 30 pages with very brief instructions and has several screen shots. But don't let the brief manual fool you. You don't really need a lot of instructions. It is a robust program and has extensive help on disk.

A few reasons why they don't back up and why they should

Here are a few of the lame excuses used by some people who don't back up their software.

Don't have the time

This is not a good excuse. If your data is worth anything at all, it is worth backing up. It takes only a few minutes to back up a large hard disk with some of the newer software. It may take just seconds to copy all of the files to a directory on another logical drive of the disk or to another hard drive.

Too much trouble

It can be a bit of trouble unless you have an expensive tape automated backup system or a second hard disk. If you back up to floppies, it can require a bit of disk swapping, labeling, and storing. But with a little organizing, it can be done easily. If you keep all of the disks together, you don't have to label each one. Just stack them in order, put a rubber band around them, and use one label for the first one of the lot.

It is a bit of trouble to make backups. But if you don't have a backup, consider the trouble it would take to re-do the files from a disk that

has crashed. The trouble that it takes to make a backup is infinitesimal.

 # Don't have the necessary disks, software, or tools

If you use floppy disks, depending on the amount of data to be backed up, and the software used, it may require 50 to 100 disks. But it may take only a few minutes and just a few disks to make a backup of only the data that has been changed or altered. In most cases, the same disks can be reused the next day to update the files.

 # Failures and disasters only happen to other people

People who believe this way are those who have never experienced a disaster. There is nothing you can say to convince them. They just have to learn the hard way.

Outside of ordinary care, there is little one can do to prevent a general failure. It could be a component on the hard disk electronics or in the controller system, or any one of a thousand other things. Even things such as a power failure during a read/write operation can cause data corruption.

 # Theft and burglary

Computers are easy to sell so they are favorite targets for burglars. It would be bad enough to lose a computer, but many computers have hard disks that are filled with data that is even more valuable than the computer.

Speaking of theft, it might be a good idea to put your name and address on several of the files on your hard disk. It would also be a good idea to scratch identifying marks on the back and bottom of the case. You should also write down the serial numbers of your monitor

and drives. I heard of a story where a man took a computer to a pawn shop. The dealer wanted to see if it worked, so he turned it on. A name came up on the screen that was different than the name the man had given to the dealer. He called the police and the man was arrested for burglary. The owner of the computer was very happy to get it back. He was also quite fortunate. Most burglaries don't have a happy ending.

Another good idea is to store your backup files in an area away from your computer. This way there would be less chance of losing both computer and backups in case of a burglary or fire. You can always buy another computer, but if you had a large database of customer orders, files, and history, how could you replace that?

An article in a recent *Information Week Magazine* says that PC theft has increased over 400% since 1991. (*Information Week Magazine* is free to qualifying subscribers. See Chapter 17 for address.)

Archival

Another reason to back up is for archival purposes. No matter how large the hard disk is, it will eventually fill up with data. Quite often, there are files that are no longer used or that are only used once in a great while. I keep copies of all the letters that I write on disk. I have hundreds of them. Rather than erase the old files or old letters, I put them on a disk and store them away.

Data transfer

There are often times when it is necessary to transfer a large amount of data from one hard disk on a computer to another. It is quite easy to use a good backup program to accomplish this. Data on a disk can be used to distribute data, company policies and procedures, sales figures, and other information to several people in a large office or company. The data can also be easily shipped or mailed to branch offices, customers, or to others almost anywhere. If more companies used disks in this manner, we could save thousands of trees that are cut down for paper.

 # Types of backup

There are two main types of backup, the image and file oriented. An *image backup* is an exact bit-for-bit copy of the hard disk copied as a continuous stream of data. This type of backup is rather inflexible and does not allow for a separate file backup or restoration. The *file oriented* type of backup identifies and indexes each file separately. A separate file or directory can be backed up and restored easily. It can be very time-consuming to have to back up an entire 40 megabytes or more each day. But with a file oriented type system, once a full backup has been made, it is necessary only to make incremental backups of those files that have been changed or altered.

DOS stores an *archive attribute* in each file directory entry. When a file is created, DOS turns the archive attribute flag on. If the file is backed up by using DOS BACKUP or any of the commercial backup programs, the archive attribute flag is turned off. If this file is later altered or changed, DOS turns the attribute back on. At the next backup, you can have the program search the files and look for the attribute flag. You can then back up only those that have been altered or changed since the last back up. You can view or modify a file's archive attribute by using the DOS ATTRIB command.

There are several very good software programs on the market that let you use a 5¼" or 3½" disk drive to back up your data. Again, you should have backups of all your master software, so you don't have to worry about backing up that software *every day*. Since DOS stamps each file with the date and time it was created, it is easy to back up only those files that were created after a certain date and time.

Once the first backup is made, all subsequent backups need to be made of only data that has been changed or updated. Most backup programs can recognize whether a file has been changed since the last backup. Most of them can also look at the date that is stamped on each file and back up only those within a specified date range. So it may take only a few minutes to make a copy of only those files that are new or have been changed. And of course, it is usually not necessary to back up your program software. You do have the original software disks safely tucked away, don't you?

Backup.com

Early versions of MS-DOS included a Backup.com that was very slow and rather difficult to use. MS-DOS 6.0 and later versions have MSBackup for DOS and Windows Backup that are fast and easy to use. The MS-DOS backup can now compete with some of the commercial backup programs.

The MSBackup and Windows Backup can let you make full, incremental, or differential backups.

DR DOS and IBM PC DOS also have backup commands that are as good as or better than the MS-DOS commands.

The XCOPY command can also be used for backup. There are several switches that can be used with XCOPY. (A switch is a /.) For instance, XCOPY C:*.* A:/A copies only those files that have their archive attribute set to on. It does not reset the attribute flag. XCOPY C:*.* A:/M copies the files, then resets the flag. Whenever a disk on A: is full, you merely have to insert a new floppy and hit F3 to repeat the last command. This continues to copy all files that have not been backed up. XCOPY C:*.* A:/D:01-15-96 copies only those files created after January 15, 1996. There are several other very useful switches that can be used.

Check your MS-DOS, DR DOS, or IBM PC DOS manuals for more details on backup. All of these systems have built-in on-line help for all commands.

The MSBackup, Windows Backup, and Xcopy commands cannot be used with most tape backup systems. Tape backup systems usually have their own proprietary backup software.

Here are just a few commercial backup programs. There are many others.

 # Norton Backup for Windows

Norton Backup for Windows 3.0 from Symantec, at (800) 441-7234/(503) 334-6054, is very easy to use. It also supports most tape and SCSI drives. Norton Desktop for Windows combines Norton Backup for Windows plus other Norton Utilities.

 # PC Tools Backup 2.0 for Windows

PC Tools Backup 2.0 for Windows from Central Point Software, at (800) 964-6896/(503) 690-8088, is one of the few backup programs that can check for viruses. PC Tools is now a part of Symantec. This gives Symantec three of the most popular backup programs in existence. They will continue to market them separately for the time being.

 # Back-It 4 and Back-It 2.0 for Windows

Back-It 4 and Back-It 2.0 for Windows from Gazelle Systems, at (800) 786-3278/(801) 377-1288, are very good inexpensive backup programs. Back-it for Windows 2.0 has a list price of $50 at this time. The program checks for viruses.

 # XTree

XTree from the XTree Company, at (805) 541-0604, is an excellent shell program for disk and file management. It has several functions that make computing much easier. You can use it to copy files from one directory or disk to another very easily. I often use it to make backups when I only have a few files to back up. XTree is now a division of Central Point and PC Tools, which is now a division of Symantec.

 # Tape

There are several tape backup systems on the market. Tape backup is easy, but it can be relatively expensive, $250 to over $500 for a drive

unit and $10 to $20 for the tape cartridges. Some of them require the use of a controller that is similar to the disk controller. So they will use one of your precious slots, but there are some SCSI systems can be daisy-chained to a SCSI controller. There are also enhanced IDE tape systems that can be controlled by an EIDE interface.

Unless the tape drives are external models, they also require the use of one of the disk mounting areas. Since it is only used for backup, it will be idle most of the time.

There are some tape systems that run off the printer parallel port. These systems don't require a controller board that takes up one of your slots. Another big plus is that it can be used to back up several different computers by simply moving it from one to the other.

Like floppy disks, tapes have to be formatted before they can be used. But unlike a floppy disk, it may take over 2 hours to format a tape. You can buy tape that has been preformatted, but they cost quite a bit more than the unformatted tapes.

Tape systems are very slow, so the backups should be done at night or during off hours. Most systems can be set up so the backup is done automatically. If you set it on auto, you won't have to worry about forgetting to back up, or wasting the time doing it.

A disadvantage of tape is that data is recorded sequentially. If you want to find a file that is in the middle of the tape, it has to search until it finds it. Since disk systems have random access; they are much faster than tape.

DAT

Several companies are offering the digital audio tape (DAT) systems for backing up large computer hard disk systems. DAT systems offer storage capacities as high as 1.3 gigabytes on a very small cartridge. The DAT systems use a helical scan type recording that is similar to that used for video recording. The DAT tapes are 4 millimeters wide, which is about 0.156 inch.

Removable disks

One of the better ways for data backup and data security is to back up to a disk that can be removed and locked up. There are several different systems and companies that manufacture such systems.

Bernoulli drives

The Bernoulli systems from Iomega use a 5¼" floppy disk cartridge. They call them *Bernoulli* systems because the drives conform to *Bernoulli Effect*, the aerodynamic principles discovered by Daniel Bernoulli in the late 1700s. The Iomega floppy drives can be spun up to almost the speed of a hard disk. The floppy drive heads do not directly contact the floppy disk because of the Bernoulli Effect.

The Iomega Company has several different models. Disk compression can be used with the floppies, so their 150MB floppy can actually store about 300MB. These drives can be used instead of a hard drive for most purposes.

One disadvantage is that the Bernoulli drives are rather expensive and the cartridges are also a bit costly.

The Iomega Zip drive

The Iomega Zip drive uses a 3½" disk that is similar to a floppy. But this 3½" disk can store 100MB. This system is much less expensive than the Bernoulli. At this time, the Zip drives cost less than $200 and the disks cost less than $20. With a few disks, you would never have to worry about running out of hard drive space.

The Zip system is ideal for backup or for any type of data storage.

SyQuest Corporation

The SyQuest Corporation manufactures drives with removable disks that can store up to 270MB. Of course, data compression can be used to almost double this amount of storage.

PCMCIA

The Personal Computer Memory Card International Association (PCMCIA) cards were originally developed to add memory to portable computers, but many desktops are now using the cards. Several different products have been developed using the card format such as modems, faxes, network cards, and hard disk drives. These very small hard disk drives may have a capacity up to 400MB or more. They are ideal for making backups.

Magneto-optical drives

The magneto-optical drives (MO) are rather expensive, but the removable cartridges are low cost. They are a good choice for use as a normal hard drive and for backup.

Recordable CD-ROM

When they first came out, the recordable CD-ROM systems were very expensive at about $7000. Some companies are now selling them for less than $2000 and the prices are still dropping.

If you have a lot of data that needs to be permanently backed up, a CD-ROM can store over 600MB. An advantage of CD-ROM over magnetic systems is that data on a CD-ROM will last for many years. Magnetic data deteriorates and may become useless within ten years. Unlike the magnetic systems, the data on a CD-ROM cannot be erased, changed, or altered. If the data needs to be changed, just record it onto another disc.

At this time, the blank discs cost about $20 each, but the price will soon come down.

Second hard disk

The easiest and the fastest of all methods of backup is to have a second hard disk. It is very easy to install a second hard disk. The

EIDE interfaces can control up to four hard drives. You can add as many as seven hard drives to a SCSI interface.

A good system is to have an IDE drive for the C: boot drive and one or more SCSI drives. You can back up several megabytes of data from one hard drive to another very easily and quickly. The chances are very good that both systems would not become defective at the same time. So if the same data is stored on both systems, it should offer very good *RAID-like* protection.

 # RAID systems

RAID is an acronym for *redundant arrays of inexpensive disks*. There is some data that is absolutely critical and essential. In order to make sure that it is saved, data is written to two or more hard disks at the same time. Originally, five different levels were suggested, but only three levels, 1, 3, and 5, are in general use today.

Some RAID systems allow you to *hot swap* or pull and replace a defective disk drive without having to power down. You don't lose any information because the same data is being written to other hard disk drives.

To prevent data losses due to a controller failure, some RAID systems use a separate disk controller for each drive. A mirror copy is made of the data on each system. This is called *duplexing*. Some systems use a separate power supply for each system. And all systems use uninterruptible power supplies.

RAID systems are essential for networks or any other area where the data is critical and absolutely must be preserved. But no matter how careful you are and how many backup systems you have, you may still occasionally lose data through accidents or some other act of God. You can add more and more to the backup systems to make them fail-safe, but eventually you will reach a point of diminishing returns.

Depending on how much is spent and how well it is engineered, the system should be *system fault tolerant (SFT)*, that is, it will remain fully operational regardless of one or more component failures.

Uninterruptible power supplies

If you have a power failure or brownout while working on a file, you could lose a lot of valuable data. In areas where there are frequent electrical storms, it is essential that you have an uninterruptible power supply (UPS). The basic UPS is a battery that is constantly charged by the 110-volt input voltage. If the power is interrupted, the battery system takes over and continues to provide power long enough for the computers to save the data that might happen to be in RAM, then shut down.

There are several companies that manufacture quite sophisticated UPS systems for almost all types of computer systems and networks. Of course, for a single user, you only need a small system. On a network or for several computers, it requires a system that can output a lot of current.

There are several UPS companies. Here are just a few:

- ➤ Acme Electric Corp.   (716) 968-2400
- ➤ American Power Conversion   (800) 788-2208
- ➤ Best Power Technology   (800) 356-5794
- ➤ Deltec Corp.   (619) 291-4211
- ➤ Sola Electric   (800) 289-7652
- ➤ Tripp-Lite Mfg.   (312) 329-1777

Again, if your data is worth anything at all, it is worth backing up. It is much better to have a backup copy than to be sorry.

Input devices

 B EFORE you can do anything with a computer, you must input data to it. There are several ways to input data such as from a keyboard, a disk, by modem, mouse, scanner, bar code readers, voice recognition input, FAX, online from a bulletin board, mainframe, or a network.

Keyboards

By far the most common way to get data into the computer is by way of the keyboard. For most common applications, it is impossible to operate the computer without a keyboard.

The keyboard is a most personal connection with your computer. If you do a lot of typing, it is very important that you get a keyboard that suits you. Not all keyboards are the same. Some have a light mushy touch, some heavy. Some have noisy keys, others silent with very little feedback.

A need for standards

Typewriter keyboards are fairly standard. There are only 26 letters in the alphabet and a few symbols so most *QWERTY* typewriters have about 50 keys. But I have had several computers over the last few years and every one of them have had a different keyboard. The main typewriter characters aren't changed or moved very often, but some of the very important control keys like the ESC, the CTRL, the PRTSC, the \, the Function keys, and several others are moved all over the keyboard. IBM can be blamed for most of the changes.

There are well over 400 different keyboards in the U.S. Many people make their living by typing on a keyboard. Many of the large companies have systems that count the number of keystrokes that an employee makes during a shift. If the employee fails to make a certain number of keystrokes, that person can be fired. Can you imagine the problems if the person has to frequently learn a new keyboard? I am not a very good typist in the first place. I have great difficulty using different keyboards. There definitely should be some sort of standard.

Figure 9-1 shows three keyboards, each of them have a different key arrangement. The keyboard at the top is a Focus FK 5001. It is the one that I use most often. It has the all-important Function keys at the left of the keyboard where they are most handy for WordStar and WordPerfect users. It also has a duplicate set of Function keys along the top. This keyboard also has a built-in calculator at the right. When the calculator is turned off, the keypad works just like all other keyboards. This keyboard also has a slot at the top of the keyboard for holding program templates. It comes with several templates, such as WordStar, WordPerfect, Microsoft Word, Lotus 1-2-3, and dBASE IV. These templates have all of the basic commands and are very helpful. The keyboard at the top has a built-in trackball. It also has keys that are positioned differently than the others.

Innovation, creating something new that is useful and needed and makes life better or easier, is great. That type of innovation should be encouraged everywhere. But many times changes are made just for the sake of differentiation without adding any real value or functionality to the product. This applies not only to keyboards, but to all technology.

IBM hasn't introduced a new keyboard design in the last couple of years. Dare we hope that we finally have a design that will last a while?

How a keyboard works

The keyboard is actually a computer in itself. It has a small microprocessor with its own ROM. The computerized electronics of

Figure 9-1

Three keyboards with different key arrangements

the keyboard eliminates the bounce of the keys, can determine when you hold a key down for repeat, can store up to 20 or more keystrokes, and can determine which key was pressed first if you press two at a time.

In addition to the standard BIOS chips on your motherboard, there is a special keyboard BIOS chip. Each time a key is pressed a unique signal is sent to the BIOS. This signal is made up of a direct current voltage that is turned on and off a certain number of times, within a definite time frame, to represent zeros and ones.

Each time a 5-volt line is turned on for a certain amount of time, it represents a 1, when it is off for a certain amount of time it represents a 0. In the ASCII code, if the letter A is pressed, the code for 65 will be generated, 1 0 0 0 0 0 1.

 # Reprogramming key functions

Most word processors, spreadsheets, database, and other software programs usually designate certain keys to run various *macros*. A macro is a word, or several words, that can be input by just pressing one or more keys. By pressing a certain key or a combination of keys, you could have it input your name and address or any other group of words that you use frequently. These programs also use the function keys to perform various tasks such as moving the cursor, underlining, boldfacing, and many other functions. The problem is that there is no standardization. Changing from one word processor or software program to another is about like having to learn a new foreign language. It sure would be nice if you could go from one program to another as easily as you can drive different automobiles.

 # Keyboard sources

Keyboard preference is strictly a matter of individual taste. The Key Tronic Company of Spokane, (509) 928-8000, also makes some excellent keyboards. They are the IBM of the keyboard world. Their keyboards have set the standards. The Key Tronic keyboards have been copied by the clone makers, even to the extent of using the same model numbers.

Quality keyboards use a copper-etched printed circuit board and keys that switch on and off. The keys of quality keyboards have a small spring beneath each key to give them a uniform tension. Key Tronic offers several models. On some models they can even let you change the little springs under the keys to a different tension. The standard is 2 ounces, but you can configure the key tension to whatever you like. You can install 1, 1.5, 2, 2.5, or 3 ounce springs for an extra fee. They can also let you exchange the positions of the CapsLock and Ctrl keys. The Key Tronic keyboards have several other functions that are clearly described in their large manual. Call them for a copy.

Many of the less expensive keyboards are of very poor quality and workmanship. Instead of an copper-etched printed circuit board, many use a piece of plastic, then use conductive paint for the connecting lines. Instead of springs beneath each key, they use a rubber cup. The bottom of each key is coated with a carbon conductive material. When the key is depressed, the carbon allows an electrical connection between the painted lines. But despite the poor quality, the keyboards work fairly well.

I recently saw new clone keyboards being sold at a swap meet for $10 each. The keyboards looked very much like the Key Tronic 101 key types. The assembly snapped together instead of using metal screws. They also had several other cost saving features. But there is quite a lot of electronics in a keyboard. I don't know how they can possibly make a keyboard to sell for $10. At that price, you could buy two or three of them. If you ever had any trouble with one, just throw it away and plug in a new one.

There are several keyboard manufacturers with hundreds of different models. Prices range from $10 to $400 or more. Look through any computer magazine.

Specialized keyboards

Several companies have developed specialized keyboards. I have listed only a few of them here.

Quite often I have the need to do some minor calculations. The computer is great for calculations. There are several programs such as SideKick, Windows, and WordStar with built-in calculators. But most of these programs require the computer to be on and be using a file. A keyboard that is available from Jameco, (415) 592-8097, has a built-in solar powered calculator where the number pad is located. The calculator can be used whether the computer is on or not.

The Focus Electronic Corp., (818) 820-0416, has a series of specialized keyboards. They have keyboards with function keys in both locations, extra * and \ keys, and several other goodies. Their FK-9000 has a built-in calculator with a small battery in the keyboard

so it can also be used whether the computer is on or not. The keyboard has 8 cursor arrow keys. With these keys the cursor can be moved right or left, up or down, and diagonally up or down from any of the four corners of the screen. The speed of the cursor movement can be varied by using the 12 function keys. These 8 cursor keys can do just about everything that a mouse can do.

Besides their standard keyboards, Key Tronic has developed a large number of specialized ones. Instead of a key pad, one has a touch pad. This pad can operate in several different modes. One mode lets it act like a cursor pad. By using your finger or a stylus, the cursor can be moved much the same as with a mouse. It comes with templates for several popular programs such as WordStar, WordPerfect, DOS, and Lotus 1-2-3.

Another Key Tronic model has a bar code reader attached to it. This can be extremely handy if you have a small business that uses bar codes. This keyboard would be ideal for a computer in a point of sale (POS) system.

Carpal tunnel syndrome

Businesses spend billions of dollars each year for employee health insurance. Of course, the more employee injuries, the more the insurance costs. Carpal tunnel syndrome (CTS) has become one of the more common complaints. CTS causes pain and/or numbness in the palm of the hand, the thumb, index and ring fingers. The pain may radiate up into the arm. Any movement of the hand or fingers may be very painful. CTS is caused by pressure on the median nerve where it passes into the hand through the carpal tunnel and under a ligament at the front of the wrist. Either one or both hands may be affected. Treatment often requires expensive surgery that may or may not relieve the pain.

CTS most commonly affects those people who must use a computer for long periods of time. Keying in data is a very important function in this computer age. That is the job of many employees, eight hours a day, every day. CTS is usually caused by the way the wrist is held while typing on the keyboard. There are several pads and devices to

help make the typing more comfortable. I have a foam rubber pad that is the length of the keyboard and is about four inches wide and three quarters of an inch thick. I can rest and support my wrists on this pad and still reach most of the keys. Many of the vendors give them away at shows like COMDEX.

Repetitive Strain Injury (RSI) is about the same as CTS. Many employees are asking for workers compensation insurance and taking companies to court because of RSI. At the time of this writing, there are several cases in court against IBM, Apple, and several other large computer manufacturers. CTS and RSI have cost millions of dollars in loss of work days. They have become serious problems.

Before the computer revolution thousands and thousands of people, mostly women, sat at a typewriter eight or more hours a day typing on keyboards that are similar to computer keyboards. Yet, there were few, if any, cases of CTS or RSI ever reported. It is a disorder that has become prevalent only in the last few years. It could be that typewriter keyboards have more slant and were usually placed at a different height. Another factor may have been that the typewriter limited the typist's speed and repetition. Some data input workers can do as many as 13,000 keystrokes per hour.

The Key Tronic Company, at (509) 923-8000, has an ergonomic keyboard that breaks in the middle and each half can be elevated from the center. The center can be separated and angled to fit the angle of your hands. The B and N keys may be separated by as much as an inch or more, while the Y and T keys may be touching. The elevation and the angle should help prevent CTS and RSI. This Key Tronic keyboard is rather expensive at about $300. Figure 9-2 shows a fairly low cost ergonomic keyboard for about $40. The Key Tronic company developed a similar keyboard for Microsoft who sells it for $99. Several other companies have also developed ergonomic keyboards that should help reduce injuries.

Some of the ergonomic keyboards are a bit expensive, but they are a lot less expensive than having to go to a doctor for a painful operation that may or may not be successful. Other than surgery, the other alternative is to rest the hands and miss several months of work. If you work for a large company, the company might save money by installing these

Figure 9-2

An ergonomic keyboard

ergonomic keyboards. Many people are now suing the companies for CTS and RSI. Of course, the insurance companies are increasing their rates to help pay for any damages that may be awarded.

Mouse systems

One of the biggest reasons for the success of the Macintosh is that it is easy to use. With a mouse and icons, all you have to do is point and click. You don't have to learn a lot of commands and rules. A person who knows nothing about computers can become productive in a very short time. The people in the DOS world finally took note of this and began developing programs and applications such as Windows for the IBM and compatibles.

There are now dozens of companies who manufacture mice. There are some mice that may cost up to $100 or more; others may cost less than $10. What is the difference in a mouse that costs $100 and one that costs $10? The answer is $90. The low-cost mouse does just about everything that most people would need from a mouse. After all, how much mouse do you need just to point and click? Of course, if you are

doing high-end type drafting, designing, and very close tolerance work, then you probably need one that has the better resolution.

 # The ball type mice

The vast majority of all mice today are the ball type. The mouse has a small round rubber ball on the underside that contacts the desktop or mouse pad. As the mouse is moved, the ball turns. Inside the mouse, two flywheels contact the ball, one for horizontal and one for vertical movements. The flywheels are mounted between two light sensitive diodes. The flywheels have small holes in the outer edge. As they turn light shines through the holes or is blocked where there are no holes. This breaks the light up into patterns of 1s and 0s. The ball picks up dirt so it should be cleaned often.

 # Mouse interfaces

You can't just plug in a mouse and start using it. The software, whether Windows, WordPerfect, or a CAD program, must recognize and interface with the mouse. So mouse companies develop software drivers to allow the mouse to operate with various programs. The drivers are usually supplied on a disk. The Microsoft Mouse is the closest to a standard so most other companies emulate the Microsoft driver. Most mice today come with a small switch that allows you to switch between the Microsoft emulation or the IBM PC. If the switch is not in the proper position, it may not work.

The mouse plugs into a serial port, COM1 or COM2. This may cause a problem if you already have two serial devices using COM1 and COM2. DOS also allows for COM3 and COM4. These two ports must be shared with COM1 and COM2, but they must have special software in order to be shared.

The serial ports on some systems use a DB25 type socket connector with 25 contacts. Others may use a DB9 socket with 9 contacts. Many of the mice now come with the DB9 connector and a DB25 connector adapter. The DB25 connector looks exactly like the DB25 connector used for the LPT1 parallel printer port except that the

serial port connect is a male type connector with pins, the LPT1 printer port is a female with sockets.

There may be times when you have a cable that is a male when you need a female or vice versa. (A male connector is one that has pins, a female connector has sockets.) You can buy DB25 *gender bender* adapters that can solve this type of problem. If you simply need an extension so you can plug two similar cables together, that type of straight through adapter is also available. There are many different kinds of combinations. The Cables To Go Company, at (800) 225-8646, has just about every cable and accessory that you would ever need. The Dalco Electronics Company, at (800) 445-5342, also has many types of cables, adapters, and electronic components.

Before you buy a mouse, you might check the type of serial port connector you have and order the proper type. You can buy an adapter for about $3.

Loading the mouse driver

Mice usually come with software drivers that must be loaded into the system before the mouse will operate. The driver file for many of them is fairly small. I usually just install the mouse driver in the root directory C:>\, then put a line in my autoexec.bat file to load it each time the system boots up.

When you install Windows, it asks what kind of mouse you have. It then automatically loads the mouse driver each time you load Windows.

Trackballs

A trackball is a mouse that has been turned upside down. Like the mouse, the trackballs also require a serial port, or a slot if they are of the bus type.

One advantage of the trackball is that you don't need the square foot of desk space that a mouse requires. The trackballs are usually larger than the ball in a mouse, so it is possible to have better resolution.

They are often used with CAD and critical design systems. There are several companies who manufacture trackballs. Look through the computer magazines for ads.

Keyboard/trackball combination

Several companies have keyboards with a trackball built into the right hand area. This gives a person the mouse benefits and capabilities, without using up any desk real estate. The trackball is compatible with the standard Microsoft and Mouse Systems. In Fig. 9-1 the middle keyboard from Chicony has a built-in trackball.

Touch screens and light pens

Some fast food places now have a touch screen with a menu of several items. You merely touch the item that you want and the order is transmitted to the executive chef who is usually a young high school kid. The same type system is sometimes found in kiosks in shopping malls and large department stores. The touch system is accurate, saves time and money, and is convenient.

The touch screen operation is similar to using a mouse and pointing. Most of them have a frame installed on the bezel of the monitor. Beams of infrared light criss-cross the front of the monitor screen. For ordinary text, most monitors are set up so they have 80 columns left to right and 25 rows from top to bottom. Columns of beams originate from the top part of the frame and pass to the bottom frame. Rows of beams originate from the left portion of the frame and pass to the right frame. If one of the beams is interrupted by an object, such as a finger or pencil, the computer can determine exactly whatever character happens to be in that portion of the screen.

Joysticks

Joysticks are used primarily for games. They are serial devices and need an interface. Many of the multifunction boards that have COM ports also provide a game connector for joysticks.

Joysticks are fairly reasonable and may cost from $10 to $30. There are usually several ads for them in magazines such as the *Computer Shopper*.

 # Digitizers and graphics tablets

Graphics tablets and digitizers are similar to a flat drawing pad or drafting table. Most of them use some sort of pointing device that can translate movement into digitized output to the computer. Some are rather small, some may be as large as a standard drafting table. They may cost as little as $150 up to over $1500. Most of them have a very high resolution, are very accurate, and are intended for precision drawing.

Some of the tablets have programmable overlays and function keys. Some work with a mouse-like device, a pen light, or a pencil-like stylus. The tablets can be used for designing circuits, for CAD programs, for graphics designs, freehand drawing, and even for text and data input. The most common use is with CAD type software. The Wacom Technology Corp. at (206) 750-8882 also has a digitizer pad that uses a cordless, batteryless, pressure sensitive pen.

Most of the tablets are serial devices, but some of them require their own interface board. Many of them are compatible with the Microsoft and Mouse Systems.

The CalComp Company, (800) 932-1212, has developed several models. These tablets use a puck that is similar to a mouse except that it has a magnifying glass and cross-hairs for very high resolution. They have both corded and cordless pucks. Call CalComp for a brochure and more information.

 # Signature capture

It is very easy to generate a fax with a computer, but most letters and memos need a signature. The Inforite Company, at (800) 366-4635, has a small pad and a stylus that let you input a signature into a file. The signature can then be attached to a fax or to other documents.

With the Inforite, you can add notes, comments, or drawings to other documents in the computer.

 # Pressure-sensitive graphics tablets

Several companies have developed pressure sensitive tablets. Wacom has developed several different models. The Wacom tablets use an electromagnetic resonance system. This allows the use of a special stylus that requires no wires or batteries. The tablet has a grid of embedded wires that can detect the location of the stylus and the pressure that is applied. The tablets sense the amount of pressure and may draw a thin line or a heavy line in response.

The tablets can be used with different graphics software programs to create sketches, drawings, designs, and art.

Here are some of the companies who manufacture pressure-sensitive tablets:

➤ Wacom Technology	(800) 922-6613
➤ Communication Intelligence	(800) 888-9242
➤ Kurta Corp.	(602) 276-5533
➤ Summagraphics	(800) 337-8662

Call the companies for brochures or more information.

 # Scanners and optical character readers

Most large companies have mountains of memos, manuals, documents, and files that must be maintained, revised, and updated periodically. If a document is bound, the whole manual or document may have to be retyped and reissued. If a manual or document is in a loose-leaf form, then only those pages that have changed will need to be retyped.

How scanners and OCRs work

Optical character readers (OCR) can scan a line of printed type, recognize each character, and input that character into a computer just as if it were typed in from a keyboard. A beam of light sweeps across the page and the characters can be determined by the absorption and reflection of the light. One problem with the early scanners was that they could only recognize a few different fonts. They could not recognize graphics at all. The machines today have much more memory and the technology has improved to where the better scanners can recognize almost any font or type.

Optical character readers have been around for several years. When they first came out they cost from $6000 to more than $15,000. Many full page scanners are now fairly inexpensive, starting at about $500. Some handheld ones, that are rather limited, may be as low as $100. The more expensive models usually have the ability to recognize a large number of fonts and graphics.

 # The Logitech ScanMan

The Logitech ScanMan (Fig. 9-3) is a very versatile compact scanner. It attaches to the parallel port of the computer so it doesn't need a separate board. It scans in 256 shades of gray to input character data, drawings, or even photos into the computer. If you need a copy of a page, scan it into the computer then print it out. It can input printed text, signatures, drawings, or graphic images to a fax/modem board or to a hard disk.

 # What to look for when buying a scanner

What to look for depends on what you want to do with your scanner. And of course, how much you want to pay. There are several manufacturers of scanners and hundreds of different models, resolutions, bus types, and prices. A monochrome scanner is fine for

Figure 9-3

The ScanMan scanner from Logitech

text. Many monochrome scanners are relatively inexpensive. They may recognize text and graphic images in up to 256 different shades.

If you are buying a color scanner, there are a lot more options to consider. Some lower-priced ones may have to make three passes, once each for red, green, and blue. For each pass, light is sent through filters that can recognize 256 levels of red, green, or blue.

The less expensive scanners may have a resolution of only 300 or 400 dots per inch (dpi). But they may use interpolation software that fills in the spaces between the dots to give two or three times the true resolution. As you might expect, some ads may list the interpolated resolution in large letters and the true resolution in small letters if it is mentioned at all.

The more expensive color scanners can capture all three colors in one pass. They may also scan at a true 24-bit color depth to yield 16.7 million colors. That means that there can be 8 bits of color information about each of the red, green, or blue colors.

You should try to find a system that conforms to the *TWAIN* specification. The word TWAIN is an acronym for *Technology Without An Interesting Name*. (Mark Twain would have appreciated this acronym.) It is an Application Programming Interface (API) specification that was jointly developed by Aldus, Caere, Eastman Kodak, Hewlett-Packard, and Logitech. A different device driver is needed for each of the hundreds of different printers. Before TWAIN, you needed a different device driver from every manufacturer for each model and type of scanner. TWAIN helps to standardize some of the device drivers. We really need something like TWAIN for printers.

Some of the less expensive scanners use a proprietary interface board. It is much better to buy one that uses the SCSI interface. There are many manufacturers of scanners. Look at the ads in any of the computer magazines listed in Chapter 17.

OCR software

The OCR capabilities of a scanner allow it to recognize each character of a printed document and input that character into a computer just as if it were typed in from a keyboard. Once the data is in the computer, a word processor can be used to revise or change the data, then print it out again.

Faxes are received as graphical documents. It requires a lot of disk space to store a Fax. But a scanner can convert them to text that takes up much less disk space. Some of the OCR software, such as WordScan Plus from Calera, can work with a large number of different scanners. It can read degraded text by reading it in context. It has a large internal dictionary that helps in this respect. It yields excellent OCR accuracy.

Once data is entered into a computer it can be searched very quickly for any item. Many times I have spent hours going through printed manuals looking for certain items. If the data had been in a computer, I could have found the information in just minutes.

Several companies have developed advanced software to work with their scanners, and in some cases, those manufactured by other companies.

Here is a brief list of the companies who have OCR software:

> Caere Corp., (800) 535-7226, OmniPage Professional
> Calera Corp., (800) 544-7051, WordScan Plus
> Logitech Corp., (510) 795-8500, Catchword Pro
> Ocron, Inc., (408) 980-8900, Perceive
> Recognita Corp., (408) 241-5772, Recognita Plus
> Delrina Company, (408) 363-2345, WinFax PRO

 # Business card scanners

If you depend on business cards to keep in contact with prospective buyers or for other business purposes, you may have several files full of cards. Or you can take each card and enter the information into your computer database. There is an easier way. Some companies have developed card scanners that can read the information off a business card and input it to a computer.

At this time they are still a bit expensive, but if you depend on business cards, they are well worth it. Like most computer products, the prices will come down very soon.

Here are four of the companies that offer business card scanners:

> CypherScan 1000   CypherTech, Inc.   (408) 734-8765
> Scan-in-Dex   Microtek Labs   (800) 654-4160
> Cognitive BCR   Cognitive Technology   (415) 925-2367
> CardGrabber   Pacific Crest Tech.   (714) 261-6444

Installing a scanner

Most scanners come with a plug-in board and software drivers. Most of them are serial-type devices, so they require the use of one of your COM ports and one of your motherboard slots. You may have to set switches or jumpers to configure the board so it does not conflict with other devices in your system.

Voice recognition input

Another way to input data into a computer is to talk to it with a microphone. Of course, you need electronics that can take the signal created by the microphone, detect the spoken words, and turn them into a form of digital information that the computer can use.

The early voice data input systems were very expensive and limited. One reason was that the voice technology required lots of memory. But the cost of memory has dropped considerably in the last few years, and the technology has improved in many other ways. Eventually, the voice input technology will replace the keyboard for many applications.

Voice technology usually involves *training* a computer to recognize a word spoken by a person. When you speak into a microphone, the sound waves cause a diaphragm, or some other device, to move back and forth in a magnetic field and create a voltage that is analogous to the sound wave. If this voltage is recorded and played through a good audio system, the loudspeaker responds to the amplified voltages and reproduces a sound that is identical to the one input to the microphone.

A person can speak a word into a microphone that creates a unique voltage pattern for that word and that particular person's voice. The voltage is fed into an electronic circuit, and the pattern is digitized and stored in the computer. If several words are spoken, the circuit digitizes each one of them and stores it. Each one of them has a distinct and unique pattern. Later, when the computer hears a word, it searches through the patterns that it has stored to see if the input word matches any one of its stored words.

Of course, once the computer is able to recognize a word, you can have it perform some useful work. You could command it to load and run a program, or perform any of several other tasks.

Because every person's voice is different, ordinarily the computer would not recognize the voice of anyone who had not trained it. Training the computer might involve saying the same word several

times so the computer can store several patterns of the person's voice. Some of the new systems now recognize the voices of others who have not trained the computer.

 # Uses for voice recognition

Here are just a few uses: Letters, reports, and complicated business and technical text. Voice recognition can be used by doctors, nurses, lawyers, reporters, loan officers, auditors, researchers, secretaries, business executives, language interpreters, and writers.

Computer voice recognition is very useful whenever you must use both hands for doing a job, but still need a computer to perform certain tasks. Voice recognition is also useful on production lines where the person does not have time to manually enter data into a computer. It can also be used in a laboratory where a scientist is looking through a microscope and cannot take his or her eyes off the subject to write down the findings or data. There might be times when the lighting must be kept too dim to input data to a computer manually. In other instances, the person might have to be several feet from the computer and still be able to input data through the microphone line or even with a wireless mike. The person might even be miles away and be able to input data over a telephone line.

Voice recognition and a computer can help many of those who have physical limitations to become productive and independent.

The Carnegie Mellon Institute is working on a system that would allow a person using English to call someone in Germany and the spoken conversation could be understood. The spoken English would be translated into German and the spoken German would be translated into English. The system would recognize the spoken word then use computerized speech to translate it for the parties. So the parties would actually be talking to a computerized mechanical interpreter. Similar systems are being developed for Japanese and other foreign languages.

The same type of system can be built into small handheld foreign language interpreters. Speak an English word into the machine and it gives you the equivalent spoken foreign word.

Many luxury automobiles now come with cellular phones with voice activated dialing. This lets the driver keep his or her eyes on the road while the number is being dialed.

The designers of computers are constantly looking for new ways to differentiate and improve their product. In the very near future, you can be sure that many of them will have voice recognition built in.

Chips that use very large scale integration (VLSI) are combining more and more computer functions onto single chips. They are making computers smaller and smaller. We now have some very powerful computers that can fit in a shirt pocket. One of the big problems is that there is not room for a decent keyboard. To fit them all on a keyboard, the keys have to be very small. You can only use a single finger to type on the keyboards. Even then if your fingers are very large, you may end up pressing two keys at once. A solution would be to build in voice recognition so the keyboard would not be needed.

Limitations

For most systems, the computer must be trained to recognize a specific discrete individual word. So the computer vocabulary is limited to what it is trained to recognize, the amount of memory available, and the limitations imposed by the software and hardware.

There are many basic systems available today that are very good at recognizing discrete words. But ordinarily, when we speak, many words meld together. There are not many systems around that can recognize continuous speech.

Another problem is homonyms, or words that are pronounced the same, and sometimes spelled the same, but have different meanings. For instance, him, hymn, and hem are all pronounced about the same, but have very different meanings. Another instance is the words to, too, and two. Many people misspell and confuse the words there and their, your and you're, and it's and its.

A lot of our words have many different meanings such as the word set, run, round, date, and many, many others.

One of the solutions to this problem would be to have software and hardware with enough intelligence not only to recognize the words, but recognize the meaning due to the context in which they are used. That requires more intelligence than some human beings have.

 # Security systems

The voice of every person is as distinct and different as fingerprints. Voice prints have been used to convict criminals. Since no two voices are alike, a voice recognition system could be used to practically eliminate the need for keys. Most automobiles already have several built-in computerized systems. You can be sure that sometime soon you will see autos that have a voice recognition system instead of ignition keys. Such a system could help reduce the number of car thefts and carjacking.

A voice recognition system could also be used for any place that required strict security. If they installed voice recognition at Fort Knox they could probably eliminate many of their other security measures.

In most of the older systems, the computer had to be trained to recognize a specific word. Memory limitations and computer power were such that the vocabulary was quite limited. Today, we have computers with lots of memory and power. Since every word is made up of only 42 phonemes, several companies such as IBM, Verbex Voice Systems, and Dragon Systems are working on systems that will use a small sample of a person's voice that contains these phonemes. Using the phonemes from this sample, the computer could then recognize any word that the person speaks.

 # Basic systems

The Verbex Voice Systems, at (800) 275-8729, has developed a fairly sophisticated system that can almost obsolete the keyboard. Their Listen for Windows uses special software and a 16-bit plug-in board with a digital signal processor (DSP) on it. After a bit of training, this system can recognize continuous speech. Of course, it is still not

perfect, so at times you must slow down, speaking discrete words and making corrections for words it does not understand. Call Verbex for more information and current pricing.

The Covox Company, at (503) 342-1271, has a less-expensive voice recognition system that recognizes discrete words. The Voice Master is an 8-bit plug-in bus card. The Voice Master System II is an external system that plugs into the parallel port. The Voice Master can practically replace the keyboard. It works with most of the major word processors.

The software is loaded as a terminate and stay resident (TSR) that requires about 20K. When the *hot keys* (the two shift keys) are pressed, a menu pops up. Then, type in the command or macro that you want performed, then say the command or name for the macro three times. This trains the software to recognize the command. Up to 1023 commands or words for a macro can be stored.

The internal Voice Master bus card and the parallel port Voice Master System II both come with headset microphones. An advantage of the parallel port System II is that it does not require you to open your computer. It also does not require the use of a precious slot. And it can also be used on notebook and laptops or any ISA type computer that has a parallel port. The Voice Master system is fairly low priced. Call the Covox Company for current prices.

Computers and devices for the disabled

Several computer devices have been developed that can help the disabled person live a better life. Just because they have a physical impairment, doesn't mean that they have a brain impairment. Nature often compensates. For instance, the hearing and tactile senses of many blind people are much more acute than those who can see.

There are devices that allow the blind, the deaf, the quadriplegic, and other severely disabled persons to communicate. There are special braille keyboards and keyboards with enlarged keys for the blind. The

EyeTyper from the Sentient Systems Technology of Pittsburgh, Pennsylvania, has an embedded camera on the keyboard that can determine which key the user is looking at. It then enters that key into the computer. Words Plus of Sunnyvale, California, has a sensitive visor that can understand input from a raised brow, head movement, or eye blinks.

The Speaking Devices Corp., (408) 727-5571, has a telephone that can be trained to recognize an individual's voice. It can then dial up to 100 different numbers when the person tells it to. The same company has a tiny ear phone that also acts as a microphone. These devices would be ideal for a person who can speak, but cannot use his or her hands.

Devices for the disabled can allow many people to lead active, useful, and productive lives. Some have become artists, programmers, writers, and scientists. These communication devices have allowed them a bit of freedom from the harsh prison of their disabilities.

IBM has a number of products, they call the *Independence Series*, that are designed to aid those people with physical disabilities. They have a DOS-based utility, AccessDOS, that can be used to add functions to the keyboard, mouse, and sound boards. Call IBM, at (800) 426-4832, for more information.

Several organizations can help in locating special equipment and lend support. If you know someone who might benefit from the latest technology and devices for the handicapped, contact these organizations:

- ➤ AbleData   (800) 344-5405
- ➤ Accent on Information   (309) 378-2961
- ➤ Apple Computer   (408) 996-1010
- ➤ Closing The Gap, Inc.   (612) 248-3294
- ➤ Direct Link for the Disabled   (805) 688-1603
- ➤ Easter Seals Systems Office   (312) 667-8626
- ➤ IBM National Support Center   (800) 426-2133
- ➤ American Foundation for the Blind (212) 620-2000

➤ Trace Research and Development Center (608) 262-6966

➤ National ALS Association (818) 340-7500

Some of these organizations are glad to accept your old computers. Of course, you can write it off your income tax as a donation. You will be helping them and yourself. And you will feel better helping someone else.

CHAPTER 10

Monitors

T HERE are many different types of monitors with many different qualities and prices. A few of the monitor basics will be discussed to help you make a better decision in buying your monitor.

⇨ The CRT

A monitor is similar to a television. The main component is the cathode ray tube (CRT) or picture tube. In some respects, the CRT is like a dinosaur that is left over from the vacuum tube era. Before the silicon age of semiconductors, vacuum tubes operated almost all electronic devices. Like all vacuum tubes, the CRTs use enormous amounts of power and generate lots of heat.

Vacuum tubes have three main elements: the cathode, grid, and plate. These elements correspond to the emitter, base, and collector of a transistor. In a vacuum tube, the cathode is made from a metallic material that causes electrons to be boiled off when heated. The cathode is heated by the filament that is made from resistive wire similar to that used in light bulbs. Also, very much like light bulbs, the filaments burn out and cause the tube to fail. Burned out filaments are the single greatest cause of failure in vacuum tubes. The filaments of computer CRTs are designed a bit better now so they don't burn out as often as they did in the early days.

If a positive direct current (dc) voltage is placed on the plate of a vacuum tube, the negative electrons boiled off from the heated cathode will be attracted to the plate. A control grid is placed between the cathode and plate. The grid acts like a valve that can be opened and closed. (The British call vacuum tubes *valves*.) If a small negative voltage is placed on the grid, it will repel the negative

electrons and keep them from reaching the plate. Zero voltage or a small positive voltage on the grid will let the electrons go through to the plate. The plate in a vacuum tube may have as much as 400 volts on it. As the analog voltage swings up and down on the grid, it acts as a switch that allows the large voltage from the plate to pass through the vacuum tube. A voltage as small as a millionth of a volt on the grid of a vacuum tube can create a much larger exact voltage replica on the output of the plate. Figure 10-1 is a diagram of a vacuum tube circuit.

With the proper voltages on the emitter, base, and collector, a transistor operates much like a vacuum tube, acting as a switch or as an amplifier. Figure 10-2 shows a diagram of a transistor circuit. A transistor is much, much smaller, uses less voltage, creates very little heat, and lasts a lifetime; a vacuum tube may be quite large, requires a lot of space and energy, produces a lot of heat, and eventually burns out.

Figure 10-3 is a diagram of a basic cathode ray tube (CRT). Like the vacuum tube, the CRT has a filament that heats up a cathode to produce electrons. It also has a grid that can shut off the passage of the electrons or let them pass through. The corresponding plate of the CRT is the back of the picture screen, which has about 25,000 volts on it to attract the electrons from the cathode. The back of the screen is coated with a phosphor. Because of the high attracting voltage, the electrons slam into the phosphor and cause it to light up and glow.

Figure 10-1

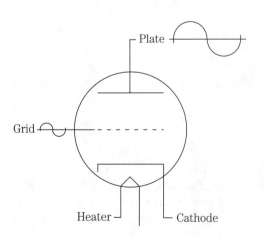

A diagram of a vacuum tube circuit

Figure 10-2

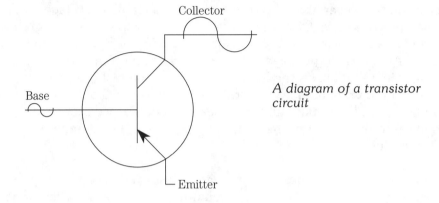

A diagram of a transistor circuit

Figure 10-3

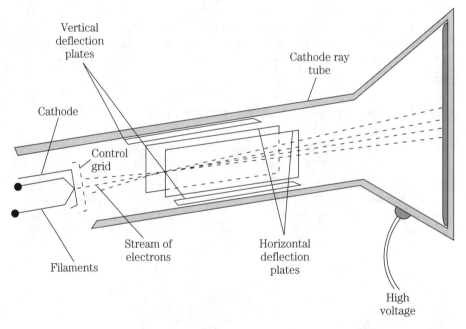

A diagram of a basic CRT. Note that it has many of the same components of the old obsolete vacuum tube.

A very small thin beam of electrons is formed. This electronic beam acts very much like a piece of iron in a magnetic field. If four electromagnets are placed around the neck of the CRT, one on top, one on the bottom and one each side, the beam of electrons can be directed to any area of the screen by varying the polarity of the voltage fed to the electromagnets. If we wanted the beam to move to

the right, we would increase the plus voltage on the right magnet. If we wanted the beam to move up, we would increase the plus voltage on the top magnet. With these electromagnets, we can move the beam to any spot on the screen.

The small input signal voltage on the grid of the CRT turns the electron beam on and off to cause portions of the screen to light up. The beam can be caused to move and write on the screen just as if you were writing with a pencil. Alphabetic characters, numbers, or any kind of graphics, can be created in an exact replica of the input signal.

The present-day CRTs are like an ancient dinosaur. Many laptops and notebook computers have excellent color screens using transistors. The active matrix type uses thousands of transistors to light up each individual pixel. But these active matrix systems are very expensive because just one transistor out of many thousand can ruin the whole panel. Other less costly systems are being developed. Eventually, we will have large low energy flat screens that can produce a good high resolution picture. Soon, even the large television CRTs will be replaced with flat screens that can be hung on a wall.

Monochrome vs. color

In a monochrome television or a monitor, there is a single *gun* that shoots the electrons toward the back of the screen. Color televisions and monitors are much more complicated than monochrome systems. During the manufacture of the color monitors, three different phosphors, red, green, and blue (RGB), are deposited on the back of the screen. Usually a very small dot of each color is placed in a triangular shape. If you use a magnifying glass and look at a color monitor or color television, you can see the individual dots.

The different phosphors used to make color monitors are made from rare earths. They are designed to glow for a certain period of time after they have been hit by an electron beam.

In a color television or monitor, there are three guns, each shooting a beam of electrons. The electrons from each gun have no color. But

each gun is aimed at a particular color, one to hit only the red dots, one the blue dots only, and one the green dots. They are very accurately aimed so they will converge or impinge only on their assigned color dots. To make sure that the beams hit only their target, the beam must go through the holes of a metal shadow mask. Being hit by stray electrons causes the shadow mask to heat up. The heat may cause fatigue and loss of focus. Many of the newer monitors use shadow masks made from Invar, an alloy that has good heat resistance.

By turning the guns on or off to light up and mix the different red, green, and blue dots of phosphor, any color can be generated.

The Sony Trinitron monitors and televisions use a system that is a bit different. Its three guns are in a single housing and fire through a single lens. Instead of a shadow mask, the Trinitron uses a vertical grill that allows the beams to pass through. The Trinitron system was actually invented in this country, but no one in the television industry was interested until Sony adopted it.

 # Dot pitch

If you look closely at a black and white photo in a newspaper, you can see that the photo is made up of small dots. There will be a lot of dots in the darker areas and fewer in the light areas. The text or image on a monitor or a television screen is also made up of dots very similar to the newspaper photo. You can see the dots and spaces with a magnifying glass. This is much like the dots of a dot matrix printer. The more dots and the closer together they are, the better the resolution. A good high resolution monitor will have solid, sharply defined characters and images. But the more dots and the closer together they are, the more difficult it is to manufacture a CRT. The red, blue, and green dots must be placed very accurately and uniformly in order for their specific electron beam to hit them. Most standard monitors will have a dot pitch of 0.28 millimeter (mm). The better monitors will have dots that are as close as 0.24 mm. Some of the low cost color monitors may have them from 0.39 mm to 0.52 mm. Such monitors may be all right for playing games. But they wouldn't be very good for anything else.

Pixels

Resolution is also determined by the number of *picture elements (pixels)* that can be displayed. A pixel is the smallest unit that can be drawn or displayed on the screen. A pixel can be turned on or off with a single bit. But to control the intensity and color depth, it may take several bits per pixel.

The following figures relate primarily to text, but the graphics resolution will be similar to the text. Most monitors are designed to display 80 characters in one row or line across the screen. By leaving a bit of space between each row, 25 lines of text can be displayed from top to bottom. The old color graphics monitor (CGA) could display 640×200 pixels. If we divide 640 by 80 we find that one character will be 8 pixels wide. There can be 25 lines of characters, so $200/25 = 8$ pixels high. The entire screen will have $640 \times 200 = 128,000$ pixels. The EGA has 640×350 so each cell has 8 pixels wide and 14 pixels high. The Video Electronics Standards Association (VESA) chose 640×480 to be the VGA standard and 800×600 to be the Super VGA (SVGA) standard. For SVGA it is $800/80 = 10$ pixels wide and $600/25 = 24$ pixels high. Many of the newer systems are now capable of 1024×768; 1280×1024; 1664×1200; and more. With a resolution of 1664×1200, we would have 1,996,800 pixels or almost 2 million pixels that could be lit up. We have come a long way from the 128,000 pixels possible with CGA.

 # Painting the screen

To put an image on the screen, the electron beam starts at the top left corner. Under the influence of the electromagnets, it is drawn across to the right of the screen lighting up a very thin line as it moves. Depending on what the beam is depicting, it will be turned on and off by the grid as it sweeps across the screen. When the beam reaches the right side of the screen, it is turned off and sent back to the left side. It drops down a bit and begins sweeping across the screen to paint another line. On a television set, it paints 262.5 lines in $\frac{1}{60}$ of a second. These are all of the even numbered lines. It then

goes back to the top and interlaces the other 262.5 odd numbered lines in between the first 262.5. It does this fairly fast, at a frequency of 15,750 Hz. (15,750 divided by 60 = 262.5). So it takes ¹⁄₃₀ of a second to paint 525 lines. This is called a *frame,* so 30 frames are written to the screen in one second. When one of the dots is struck by the electron beam, it lights up and remains lit up for a certain length of time depending on the type of phosphor it was made from.

When we watch a movie, we are seeing a series of still photos, flashed one after the other. Due to our persistence of vision, it appears to be continuous motion. It is this same persistence of vision phenomenon that allows us to see motion and images on our television and video screens.

 # Scan rate

It is obvious that 525 lines on a television set, especially a large screen, leaves a lot of space in between the lines. If there were more lines, the resolution could be improved. At this time, the FCC and the television industry are trying to decide on a standard for a High Definition television that would have 750 to about 1200 lines at 30 frames per second. At 750 lines, it would paint 375 lines in ¹⁄₆₀ of a second and 750 in ¹⁄₃₀ of a second. For 750 lines the horizontal frequency would be 22,500 Hz. For 1200 lines the horizontal frequency would be 36,000 Hz.

 # The vertical scan rate

The time that it takes to fill a screen with lines from top to bottom is the *vertical scan rate.* This may also be called the *refresh rate.* The phosphor may start losing some of its glow after a period of time unless the vertical scan refreshes it in a timely manner. Some of the multiscan, or multifrequency, monitors can have several fixed or variable vertical scan rates. The Video Electronics Standards Association (VESA) specifies a minimum of 70 Hz for SVGA and 72 Hz for VGA systems.

 # Interlaced vs. noninterlaced

The higher scan frequencies require that the adapter have more precise and higher quality electronics. The monitor must also be capable of responding to the higher frequencies. Which of course, requires higher costs to manufacture. To avoid this higher cost, IBM designed some of their systems with an interlaced horizontal system. Instead of increasing the horizontal frequency, they merely painted every other line across the screen from top to bottom, then returned to the top and painted the lines that were skipped. This is the same system used on television sets. Theoretically, this sounds like a great idea. But practically, it doesn't work too well because it causes a very annoying flicker. It can be very irritating to some people who have to work with this type of monitor for very long.

This flicker is not readily apparent, but some people have complained of eyestrain, headaches, and fatigue after prolonged use of an interlaced monitor. If the monitor is only used for short periods of time, by different people, then the interlaced type would probably not be a problem.

Some companies make models that use interlacing in some modes and noninterlacing in other modes. Most companies do not advertise the fact that their systems use interlacing, some may use the abbreviation *N/I* for their *noninterlaced adapters*. The interlaced models are usually a bit lower in price than the noninterlaced. You may have to ask the vendor what system he is using.

 # Multiscan

The multiscan monitors can accept a wide range of vertical and horizontal frequencies. This makes them quite versatile and flexible. Many of the early multiscans could accept both digital and analog signals. Almost all monitors sold today are the analog type.

The VGA system introduced by IBM on their PS/2 systems in 1987 used a fixed frequency instead of a multiscan adapter and monitor. A multiscan design costs more to build so many of the low cost VGAs

are designed to operate at a single fixed frequency. They are not as versatile or flexible as the multiscan, but the resolution may be as good as the multiscan.

Many companies are manufacturing monitors with multi-fixed frequencies with two or more fixed frequencies. Again, they are not quite as flexible as the true multiscan, but they can cost less. I am using a 19-inch Sampo TriSync that has three different frequencies. For my purposes, it does everything that I need to do.

The multiscan monitors may sell for as little as $250 and up to as much as $3500 or more for some of the large 19- to 30-inch sizes.

 # Adapter basics

You can't just plug a monitor into your computer and expect it to function. Just as a hard disk needs a controller, a monitor needs an adapter to interface with the computer. Our computer monitors are a bit different than a television. A television set usually has all of its controlling electronics mounted in the console or case and is assembled and sold as a single unit. A computer monitor may have some electronics within its case, but its main controller, the adapter, is usually on a plug-in board on the PC motherboard. This gives us more versatility and utility because we can use different or specialized adapters if needed.

There are several manufacturers that make monitor adapters so there is quite a lot of competition. This has helped to keep the prices fairly reasonable. Most monitors can operate with several different types of adapters. Adapters may cost as little as $40 and up to $1000 or more. Monitors may cost as little as $200 and up to $3000 or more. It would be foolish to buy a very expensive monitor and an inexpensive adapter, or vice versa. You should try to match the capabilities of the monitor and the adapter.

Most monitor adapters have text character generators built onto the board that is similar to a built-in library. When we send an A to the screen, the adapter goes to its library and sends the signal for the preformed A to the screen. Each character occupies a cell made up of a number of pixels. The number of pixels depends on the resolution of the screen and the adapter. In the case of the VGA, if all the dots within a cell were lit up, there would be a solid block of dots 10 pixels or dots wide and 24 pixels high. When an A is placed in a cell, only the dots necessary to form the outline of the A will be lit up. It is very similar to the dots formed by the dot matrix printers when it prints a character.

With the proper software a graphics adapter can allow you to place lines, images, photos, normal and various text fonts, and almost anything one can imagine on the screen. Almost all adapters sold today have both text and graphics capability.

Analog vs. digital

Most all monitors and adapters sold today are analog systems. Up until the introduction of the PS/2 with VGA, most displays used the digital system. But the digital systems have severe limitations.

The digital signals are of two states, either fully on or completely off. The signals for color and intensity require separate lines in the cables. It takes six lines for the EGA to be able to display 16 colors out of a palette of 64. The digital systems are obsolete.

The analog signals that drive the color guns are voltages that are continuously variable. It takes only a few lines for the three primary colors. The intensity voltage for each color can then be varied almost infinitely to create as many as 256 colors out of a possible 262,144. To display more than 256 colors requires the true color adapters.

Accelerator boards

The fixed-function cards have accelerator chips with several built-in graphics functions. Because they have built-in functions, they can handle many of the Windows type graphics tasks without having to bother the CPU. Since they don't often have to go back and forth to the CPU over the I/O bus at the slow speed of 8 MHz, they are usually much faster

than the dumb frame buffer type. There is a wide price range for these cards. Examples of the graphics chips used in these cards are S3 86CXXX, IIT AGX014, and the ATI 68800. Some that have a limited fixed-function may cost as little as $50 and up to $400.

Another type of adapter has its own coprocessor chip on board such as the Texas Instruments 34010 or the Hitachi HD63483. By using an on-board coprocessor, it frees up the CPU for other tasks. The coprocessor boards are usually more expensive than any of the other types of boards.

 # Video memory

Having memory on the adapter board saves having to go through the bus to the conventional RAM. Some adapter boards even have a separate plug-in daughterboard for adding more memory. With the older dumb frame buffer type cards, even with a lot of memory, the adapter had to go back and forth over the 16-bit bus to communicate with the CPU. Many of the applications, especially under Windows, may be painfully slow. An accelerator card with lots of onboard memory and a VESA local bus (VLB) or Peripheral Component Interconnect (PCI) bus system can speed up the processing considerably.

It is possible to use 8-bit boards to display color images in 256 colors. But these boards are obsolete. You will be much better off using a 16-bit board. Better yet would be a VLB or a PCI bus. Figure 4-7 in Chapter 4 shows a VLB and a PCI adapter from the Diamond Company.

You should have at least 1MB of memory to display 256 colors in 1024 × 768 resolution. Of course, the more colors displayed and the higher the resolution, the more memory is required. To display 64,000 colors at 1024 × 768 requires 2MB, and for 24-bit true color it takes about 4MB.

Graphics speed can be slowed if the graphics have to be pulled off a hard disk. You can speed up the process a bit if you have at least 8MB of RAM with a 2MB SmartDrive disk cache. Even better is 16MB of RAM with a 4MB SmartDrive disk cache.

Adapter memory chips

Many of the high resolution adapters have up to 4MB or more of Video RAM (VRAM) memory on board. The VRAM chips look very much like the older DRAM DIP memory chips, but they are not interchangeable with DRAM. The DRAM chips have a single port; they can only be accessed or written to through this port. The VRAM chips have two ports and can be accessed by one port while being written to in the other. This makes them much faster and a bit more expensive than DRAM. Some of the less expensive adapters use DRAM memory.

Many of the less expensive adapter boards are sold with only 512K of DRAM or less. They often have empty sockets for adding more memory. Some cards have space to install as much as 40MB of DRAM. It is not likely that you would need that much for ordinary use. It is very easy to install the memory chips in the sockets. Just be sure that you orient them properly. They should be installed the same way as other memory on the board. Make sure that all legs are fully inserted in the sockets.

If you expect to do any high resolution type graphics, you should have a minimum of 1MB of VRAM on the adapter, 2MB would be even better.

 # SVGA colors

The number of colors that a SVGA card can display is dependent on the resolution displayed. Here are the numbers for a low cost SVGA: 16.7 million colors at 640 × 480, only 64,000 colors at 800 × 600 and only 16 colors at 1280 × 1024.

Of course, there are adapters that can display a much greater number of colors than listed, but they are also more expensive.

 # True colors

Most of the standard low cost VGA cards are capable of only 16 colors. True colors or pure colors require video boards with lots of fast memory, a coprocessor, and complex electronics. True color means that a video board can drive a monitor to display a large number of shades in separate, distinct hues or pure colors. Remember that a pixel can be turned on or off with a single bit, but for color intensity or shades and depth, it may take several bits per pixel (see Table 10-1). A good adapter for true color may cost more than the monitor.

Table 10-1   **Pure Color**

Bits	Shades	Depth
4 or 2^4	16	
8 or 2^8	256	
15 or 2^{15}	32,768	5:5:5
16 or 2^{16}	65,536	5:6:5 or 6:6:4
24 or 2^{32}	16.7 million	8:8:8

 # Depth

True color usually refers to displays with 15-, 16-, or 24-bit depths. Depth means that each of the individual red, green, or blue (RGB) color pixels will have a large amount of information about each color. The 15-bit system will have 5 bits of information for each of the three colors. The 16-bit system may have 6 bits for red, 6 bits for green, and 4 bits for blue or a combination of 5:6:5. The 24-bit system will have 8 bits for each color.

Table 10-2 can give you an idea of how much memory is needed for the various resolutions and colors.

Memory and Resolution

Table 10-2

Bits/pixel	Color	640×480	800×600	1024×768
4	16	150K	234K	386K
8	256	300K	469K	768K
16	35,536	600K	938K	1.536MB
24	16,777,216	900K	1.406MB	2.304MB

Dithering

If a board doesn't have enough power to display the true distinct colors, it may use dithering to mix the colors to give an approximation.

Dithering takes advantage of the eye's tendency to blur colors and view them as an average. A printed black and white photo uses all black dots, but several shades of gray can be printed depending on the number of black dots per inch. A mixture of red dots with white ones can create a pink image. Gradual color transitions can be accomplished by using dithering to intersperse pixels of various colors.

VL bus and PCI bus adapters

Many of the 486 and Pentium motherboards have either a VL bus or a PCI bus. The VL bus and PCI bus adapters are much faster than the older graphics and accelerator boards because they have a 32- or 64-bit path that is used to directly communicate with the CPU. This direct path also allows them to communicate at the CPU speed or frequency. The older I/O systems were limited to the 8- or 16-bit bus and were limited to a speed of 8 MHz, no matter how fast the CPU was.

Some Windows, most graphics, and many other applications, require a lot of interaction with the CPU. So many of the true color adapters are made for motherboards with a local bus connector.

 # Sources

There are hundreds of adapter manufacturers. I hesitate to mention models because each manufacturer has dozens of different models with different features and resolutions. And they are constantly designing, developing, and introducing new models.

 # Adapter software

Most adapter cards will work with any software that you have. But many adapter vendors provide special software drivers that are necessary for high resolution and speed with certain applications. Make sure that the adapter has drivers for all popular graphics type software.

 # MPEG boards

The Motion Pictures Expert Group (MPEG) devised a specification for compressing graphics and video. Ordinarily, a single frame in a moving picture requires about 25MB to digitize and store. The MPEG system allows a compression up to 100 to 1, so it is possible to store as much as 72 minutes on a 650MB CD-ROM. Several companies have developed plug-in boards that will allow you to capture and play back video from several different sources such as a VCR, Camcorder, CD-ROM, TV, Laser Disk, and others. Some cards have built-in sound systems and some can even be supplied with a television tuner so you can watch television on your monitor.

Here are a couple of companies. Call them for brochures and information: Prolink, (213) 780-7978; High Technology, (800) 697-8001.

 # Choosing a monitor

The primary determining factors for choosing a monitor should be its intended use and the amount of money you have to spend. If you can

afford it, buy a large 21-inch monitor with super high resolution and a good SVGA board to drive it.

The stated screen size of a monitor is very misleading and almost fraudulent. The stated size is a diagonal measurement. There is a border on all four sides of the screen. The usable viewing area on a 14-inch monitor is about 9.75 inches wide and about 7.75 inches high. One reason is because the screen is markedly curved near the edges on all sides. This curve can cause distortion so the areas are masked off and not used.

If you expect to do any kind of graphics or CAD/CAM design work, you will definitely need a good large screen color monitor, with very high resolution. A large screen is almost essential for some types of design drawings so as much of the drawing as possible can be viewed on the screen.

You will also need a high resolution monitor for close tolerance designs. For instance, if you draw two lines to meet on a low resolution monitor, they may look as if they are perfectly lined up. But when the drawing is magnified or printed out, the lines may not be anywhere close to one another.

Most desktop publishing (DTP) is done in black-and-white print. The high-resolution paper-white monochrome monitors may be all you need for these applications. These monitors can usually display several shades of gray.

Many of these monitors are the portrait type, that is, they are higher than they are wide. You find many of this style used for desktop publishing and other special applications. Many of them have a display area of 8½ by 11 inches. Instead of 25 lines, they have 66 lines, which is the standard for an 11-inch sheet of paper. Many have a phosphor that will let you have black text on a white background so the screen looks very much like the finished text. Some of the newer color monitors have a mode that lets you switch to pure white with black type.

Most monitors are wider than they are tall. These are called landscape styles. Some of the 19-inch and larger landscape type

monitors can display two pages of text side by side if the software allows it.

 # What to look for

If possible, go to several stores and compare various models. Turn the brightness up and check the center of the screen and the outer edges. Is the intensity the same in the center and the outer edges? Check the focus, brightness, and contrast with text and graphics. There can be vast differences even in the same models from the same manufacturer. I have seen monitors that displayed demo graphics programs beautifully, but were not worth a damn when displaying text in various colors. If possible, try it out with both text and graphics.

Ask the vendor for a copy of the specs. Check the dot pitch. For good high resolution, it should be no greater than 0.28 mm., even better would be 0.26 mm. or 0.24 mm.

Check the horizontal and vertical scan frequency specs. For a multiscan, the wider the range, the better. A good system could have a horizontal range from 30 kHz to 40 kHz or better. The vertical range should be from 45 Hz to 70 Hz or higher.

 # Controls

You might also check for available controls to adjust the brightness, contrast, and vertical/horizontal lines. Some manufacturers place them on the back or some other difficult area to get at. It is much better if they are accessible from the front so you can see what the effect is as you adjust them.

 # Glare

If a monitor reflects too much light, it can be like a mirror and be very distracting. Some manufacturers have coated the screen with a silicon formulation to cut down on the reflectance. Some have etched the screen for the same purpose. Some screens are tinted to help cut down on glare. If possible, you should try the monitor under various lighting conditions.

If you have a glare problem, several supply companies and mail order houses offer glare shields that cost from $20 up to $100.

 # Cleaning the screen

Since about 25,000 volts of electricity hit the back side of the monitor face, it creates a static attraction for dust. This dust can distort images and make the screen difficult to read.

Most manufacturers should have an instruction booklet that suggests how the screen should be cleaned. If you have a screen that has been coated with silicon to reduce glare, you should not use any harsh cleansers on it. Usually, plain water and a soft paper towel will do fine.

 # Monitor radiation

Almost all electrical devices emit very low frequency (VLF) magnetic and electrical fields. There have been no definitive studies that prove that this radiation is harmful to a person. In some cases, the emissions are so weak that they can hardly be measured. However, the government of Sweden developed a set of guidelines to regulate the strength of emissions from video display terminals (VDTs).

Several people in this country are also concerned that the VDT radiation might be a problem, so many monitor manufacturers now add shielding to control the emission. If you are worried about VDT emissions, look for monitors that are certified to meet MPR II specifications.

Incidentally, if you use a hair dryer, you will get much more radiation from that than from a monitor.

 # Green monitors

The monitor may use 100 to 150 watts of energy. The EPA Energy Star program demands that the energy be reduced to no more than 30 watts when they are not being used.

I sometimes sit in front of my monitor for 10 or 15 minutes, doing research, or more likely with writers block. All this time the monitor is burning up lots of watts of energy. Many of the new monitors meet the Energy Star specifications, so when there is no activity, they go into a sleep mode where they use very little energy. A small amount of voltage is still applied to the monitor and it will come back on line almost immediately.

None of my monitors comply with the Energy Star specification. But I am saving energy by using the PC ener-g saver from the NEI Company, at (800) 832-4007. It allows me to plug in my monitor and printer power cords. It also has a connection for the keyboard to be plugged in. Using software that comes with the unit, you can set the PC ener-g saver to shut down your monitor and printer if there is no activity from the keyboard. You can set the time interval for no activity from just a few seconds up to several minutes. As soon as any key on the keyboard is pressed or the mouse is moved, the monitor comes back on. It comes back to the same place where you were working when it shut down. To reactivate the printer, just send it a print command.

 # Software for monitor testing

If you are planning to buy an expensive, high-resolution monitor, you might want to buy a software program called DisplayMate for Windows from Sonera Technologies, at (908) 747-6886. It is a collection of utilities that can perform several checks on a monitor. It lets you measure the resolution for fine lines, the clarity of the image, distortion, has gray and color scales, and a full range of intensities and colors. The software can actually help tweak and fine tune your monitor and adapter. The setup also helps a person set the controls

for the optimum values. If you plan to spend $1500 or so for a monitor, it could be well worth it to test the monitor first.

 # Other resources

The monitor is a very important part of your computer system. I couldn't possibly tell you all you need to know in this short chapter. One of the better ways to keep up on this ever-changing technology is to subscribe to one or more computer magazines. They frequently have articles about monitors. Of course, they also have many ads for monitors and adapters. I have listed several computer magazines in Chapter 17.

CHAPTER 11

Communications

T ELEPHONES are an important, and sometimes, critical part of our life. By adding a modem to your computer, you can use your computer and the telephone line to access online services, bulletin boards, the Internet, and to communicate with anyone else in the world who also has a computer and modem.

Many of the modem boards are now integrated with fax capability. A modem board with a fax may not cost much more than the modem alone. Communicating by fax is fast and efficient.

Reaching out

More than 100 million personal computers are installed in homes, offices, and businesses worldwide. About half of them have a modem or some sort of communications capability. This capability of the computer is one of its most important aspects.

If your computer has a modem, you can access over 10,000 bulletin boards in the United States. You can take advantage of electronic mail, faxes, up-to-the-minute stock market quotations, and a large number of other online services such as home shopping, home banking, travel agencies, business transactions, and many databases and other data services. And even dating services.

For some types of work, a person can use a modem and work from home. Someone has called this *telecommuting*. It is a whole lot better than commuting by auto and sitting in traffic jams on the crowded freeways.

Communications covers a wide range of activities and technologies. Many books have been written that cover all phases of

communications. Just a few of the many technologies are discussed in this chapter.

The Internet and World Wide Web

One of the hottest topics at the moment is the Internet or World Wide Web. The Internet started off as a government project in 1973 with the Advanced Research Projects Agency (ARPA), an agency of the Department of Defense (DOD). It was a network designed to facilitate scientific collaboration in military research among educational institutions. ARPAnet had some similarities to peer-to-peer networking. It allowed almost any system to connect to another through an electronic gateway.

The ARPAnet is no longer primarily concerned with military research. It is now known as the Internet or the World Wide Web (WWW). It is now possible to access the Internet or WWW from several online services. Here are some voice numbers: CompuServe at (800) 848-8990, Prodigy at (800) 776-3449, America Online at (800) 827-6364, and Delphi at (800) 695-4005. Many other services also provide access. Many books have been written about the Internet. Three very good ones, published by Osborne/McGraw-Hill, at 1-800-227-0900, are *Internet Essentials and Fun List*; *Internet, the Complete Reference*; and the *Internet Yellow Pages*. If you are just getting started, the *Internet Complete Reference* would help you immensely. It has more than 800 pages of information about getting on the net. It has addresses and numbers of hundreds of local, state, national, and international access gateways. There are valuable helpful hints on almost every page. There are several other books about the Internet offered by other publishers.

There are now millions of people who access the Internet. There is something on the Internet for everyone. There are encyclopedias, up-to-the-minute news, people chatting with one another, online romance, and X-rated photos and talk. You can post notes or send E-mail. If you don't know where to find something you can use Gopher, Archie, Veronica, and Jughead to search for you. These

comic-book character names are search software that can help you find almost anything on the 'net.

The vast majority of people are good and honest. But when you get this many people communicating with one another, there will always be a few who will try to take advantage of others. Just be careful.

 # Modems

A modem is an electronic device that allows a computer to use an ordinary telephone line to communicate with other computers that are equipped with a modem. Modem is a contraction of the words *modulate* and *demodulate.* The telephone system transmits voice and data in analog voltage form. Analog voltages vary continuously up and down. Computer data is usually in a digital voltage form, which sends a series of on and off voltages.

The modem takes the digitized bits of voltage from a computer and modulates, or transforms, it into analog voltages to transmit it over telephone lines. At the receiving end, a similar modem demodulates the analog voltage and transforms it back into a digital form.

 # Transmission difficulties

Telephone systems were originally designed for voice and have a very narrow bandwidth. A person with perfect hearing can hear from 20 cycles per second, or *hertz (Hz)*, all the way up to 20,000 Hz. For normal speech, we only use about 300 Hz up to 2000 Hz.

The telephone analog voltages are subject to noise, static, and other electrical disturbances. Noise and static take the form of analog voltages. So do most of the other electrical disturbances such as electrical storms and pulses generated by operating electrical equipment. The analog noise and static voltages are mixed in with any analog data voltages that are being transmitted. The mixture of the static and noise voltages with the data voltages can corrupt and severely damage the data. The demodulator may be completely at a loss to determine which voltages represent data and which are noise.

→ Baud rate

These problems, and the state of technology at the time, limited the original modems to about 5 characters per second (cps), or a rate of 50 *baud*.

We get the term *baud* from Emile Baudot (1845–1903), a French inventor. Originally, the baud rate was a measure of the dots and dashes in telegraphy. It is now defined as the actual rate of symbols transmitted per second. For the lower baud rates, it is essentially the same as bits per second. Remember that it takes 8 bits to make a character. Just as we have periods and spaces to separate words, we must use one *start bit* and one *stop bit* to separate the on/off bits into characters. A transmission of 300 baud would mean that 300 on/off bits are sent in one second. For every 8 bits of data that represents a character, we need one bit to indicate the start of a character and one bit to indicate the end. We then need another bit to indicate the start of the next character. So counting the start/stop bits, it takes 11 bits for each character. If we divide 300 by 11, it gives us about 27 cps.

Some of the newer technologies may actually transmit symbols that represent more than one bit. For baud rates of 1200 and higher, the cps and baud rate can be considerably different.

There have been some fantastic advances in the modem technologies. A few years ago, the 2400 baud systems were the standard. Today they are obsolete. The industry has leaped over the 4800 and 9600 baud systems to the 14.4K systems. These units incorporate the V.42bis compression standard. This allows them to use 4:1 data compression and thus transmit at 57,600 bits per second (bps). Many people are still using the 14.4K systems, but they are now obsolete and have been displaced by the 28.8K V.34 systems.

When communicating with another modem, both the sending and receiving unit must operate at the same baud rate and use the same protocols. Most of the faster modems are downward-compatible and can operate at the slower speeds. If you use a modem frequently, a high-speed modem can quickly pay for itself. We have sure come a long way since those early 50-baud standards.

 # How to estimate connect time

You can figure the approximate length of time that it will take to transmit a file. For rough approximations of cps you can divide the baud rate by 10. For instance, a 14.4K modem would transmit at about 1400 cps. Look at the directory and determine the number of bytes in the file. Divide the number of bytes in the file by the cps to give a rough approximation.

 # Data compression

One way to reduce modem phone charges is to use file compression. Bulletin boards have been using a form of data compression for years. There are several public domain programs that squeeze and unsqueeze data. The newer modems take advantage of compression using the standard V.42bis for 4 to 1 compression. Using 4 to 1 compression, a 14.4K modem can send at 57,600 bps.

With a 14.4K baud modem, and 4 to 1 compression, a 40K file that takes 3.6 minutes when transmitted at 2400 baud, can be sent in less than one second.

The 14.4K modem is practically obsolete. At the moment, the V.34 28.8K modem is the fastest modem available, unless you have a digital ISDN system.

The major online service companies such as CompuServe, Prodigy, America On Line, Delphi, and others, charge for connect time to their service. The connect time is much less with some of the high speed modems. In order to keep their revenue up, some companies charge more if you use a high speed modem.

 # Protocols

Protocols are procedures that have been established for exchanging data, along with the instructions that coordinate the process. Most

protocols can sense when the data is corrupted or lost due to noise, static, or a bad connection. It automatically resends the affected data until it is received correctly.

There are several protocols, but the most popular ones are Kermit (named for Kermit the frog), Xmodem, and Ymodem. These protocols transmit a block of data along with an error-checking code, then wait for the receiver to send back an acknowledgement. It then sends another block and waits to see if it got through okay. If a block does not get through, it is resent immediately. Protocols such as Zmodem and HyperProtocol send a whole file in a continuous stream of data with error checking codes inserted at certain intervals. They then wait for confirmation of a successful transmission. If the transmission is unsuccessful, then the whole file must be resent.

Both the sending and receiving modems must both use the same protocol and baud rate. You cannot send a file at 28.8K to someone who only has a 2400 baud modem. However, the faster modems are able to shift down and send or receive at the lower speeds.

ITU recommended standards

The communications industry is very complex. So there have not been many real standards. There are many different manufacturers and software developers. Of course, all of them want to differentiate their hardware or software by adding new features.

A United Nations standards committee was established to help create worldwide standards. If every country had different protocols and standards, it would be very difficult to communicate. The original committee was called the Comite Consultatif Internal de Telegraphique et Telephone (CCITT). The name has now been changed to International Telecommunications Union (ITU). This committee has representatives from over 80 countries and several large private manufacturers. The committee makes recommendations only. A company is free to use or ignore them. But more and more companies are now adopting the recommendations.

All ITU recommendations for small computers have a V or X prefix. The V series is for use with switched telephone networks, which is almost all of them. The X series is for systems that do not use switched phone lines. Revisions or alternate recommendations have bis (second) or ter (third) added.

The V prefixes can be a bit confusing. For instance, a V.32 modem can communicate at 4800 or 9600 bps. It can communicate with any other V.32 modem. A V.32bis can communicate at 14,400 bps. The V.32bis standard is a modulation method and is not a compression technique. The V.34 standard is for 28.8K modems.

A V.42bis standard is a method of data compression plus a system of error-checking. A V.42bis can communicate with another V.42bis at up to 57,600 bps by using compression and error-checking.

 # Communications software

In order to use a modem, it must be driven and controlled by software. There are dozens of communication programs that can be used. Crosstalk, (404) 998-3998, was one of the earlier modem programs.

ProComm Plus from DataStorm, at (314) 474-8461, is an excellent communications program. Qmodem from Mustang Software Company, at (805) 873-2500, is another very good program. At one time, both ProComm and Qmodem were low-cost shareware programs. They were among the most popular communication programs available. Both of them are now commercial programs, but are still reasonably priced.

Mustang Software also provides software for setting up bulletin boards. If you would like to start your own BBS contact them for the details.

One of the most comprehensive communications programs is the Delrina WinComm PRO from Delrina, at (800) 268-6082. It operates under Windows and handles both modem and fax communications. It can be used to access all of the online services, other modems, and can even be set up as a mini-BBS to let other users log on to your computer. You can set up passwords and access privileges. Since it works under Windows, a mouse can be used to point and click on the many icons and buttons. WinComm PRO is much like the plug and play software in that it can automatically detect and avoid port conflicts. Call Delrina and ask for a brochure. It is one of the better communication software packages available.

 # Low-cost communication software

If you buy a modem or modem/fax board, many companies include a basic communications program. If you subscribe to one of the large online services, such as CompuServe or Prodigy, they provide special software for their connections.

You can get copies of communication shareware programs from bulletin boards or from any of the several companies that provide shareware and public domain software. Shareware is not free. You may try it out and use it, but the developers ask that you register the program and send in a nominal sum. For this low cost, they usually provide a manual and some support. Some of the shareware companies are listed in Chapter 17.

 # Basic types of modems

There are two basic types of modems: the external desktop and the internal. Each type has some advantages and disadvantages.

A disadvantage is that the external type requires some of your precious desk space and a voltage source. It also requires an external cable from a COM port to drive it. The good news is that most external models have LEDs that light up and let you know what is happening during your call.

Both the external and the internal models have speakers that let you hear the phone ringing or if you get a busy signal. But the internal modem may have a very small speaker and you may not even be able

to hear the dial tone and the ringing. Some of the external models have a volume control for the built-in speaker.

The internal modem is built entirely on a board, usually a half or short board. The good news is that it doesn't use up any of your desk real estate, but the bad news is that it uses one of your precious slots. It also does not have the LEDs to let you know the progress of your call. Of course, seeing the LEDs flashing might not be important to you. The only thing most people care about is whether it is working or not. The fewer items to worry about, the better.

Even if you use an external modem, if your motherboard does not have built-in COM ports, you need an I/O board that requires the use of one of your slots for a COM port. The external modems may cost up to $100 more than an equivalent internal modem. By far, the most popular modems are the internal types.

 # Hayes compatibility

One of the most popular early modems was made by Hayes Microcomputer Products. They became the IBM of the modem world and established a *de facto* standard. There are hundreds of modem manufacturers. Except for some of the very inexpensive ones, almost all of them are Hayes compatible.

 # Installing a modem

If you are adding a modem on a board to a system that is already assembled, the first thing to do is to check your documentation and set any jumpers or switches needed to configure the board. There are usually jumpers or small switches that must be set to enable COM1 or COM2. Once the switches and jumpers have been set to configure the modem, remove the computer cover. Find an empty slot and plug the board in.

Normally, most systems only allow for two COM ports. If you have an I/O board in your system with external COM ports and you have

built-in COM ports on your motherboard, you can only use two of them. You must set the switches or jumpers to configure your system for whichever port that will be used by the modem and the port used by a mouse or other device. Any port on the motherboard or on a plug-in board that is not being used should be disabled. Ordinarily jumpers are used to enable or disable the ports.

If you are installing an external modem, you must go through the same procedure to make sure the COM port is accessible and does not conflict. If you have a mouse, a serial printer, or some other serial device, you will have to determine which port they are set to. You cannot have two serial devices set to the same COM port unless you have special software that allows them to share the port.

A simple modem test

It is often difficult to determine which COM port is being used by a device. You can use the AT command to determine if your modem is working with this simple test:

Switch to your communications software directory. At the DOS prompt C:> type the following using uppercase: ECHO AT DT12345>COM1:. The AT is for modem attention, the DT is for dial tone. If you have a pulse phone system, the command would be AT DP12345. If the modem is set properly, you will hear a dial tone, then the modem will dial 12345. The modem will then emit a continuous busy signal. You can stop the busy signal by invoking the command ECHO ATHO. The HO tells it to hang up.

If two devices are both set for the same COM port there will be a conflict. The computer will try for a while, then give an error message and the familiar Abort, Retry, Ignore, Fail? If the modem is connected to COM1 and you invoke the command ECHO AT DT12345>COM2, you will get the message, Write fault error writing device COM2. Abort, Retry, Ignore, Fail?

You may not get any message and not hear the dial tone if the COM ports on both the I/O board and motherboard are enabled. You must disable those ports that are not used.

A diagnostic program such as Check-It Pro from TouchStone, at (714) 969-7746, can determine which ports are being used. It also does several other very helpful diagnostic tests. Another good program for finding port conflicts is the Port Finder from the mcTronic Systems, at (713) 462-7687.

It is very important that you keep any documentation that you get with your various plug-in boards. Many of the I/O boards have dozens of pins and jumpers. If you don't have the documentation, you may never be able to determine how it should be configured. It is also necessary that you write down and keep a log of which ports and addresses are enabled. It can save a lot of time. Eventually, we will have true plug and play hardware, which will make life so much easier.

Plug in the modem board and hook it up to the telephone line. Unless you expect to do a lot of communicating, you may not need a separate dedicated line. The modem may have an automatic answer mode. In this mode it will always answer the telephone. Unless you have a dedicated line, this mode should be disabled. Check your documentation. There should be a switch or some means to disable it.

There should be two connectors at the back end of the board. One may be labeled for the line in and the other for the telephone. Unless you have a dedicated telephone line, you should unplug your telephone, plug in the extension to the modem and line, then plug the telephone into the modem.

After you have connected all of the lines, turn on your computer and try the modem before you put the cover back on. Use the simple test that was mentioned above.

Make sure you have communications software then call a local bulletin board. Even if you can't get through, or have a wrong number, you should hear the dial tone, then hear it dial the number.

 # Bulletin boards

If you have a modem, you have access to several thousand computer bulletin boards. At one time, most bulletin boards were free of any

charge. You only had to pay the phone bill if they are out of your calling area. But there have been a lot of low-down scum who have uploaded software with viruses, pirated commercial software has been loaded onto some of them, stolen credit card numbers have been posted and many other loathsome and illegal activities. Because of this, the Sysops (systems operators) have had to spend a lot of time monitoring their BBS. Many of the bulletin boards now charge a nominal fee to join, some just ask for a tax deductible donation.

Some of the bulletin boards are set up by private individuals and some by companies and vendors as a service to their customers. Some are set up by users groups and other special interest organizations. There are over 100 boards nationwide that have been set up for doctors and lawyers. You probably won't be surprised to know that there are gay bulletin boards in the San Francisco area and other areas. There are also X-rated boards and several for dating.

Many of the bulletin boards are set up to help individuals. They usually have lots of public domain software and a space where you can leave messages for help, advertising something for sale, or just plain old chit-chat.

If you are just getting started, you probably need some software. There are all kinds of public domain and shareware software packages that are equivalent to almost all of the major commercial programs. And the best part is that the public domain software is free and the shareware is practically free.

Viruses

A few years ago, you could access a bulletin board and download all kinds of good public domain or shareware software. You never had to worry about the software destroying your data. Because a few sick psychopaths have created computer viruses, you now have to use safeguards. You now must be quite selective and careful about where you get your software and who you get it from.

A computer virus is not a living thing, it cannot harm you, only the data in a computer or on a disk. But you may have invested a large

part of your life creating that data. A computer virus is usually a bit of program code, hidden in a piece of legitimate software. The virus is usually designed to redirect, corrupt, or destroy data. The computer virus may resemble an organic virus in that it can cause a wide variety of virus-type symptoms in the computer host.

The virus code may be written so it can replicate or make copies of itself. When it becomes embedded on a disk, it can attach itself to other programs that it comes in contact with. Whenever a floppy disk is inserted into the drive, it can come away with a hidden copy of the virus.

Infected software may appear to work as it should for some time. But eventually, it may contaminate and destroy many of your files. If a virus gets on a workstation or network, it can infect all of the computers in the network. The McAfee Associates, at (408) 988-3832, has one of the best shareware anti-virus programs available. McAfee has a bulletin board, at (408) 988-4004, from which you can download the latest version. They constantly revise the program to try to keep up with the latest viruses.

PC Tools, at (503) 690-8090, Disk Technician Gold from Prime Solutions, at (619) 274-5000, Microsoft DOS 6.0, and later versions and IBM PC-DOS 7.0 all have anti-virus utilities. PC Tools, which is now a part of the Symantec Corp., constantly upgrades their anti-virus utilities also. The anti-virus utility in DOS is under the command MSAV, or MWAV for Windows.

 # Where to find bulletin boards

Several computer magazines devote a lot of space to bulletin boards and user groups. In California the *MicroTimes* and *Computer Currents* magazines have several pages of bulletin boards and user groups each month. The *Computer Shopper* magazine has the most comprehensive national listing of bulletin boards and user groups of any magazine. The *Computer Shopper* alternates each month with a listing of user groups one month and Bulletin Boards the next.

If you have a bulletin board or belong to a user group and want them listed in the *Shopper*, use your modem and submit your entry to (913) 478-3088 at 2400 bps.

Online services

One of the most popular of the large national online service companies is CompuServe, at (800) 848-8199. They provide forums for help and discussions, mail boxes, and a large variety of information and reference services. A caller can search the databases and download information as easily as pulling the data off his own hard disk. The company charges a fee for the connect time.

Prodigy, at (800) 284-5933, was unlike the other online services at first because they did not charge for connect time. They charged only a very nominal monthly rate. They have recently revised their fee structures so for certain types of service you may be charged over and above the monthly rate. They have phone service to most areas in the larger cities so there is not even a toll charge. They have an impressive list of services including home shopping, home banking, airline schedules and reservations, stock market quotations, a medical bulletin board, and many others.

America Online, at (800) 827-6364, offers all of the services provided by CompuServe and Prodigy and gives you 10 free hours just to try the service. All you need is a modem and Windows. AOL sends you a sign-on disk that has the connect software. AOL has lots of local access numbers, so in most cases it shouldn't be a toll call. After the first 10 free hours, it costs $9.95 per month. For the $9.95, you get 5 hours each month. If you go beyond the 5 hours, there is a nominal extra charge.

Delphi, at (800) 695-4005, is another popular online service. Like the other systems, you can get stock quotes, access encyclopedias, news wires, the Internet, and hundreds of other services.

 # Banking by modem

Many banks offer systems that let you do all your banking with your computer and a modem from the comfort of your home. You would never again have to drive downtown, hunt for a parking space, then stand in line for a half hour to do your banking.

Intuit, at (415) 322-0573, developed Quicken, which is an excellent financial software program. Intuit offers CheckFree, a service that allows you to pay all your bills electronically. Or it allows you to print your checks from your computer on a laser printer. This requires special checks that are imprinted with your account number in magnetic ink.

CheckFree costs about $10 a month. If you spend about 4 hours a month paying bills, $10 is not much compared to the time spent. Another advantage to CheckFree is that the bills are paid automatically, but not until they are due. This lets your account accrue interest until the last moment. If you write a lot of checks, CheckFree and Quicken can quickly pay for themselves.

Intuit is now merged with ChipSoft, at (602) 295-3070. ChipSoft is the developer of TurboTax, one of the better software packages for doing your taxes. The marriage of these two companies means that they can offer the most complete financial software available for your computer system. With a good financial program, you can get rid of the shoe boxes full of canceled checks. The data that is in your computer can automatically flow onto the TurboTax forms. It can make the onerous task that occurs on April 15 each year a bit easier to accomplish.

 # Facsimile machines

Facsimile (fax) machines have been around for quite a while. Newspapers and businesses have used them for years. The early machines were similar to the early acoustic modems. Both used foam rubber cups that fit over the telephone receiver-mouthpiece for coupling. They were very slow and subject to noise and interference. Fax machines and modems have come a long way since those days.

A page of text or a photo is fed into the facsimile machine and scanned. As the scanning beam moves across the page, white and dark areas are digitized as 1s and 0s, then transmitted out over the telephone lines. On the receiving end of the line, a scanning beam sweeps across the paper. The dark areas cause it to print as it sweeps across the paper. The finished product is a black and white image of the original. When a text file is sent by modem, the digitized bits that make up each character are converted from digital voltage to analog voltage. A modem sends and receives bits that make up each character. A fax machine or board sends and receives scanned whole pages of letters, graphics, images, signatures, etc. Since a modem recognizes individual characters, a computer program can be sent over a modem, but not over a fax. A fax sends and receives the information as digitized graphic data. A modem converts the digital information that represents individual characters into analog voltages, sends it over the line, then converts it back to individual digital characters.

There are times when a modem or fax is needed. Both units could not be in use at the same time on the same phone line. Otherwise a single phone line can be used for both fax and modems.

There are millions of facsimile machines in use today. There are very few businesses that cannot benefit from the use of a fax. It can be used to send documents, that include handwriting, signatures, seals, letterheads, graphs, blueprints, photos, and other types of data around the world, across the country, or across the room to another fax machine.

Express mail may cost from $8 to $10 or more. A fax machine can deliver the same letter for about 40 cents and do it in less than three minutes. Many of the software programs let you delay sending a fax until late at night to get the best rates. Depending on the type of business, and the amount of critical mail that must be sent out, a fax system can pay for itself in a very short time.

Most of the fax machines use thermal type paper for printing, especially the lower cost machines. The thermal paper does not provide very good resolution and it fades when exposed to light. The better, and more expensive, fax machines use ink jet or laser technology and print on plain paper.

They are usually a bit slow, but almost all of the fax machines can be used as a copier. Fax machines have a lot in common with copy machines, scanners, and printers. Several companies have added these features to machines so one machine does the work of several.

 # Fax/modem computer boards

Several companies have developed fax systems on circuit boards that can be plugged into computers. Most of the fax boards are now integrated with a modem on the same board. The modem and fax combination costs very little more than either board separately. This combination also saves having to use an extra plug-in slot.

For some time, the standard baud rate for fax was 9600. But many of the newer fax-modem boards are now capable of a 14,400 speed for both modem and fax. However, just like the modem connections, both the sender and receiver must be operating at the same speed. Also like the modem, the fax can shift down to match the receiver if it is slower.

Special software allows the computer to control the fax boards. Using the computer's word processor, letters and memos can be written and sent out over the phone lines. Several letters or other information can be stored or retrieved from the computer hard disk and transmitted. The computer can be programmed to send the letters out at night when rates are lower.

But the computer fax boards have one disadvantage. They cannot scan information that is not in the computer. Without a scanner the information that can be sent is usually limited to that which can be entered from a keyboard or disk.

However, the computer can receive and store any fax. The digitized data and images can be stored on a hard disk, then printed out.

 # Fax software

You need fax software. There are several companies who provide the software. Ordinarily, when you receive a fax, it is in graphics form so

all you can do is view it. Some of the newer Fax plus OCR software packages, such as UltraFAX from WordStar, have optical character recognition (OCR) capabilities. This software can automatically scan the incoming fax and convert it to individual characters. You can then edit the fax, combine it with a word processor file, a spreadsheet or database, or just save parts of it. You can also print it out on a laser printer for much better resolution than you normally get from a fax. A fax that has been converted to digital characters takes up much less disk space than the normal graphic form.

There are several other companies that offer Fax plus OCR. WordStar's UltraFAX is about the least expensive. Intel's Faxability Plus/OCR is fairly expensive at about twice the price of UltraFAX. They both have about the same features. Here are some of the other companies that offer Fax plus OCR software:

➤ BitFax/OCR	Bit Software	(510) 490-2928
➤ FaxMaster	Caere Corp.	(408) 395-7000
➤ WinFax Pro	Delrina Corp.	(800) 268-6082
➤ Eclipse Fax	Phoenix Tech.	(617) 551-4000
➤ DataFax	Trio Information	(800) 880-4400
➤ Faxability+OCR	Intel Corp.	(800) 538-3373
➤ UltraFAX	WordStar	(415) 382-4859

Fax-on-demand

Several companies have set up fax machines that can supply information to you 24 hours a day. You simply call them with your voice phone, tell them what documents you want, give them your fax number and the documents will be sent immediately.

Most of the companies have a catalog that lists all of their documents and the document number. You should first ask to have the catalog faxed to you. You can then determine which documents to order.

The FaxFacts Company, at (708) 682-8898, publishes a small booklet that lists several companies that have the fax-on-demand or

faxback capability. They list things such as medical, computers, travel, trade shows, and many more.

Most faxback information is free, but some companies such as Consumer Reports, at 800-766-9988, ask for a credit card number and charge a fee for articles you request. Here are just a few of the other companies who offer faxback or fax-on-demand (when you call, ask for new users instructions and navigation map):

- ➤ Borland TechFax   (800) 822-4269
- ➤ Central Point Anti-Virus   (503) 690-2660
- ➤ IBM   (800) 426-4329
- ➤ Novell Support Line   (800) 638-9273
- ➤ Symantec Corp.   (800) 554-4403
- ➤ WordStar Fax Support   (404) 514-6333

If you prefer, most will send the information to you by mail rather than by fax.

Fax/modem/phone switch

Having the modem and telephone on the same line should cause no problems unless someone tries to use the telephone while the modem is using it. Life is a lot simpler, though, if you have a switch that can detect whether the incoming signal is for a fax, a modem, or voice. Fax and modem signals transmit a high pitched tone, called the *CNG (calling) signal*. A fax/modem switch can route the incoming call to the proper device. You should be aware that some older systems do not use the CNG signals. My Command Communication system lets me manually transfer the call in that case. If I know the incoming call is a fax, I can press 1 1 and it switches to the fax machine. If it is a modem call, I can press 2 2 and it switches to the modem.

Of course, I have to be there to answer such a call. One solution to this problem for those people who have machines without the CNG signal is to have the caller punch in the 1 1 or 2 2 on his or her end

after they dial the number. I can also put this instruction on my answering machine if I am not available.

Command Communications, at (800) 288-6794, has several different model switchers that are suitable for homes, small offices, and up to large businesses. They have connections for a telephone answering device (TAD), telephone extensions, a fax machine or fax board, and a connection for an auxiliary or modem. The alternative to a switcher would be to install a dedicated telephone line for the fax machine, another for the modem, and a third line for voice. If you don't do a lot of transmissions by fax and modem, you can get by with a single telephone and a good switcher. It can pay for itself many times over.

There is another solution for the problem of those people who have machines without the CNG signal. The telephone company can set up two or more numbers with different and distinctive rings on a single line. The Command Communications switchers can be programmed to recognize the distinctive ring and route the call to the proper device. The South Tech Instruments Company, at (800) 394-5556, has a FoneFilter device that can recognize the distinctive rings and route the call to a fax, modem, or answering machine. Of course, there is a charge by the telephone company for the extra numbers added to your line. At this time, in the Los Angeles area, it costs $7.50 to set up a separate distinctive ring on your line and then $6.00 a month thereafter. This is still less expensive than adding a second line.

Telephone outlets for extensions

You need a telephone line or extension to hook up a computer modem or a fax. You may also want telephone outlets in several rooms or at one or more desks or at another computer. You can go to almost any hardware store, and even some grocery and drug stores, to buy the telephone wire and accessories needed. But you may have trouble running telephone wires to the computer, desks, and other rooms. It can be a lot of work cutting holes in the walls and running the wires up in the attic or under the floor.

There is a much simpler way. Just use the 110-volt wiring of the building. The Phonex Company, at (801) 566-0100, developed special adapters that plug into any wall plug outlet. It requires at least two adapters, one for the input telephone line, then another adapter for where you want the extension. More adapters can be plugged into any other 110-volt outlet to provide as many telephone extensions as needed. Or if you need an extension in another location, just unplug an adapter and plug it into another nearby wall outlet. Electronic circuitry in the adapters blocks the ac voltage from getting into the telephone lines, but allows voice and data to go through. The device is being marketed and sold by General Electric and Comtrad Industries, at (800) 992-2966.

 # Computerized answering machines

Many companies have replaced real live people with computerized answering machines. I can understand why the companies might want to install the computerized machines. The machines don't take coffee breaks, they don't need health insurance, vacation benefits, parking spaces, and other perks. The companies are saving money with the automated answering machines.

One telephone technology that I do like is the speaker phone. If I am put on hold, I can turn on the speaker and go about my business while waiting to talk to a live person.

 # Combination devices and voice mail

The Compex International Company, at (800) 626-8112, has an all-in-one fax, scanner, printer, and copier.

The Speaking Devices Corporation, at (408) 727-2132, has a unit with a fax, fax/phone Switch, scanner, voice mail, and caller ID.

Boca Research, at (407) 997-6227, has a 14.4K Multimedia Voice Modem that has up to 1000 password protected voice and fax mailboxes, has private and public fax on demand, remote message and fax retrieval, professionally recorded greetings, and voice prompts and personalized greetings for individual mailboxes.

Tiger Software, at (800) 888-4437, publishes a catalog that has hundreds of software and hardware items. They advertise the Vomax 2000, which is a Fax, voice, and modem system. It has one megabyte of digital storage that can store up to 20 minutes of voice mail messages or up to 50 sheets of faxes. It has message forwarding so it can call another number and play your messages. It can also call your pager and relay messages. Call Tiger Software for a catalog and more information.

Telecommuting

Millions of people risk their lives and fight frustrating traffic every day. Many of these people have jobs that could allow them to stay home, work on a computer, then send the data to the office over a modem or a fax. Even if the person had to buy their own computer, modem and fax, it still might be worth it. You could save the cost of gasoline, auto maintenance, and lower insurance. Thousands are killed on the highways. Telecommuting can be a life saver.

Being able to work at home would be ideal for those who have young children, the handicapped, or anyone who hates being stuck in traffic jams. Over 7 million PCs were purchased for the home in 1995. It is expected that about half of all PCs sold in 1996 will be for home use. A large percentage of those computers will be used for telecommuting.

Remote control software

If you are on the road or working from home and have a computer at the office, it is often necessary to access the data on that computer. There are several software packages that allow you to connect from

remote locations. You can be sitting in a distant hotel room or at a PC at home and dial up a computer at the office. You can take control across a phone line or across a network and work just as if you were sitting in front of the office computer. You can review documents, update files, edit reports, do printouts, or download files.

Here are a few software packages for remote control:

> Reachout   Ocean Isle   (800) 677-6232

> Norton pcAnywhere   Symantec

> Carbon Copy   Microcom

> Close-Up   Norton Lambert

> CO/Session   Triton

You should be able to find the above software at most software stores or find them listed in software catalogs, such as the MicroWarehouse, at 800-367-7080, or DellWare, at 800-847-4051.

All of these packages work only if the computer is turned on and booted up. Server Technology has Remote Power On/Off + AUX. This device plugs into the power line between the computer and the wall plug. The telephone line plugs into this device. When the device detects an incoming call it automatically turns on and boots up the PC. When the call is ended, it can turn off the PC. It can even let you reboot if the computer hangs up for some reason. Some companies bundle the Remote Power On/Off with the pcAnywhere and other remote software. It is available from Dellware, Micro Warehouse, and other discount catalog stores.

 # Telephony

There have been some important advances in computers and telephony in the last few years. Even greater changes can be expected soon. All of the items listed below can be used in a large business or a small office or home office (SOHO). The SOHO has become a very important element of business today.

A new magazine has recently been published that is devoted entirely to telephone computer technology. The magazine is free to qualified subscribers. If you work for a company, for yourself, use a telephone or computer, then you can probably qualify for a free subscription. Call (800) 677-3435 and ask them to send you a qualifying form.

Telephone conference

It is very simple to have a telephone conference with as few as two persons or as many as several hundred. In the conference calls, everyone on the line can talk to anyone else on the line. You can do teleconferences from home, a small, or a large office.

Fax conferences

If you have a fax machine, you can send out a graphics design, or plans or any number of business papers, have other persons review the plan or whatever, make changes or sign it, and return it. You can have an interactive meeting with others in the same building, or almost anywhere in the world, over a simple telephone line. One disadvantage is that it is not in real time. You have to send the fax, then wait for a reply.

Modem teleconferences

With a computer modem you can have a desktop conference. You send data, graphics, and other materials over the telephone line to other computers over a local area network (LAN), in the same building or almost anywhere in the world. Other persons sitting at the computer, can view the text data, spreadsheets, graphics, and other materials. The persons can change the material or interact with the other persons on the line in real time.

One of the better products that can help with a desktop conference is called TALKShow, from Future Labs, at (415) 254-9000 or Fax at (408) 736-8030. This small simple program works under Windows. Each person in the conference must have a copy of TALKShow

installed on their computer. TALKShow connects everyone together and automatically handles all of the computer communications.

The same data appears on all the computer screens that are on the line. Many live conferences use a large white board in front of the conference room. The leader writes on the board while the attendees watch, and perhaps make comments for changes. With TALKShow, each computer screen becomes a white board. Each individual can suggest changes or additions to the material on the screen. Of course, if it is the president of the company who is leading desktop conference, you may have to be careful of what you suggest.

With TALKShow, anything that appears on the screen can be saved on the hard disk or printed out.

 # National telephone directories

I live in the Los Angeles area. In Los Angeles and Orange Counties, there are over 100 suburban cities with over 12 million people. Can you imagine a single telephone directory that would list all of these people? Or how about a telephone directory that would list all of the millions of people in New York? Or Boston or San Francisco? Believe it or not there are such directories. And these directories are smaller than one that you might find in a small town. These national directories are small because they are on CD-ROM discs.

The ProPhone, from New Media Publishing, at (617) 631-9200, has seven CD-ROM discs, 6 discs for the *white pages* and one disc for businesses in the United States. There is over 600MB of data on each disc. They list the telephone numbers, the address, and zip codes. They do not have every person listed on the discs. The separate disc for business makes it very easy to look up a company anywhere in the country.

The PhoneDisc, from Digital Directory Assistance at (301) 657-8548, only has five CD-ROM discs. It has over 90 million listings of residential and businesses. It does not have a separate business disc, but lists businesses along with the general population in the white pages.

If you are in a business where you have to contact a lot of people, then you need these two directories. You may also need them if you live in the Los Angeles area.

 # ISDN

ISDN is an acronym for *Integrated Services Digital Network*. Most of the ISDN networks are made up of fiber-optic cable. Eventually, the whole world will have telephone systems that use this concept. It will be a system that will be able to transmit voice, data, video, and graphics in digital form rather than the present analog. When this happens, we can scrap our modems. We will then need only a simple interface to communicate at up to several million bits per second.

ISDN is already installed in several cities. But don't throw your modem away just yet. The new service may not be available at all locations for some time. It will be rather expensive.

 # Sources

I have not listed the names and manufacturers of modems and faxes because there are so many. Look in any computer magazine and you see dozens of ads. A recent copy of the *Computer Shopper* had ads for about 200 modem/fax boards from several different companies.

One modem company that we do want to mention is USRobotics. They manufacture a large variety of modems, especially the high end, high speed type. The company will send you a free 110-page booklet that explains about all you need to know about modems. For a free booklet, call (800) 342-5877.

 # Books

John Dvorak and Nick Anis put together a very good book they called *Dvorak's Guide to PC Telecommunications*. It was published in 1990, so it is a bit dated. But some of the information is timeless, so

it is just as good today as it was in 1990. It is published by
Osborne/McGraw-Hill, 2600 10th Street, Berkeley, California
94710.

Another good book to have is *The Complete Guide to CompuServe*
by Brad and Debra Schepp. It was also published in 1990 by Osborne
McGraw-Hill, but it also has information that is as essential today as it
was a short time ago.

CHAPTER 12

Printers

F OR the vast majority of applications, a computer system is not complete without a printer. This chapter discusses some of the features and functions of the different types of printers.

⇨ A bit of history

Johann Gutenberg started the printer revolution way back in 1436 when he developed movable type and began the printing of the first Bible. Though he started printing the first Bible, he did not complete it. He had borrowed money from a man named Johann Fust. When Gutenberg could not repay the loan, Fust took over the press and type and completed the work started by Gutenberg. So it was Fust who was first to print the Bible, not Gutenberg.

⇨ Printer life expectancy

Printers usually have a long life. As a result, I have only bought a few different printers in the last ten years. When I have needed an excuse to buy a new printer, I just passed my old ones on to my children. These old printers are all still going strong. Although printers usually last a long time, like most other industries, the printer manufacturers constantly introduce new and improved models.

There are several types of printers. There are some that are more suitable for certain applications than others. Several types are briefly discussed.

 # Dot matrix printers

There are dot matrix printers in a large number of price ranges. The print quality of the low priced 9 pin systems may be poor. The low priced ones are also limited in fonts and graphics capability. The laser printer speed is measured by the average number of pages per minute it can print. Dot matrix printers' speed is measured by the characters per second (cps) they can print. They can print much faster in the draft mode than in the NLQ mode. There are some high end dot matrix line printers that can print a whole line at a time. Some of them can print up to 1000 lines per minute. In order to get the high speed, some dot matrix may have four or more heads, with each head printing out a different line.

Many of the dot matrix printers can also print using different fonts. But the number of fonts is usually limited to less than ten. Only a few higher priced units can use scalable fonts. Some can print limited graphics, but they are usually very slow. Some of them can even print fairly good color by using low cost multicolor ribbons.

 # Advantages of dot matrix

One of the distinct advantages that dot matrix printers have over the lasers is the low cost. Some dot matrix printers cost less than $150. Of course, there are some high-end dot matrix printers, such as the very fast line printers, that may cost close to $10,000.

The dot matrix is not only lower in initial cost, they are usually lower in cost of printing per page. The *PC Magazine* estimated that it costs less than one cent per page for dot matrix printing. It costs two to three cents per page for lasers and about six cents a page for ink jets. It may cost from 50 cents to more than a dollar per page to print high resolution color graphics.

There are many applications where a dot matrix printer is needed to accomplish a task. Wide continuous sheets are necessary for some spreadsheet printouts. My LaserJet can't handle anything wider than

8½ inches. With the wide carriage on my Star dot matrix, the wide sheets are no problem.

Another advantage is the number of sheets that can be printed. Most lasers have from 100 to 250 sheet bins. The dot matrix can print up a whole box of 5000 sheets of fanfold continuous sheets. (It has been my experience though, if I start a job that requires a lot of printed sheets, as long as I stand there and watch the printer, it works perfectly. If I walk away and start doing something else, the printer immediately has a paper jam or some other problem. This is probably one of Murphy's many laws.)

Many offices and businesses still use multiple sheet forms. A laser printer can't handle these forms, but a dot matrix can easily print them.

The dot matrix can also print on odd sizes, shapes, and thicknesses of paper. There are many times when I use mine to address large manila envelopes.

The U.S. Post Office has adopted a Postnet bar code that helps sort and speed up mail. If you look at some of the envelopes that you receive in the mail, you may see the Postnet bar codes below the address. Many of the companies that send out bulk mail use this code. Several of the dot matrix printers have the Postnet bar code built-in, some others offer it as an option. The Post Office gives a discount when the envelopes have the Postnet code on them. If you do a lot of mailing, a printer with the Postnet option could save you some money.

Dot matrix color

Most major dot matrix printer manufacturers offer printers that can produce color. These dot matrix printers can use a multicolored ribbon to print out color. The ribbons are wider than the standard ribbons. The ribbons usually have different color stripes so one part is red, one green, one blue, and one black. The ribbons are fairly inexpensive and the extra cost for the color option is quite reasonable.

You need special software to print color on the dot matrix. Under the control of the software the heads move up and down and strike

whatever color stripes on the ribbon that are needed. By striking the red, green, and blue colors on the ribbon, and overprinting them when necessary, all of the colors of the rainbow can be blended and printed. The result is definitely not of photographic quality, and it is a bit slow. But if you need color to jazz up a presentation, or for accent now and then, they are great.

 # Maintenance costs

Maintenance costs of dot matrix are usually much less than that for lasers and ink jets. The main costs for a dot matrix is to replace the ribbon about every 3000 sheets. A dot matrix ribbon may cost from $3.00 to $10.00. A color ribbon may cost from $20 to $35. A laser toner cartridge also lasts for about 3000 sheets and may cost from $30.00 to $100.00 to replace.

 # Number of pins

There are still a few 9-pin dot matrix printers being sold today, but most people are buying those with a 24-pin print head. The 24-pin head has much better resolution and may cost only a few dollars more. The 24-pin printer forms characters from two vertical rows of 12 pins in each row.

There are small electric solenoids around each of the wire pins in the head. An electric signal causes the solenoid to push the pins forward. Dot matrix printers are also called *impact printers* because the pins impact against the ribbon and paper. The solenoids press one or more of the various pins as the head moves in finite increments across the paper so any character can be formed.

Figure 12-1 is a representation of the pins if it were a 7-pin print head and how it would form the letter A. The numbers on the left represent the individual pins in the head before it starts moving across the paper. The first pin to be struck would be number 7, then number 6, then 5, 4, 3, 5, and 2, 1, 2 and 5, 3, 4, 5, 6, then 7.

A 24-pin head would be similar to the 7-pin representation above, except that it would have two vertical rows of 12 pins, side-by-side, in

```
1 o              o                          Figure 12-1
2 o             o o
3 o            o   o
4 o           o     o         How a 7-pin dot matrix printer
5 o          o o o o          forms the letter A
6 o          o       o
7 o          o       o
```

Print Head moves in this direction ==>

each row. The pins in one row would be slightly offset and lower than the pins in the other row. Since the pins are offset, they would overlap slightly and fill in the open gaps normally found in a 9-pin system.

There is a lot of competition among the dot matrix and laser companies for your dollar. Some vendors are now selling laser printers for about the same price as some of the dot matrix printers. This low cost of the lasers has forced the dot matrix people to lower their prices. In addition to lower prices, many dot matrix companies are also adding more features, such as more memory and more fonts, in order to attract buyers.

 # Some disadvantages of dot matrix

Some of the disadvantages are that the dot matrix can't come close to the quality printing of a laser. In the draft mode, if the printer has a 24-pin print head, only half of the pins are hit. There is noticeable spacing between the dots. For NLQ, all of the pins are hit. In draft mode with a 9-pin head, all of the pins are hit, but there are spaces between the dots. For NLQ on a 9-pin system, the printer makes a second run with the head slightly displaced so the pins hit different spots and fill in the open spaces. So in draft mode the printing can be fairly fast, but has poor quality. In the NLQ mode, they slow down considerably but have much better quality.

Most 24-pin dot matrix printers have a resolution of 360×360 dots per inch (dpi). Until recently, the standard laser was rated at 300×300 dpi. But if you compare the dot matrix output to the laser, you can see that the laser has a much higher resolution. The reason is that the laser produces a much smaller dot than the dot matrix. So if

an A is printed out on a dot matrix, the jagged edges from the large dots are very apparent.

Most lasers can use scalable type fonts, only a very few of the high-end dot matrix printers can use scalable fonts.

Most dot matrix printers have only 8K or less of memory. A few of the high-end dot matrix printers may have as much as 64K or even up to 128K. The memory on a dot matrix can be used as a print buffer. The computer can download a file to the printer then go about its business doing other things. Laser printers use memory a bit differently. They take the file and format the whole page in memory before they start printing. Most lasers come with a minimum of 512K and you have the option to add more. For higher speed and graphics, the laser should have a minimum of 2MB.

One problem that most dot matrix printers have is that they are noisy. If you are working in an office where there are several printers going, it may cause you to buy some ear plugs. There are special enclosures that be used to make them a bit quieter. Some companies have developed some printers that are a bit less noisy, but they still can't match the laser for quiet operation.

If you can get by with a dot matrix, you should be able to find one at a very good price. Look for ads in the *Computer Shopper* or any of the other computer magazines.

Ink jets

Hewlett-Packard developed the first ink jet printer. Now there are many companies, such as Brother, Cannon, Epson, Texas Instrument, Lexmark, and several others, that are manufacturing ink jet printers. Some of the companies call them by a different name such as Canon's Bubble Jet, but they are all basically ink jets. The ink jet printers have a print output that approaches that of the laser, but at a lower cost. One very big advantage of some of the ink jets over the laser is that they can print color. Most of the ink jet manufacturers have one or more color models. Those models that can print in color

usually have a C in the model number, such as the HP DeskJet 550C or the Canon Bubble Jet BJC-600.

The ink jet printers use a system that is similar to the dot matrix printers. But instead of pins that press a ribbon onto the paper, they use a matrix of small ink jets that spray dots of ink on the paper. They also have a much larger number of ink jets; the dot matrix may have from 9 to 24 pins, the ink jet may have from 48 to 128 small jets. The head moves across the paper much like the dot matrix system. Again, much like the dot matrix system, ink from the small jets is sprayed onto the paper to form text or graphics. To print color, they have three or more color ink jets. Most of the ink jet printers come with one or more fonts, but they may be able to use several more that are available on plug-in font cartridges. Some of the ink jets can use scalable fonts.

Like the dot matrix, the speed of the ink jets is measured in characters per second. Depending on the type of print the average speed is about two pages per minute.

Some of the high-end fax machines that use ink jet technology have multiple functions. The ink jet fax machines from Ricoh Corp., HP, and other companies not only print excellent received faxes, they can be used as a copier or a computer printer.

The price of the single color ink jets is close to that of the dot matrix at $300 or less at this time. It is possible to buy different color ink cartridges and use it once in a while instead of the standard black. You could use a red or green to make up letterheads or use the color for accent. Here are a few of the companies who make low cost ink jet printers:

- ➢ Brother HJ-400   (800) 284-4357
- ➢ Canon BJ-200   (800) 848-4123
- ➢ C. Itoh CJ-300   (714) 833-1165
- ➢ Epson Stylus 800   (800) 289-3776
- ➢ HP DeskJet 500   (800) 752-0900
- ➢ Lexmark ExecJet   (800) 358-5835

> NEC Jetmate 1000   (800) 632-4636
> TI microMarc   (800) 257-3500

If you are interested in buying an ink jet printer, call the numbers above and ask them to send you a brochure and specification sheets.

⇨ Ink jet color

It is now possible to buy color ink jet printers for less than $300. Most people would like the option of being able to print color now and then. But some of the color machines can be very slow. About the best they can do is two pages per minute just printing black text. Lasers can print 4 to 8 pages per minute. A color graphics printout may take several minutes on an ink jet machine.

The ink jet color printers use a system of three different colored ink cartridges, cyan, magenta, and yellow, to print color. Some systems also have a black cartridge for standard text, some use the mixture of the three colors to make black. As the head moves across the paper, the software can have any of the various colors sprayed onto the paper. The colors can be blended much better than is possible on a dot matrix.

If you do any presentations using an overhead projector, the ink jets can handle transparencies very well. The color ink jet printers are ideal for creating low-cost colored transparencies for presentations, graphs, and schematic plotting and drawings.

Most of the ink jet cartridges are good for about 300 pages of text. They must then be replaced or refilled. The cartridges cost from $5 to $10 each.

At less than $300, the HP 540C is about the least expensive color ink jet printer you can buy at the present time. The HP DeskJet 560C and the Canon BJC-600 are a bit more expensive. They are about equivalent in speed, graphics capabilities, and cost. The HP DeskJet 1200C is a more sophisticated machine, has more memory and can print faster. HP also has a 1200C-PS that has PostScript. The IBM Jetprinter PS 4079 is also a PostScript printer and about

equivalent to the HP 1200C-PS. Of course, there are several options and features not listed above. Many of the companies have several different models of their products. Prices listed are for comparison only and may be different when you read this. Check through the ads in computer magazines.

Here are some of the color ink jet companies and their numbers:

> Canon Corp.   (800) 848-4123
> Hewlett-Packard   (800) 752-0900
> IBM Jetprinter PS 4079   (800) 358-5835

Call the companies for brochures and specifications.

The CJ10 from Canon Corp. is an all-around-do-everything color Bubble Jet copier/scanner/printer. This is an amazing machine that not only copies in color, it is also a color printer and scanner. With the available options, it can input graphics to a computer or copy and print from a still video camera, a video camera, a video player, a 35mm film projector, an intelligent editor, and other devices. It can scan almost any kind of color graphic into a computer. And it can print out almost any color graphic or text from a computer or from other input devices. This machine would satisfy just about all of the needs of an office. It can be used as a high speed plotter, for presentations, for color brochures, and thousands of other colorful uses.

The Canon CJ10 is rather expensive. The Lexmark Company, a branch of IBM, has developed a machine that is similar to the CJ10 in functions, but at a much lower cost.

There are several ink jet and color ink jet printers that I did not mention. There are many different models, from different companies with different features, functions, and prices. Look for ads in the major computer magazines.

⇨ Ink jet supplies

The original cost of a printer is not the end. If you do much printing, the cost of supplies may be more than the cost of the printer. Ink

cartridges may cost from $30 to $35. Some cartridges only last for about 300 pages. It is possible to refill some of the cartridges.

 # Laser printers

The Hewlett-Packard LaserJet was one of the first lasers. It was a fantastic success and became the *de facto* standard. There are now hundreds of laser printers on the market. Most of them emulate the LaserJet standard. Even IBM's laser printer emulates the HP standard. Laser printers are a combination of the copy machine, computer, and laser technology. They have excellent print quality, but they have lots of moving mechanical parts and are rather expensive.

Laser printers use synchronized, multifaceted mirrors and sophisticated optics to write the characters or images on a photosensitive rotating drum. The drum is similar to the ones used in repro machines. The laser beam is swept across the spinning drum and is turned on and off to represent white and dark areas. As the drum is spinning, it writes one line across the drum, then rapidly returns and writes another. It is quite similar to the electron beam that sweeps across the face of a television screen or computer monitor one line at a time.

The spinning drum is sensitized by each point of light that hits it. The sensitized areas act like an electromagnet. The drum rotates through the carbon toner. The sensitized areas become covered with the toner. The paper is then pressed against the drum. The toner that was picked up by the sensitized areas of the drum is left on the paper. The paper then is sent through a heating element where the toner is heated and fused to the paper. Except for the writing to the drum, this is the same thing that happens in a copy machine. Instead of using a laser to sensitize the drum, a copy machine takes a photo of the image to be copied. A photographic lens focuses the image onto the rotating drum, which becomes sensitized to the light and dark areas projected onto it.

 # Engine

The drum and its associated mechanical attachments is called an *engine*. Canon, a Japanese company, is one of the foremost makers

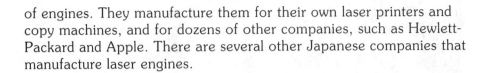

of engines. They manufacture them for their own laser printers and copy machines, and for dozens of other companies, such as Hewlett-Packard and Apple. There are several other Japanese companies that manufacture laser engines.

 # Low-cost laser printers

Because of the large number of companies manufacturing laser printers, there is lots of competition that is a great benefit to us consumers. The competition has driven prices of both lasers and dot matrix printers down. It has also forced many new improvements.

Until recently, most laser printers had a resolution of only 300 × 300. The Hewlett-Packard LaserJet IV has a resolution of 600 × 600. Some vendors are selling them for less than $1000.

Memory

If you plan to do any graphics or desktop publishing (DTP), you need to have at least 1MB of memory in the machine. Before it prints the first sheet, the printer loads the data into its memory and determines where each dot will be placed on the sheet. Of course, the more memory, the better.

Not all lasers use the same memory configuration. For some machines, you must buy a special plug-in board for the memory. Check the type of memory that you need before you buy.

Several companies offer laser memories. Here are a couple:

> ➢ ASP   (800) 445-6190
> ➢ Elite   (800) 942-0018

Page-description languages

If you plan to do any complex desktop publishing, you may need a page-description language (PDL) of some kind. Text characters and

graphics images are two different species of animals. Laser printer controllers are somewhat similar to monitor controllers. The monitor adapters usually have all of the alphabetical and numerical characters stored in ROM. When we press the letter A from the keyboard, it dives into the ROM chip, drags out the A, and displays it in a precise block of pixels wherever the cursor happens to be. These are called *bitmapped* characters. If you wanted to display an A that was twice as large, you would have to have a complete font set of that type in the computer.

Printers are very much like the monitors and have the same limitations. They have a library of stored discrete characters for each font that they can print. My dot matrix Star printer has an internal font and two cartridge slots. Several different font cartridges can be plugged into these slots. But they are still limited to those fonts that happen to be plugged in. With a PDL, the laser printer can take one of the stored fonts and change it, or scale it, to any size you want. These are *scalable fonts*. With a bitmapped font, you have one type face and one size. With scalable fonts, you may have one typeface with an infinite number of sizes. Most of the laser printers accept ROM cartridges that may have as many as 35 or more fonts. You can print almost anything that you want with these fonts if your system can scale them.

 # Speed

Laser printers can print from four to over ten pages per minute depending on the model and what they are printing. Some very expensive high-end printers can print over 30 pages per minute.

A dot matrix printer is concerned with a single character at a time. The laser printers compose, then print a whole page at a time. With a PDL, many different fonts, sizes of type, and graphics can be printed. But since the laser must determine where every dot that makes up a character, or image is to be placed on the paper before it is printed, the more complex the page, the more memory it will require and the more time needed to compose the page. It may take several minutes to compose a complex graphics. Once composed, it prints out very quickly.

A PDL controls and tells the laser where to place the dots on the sheet. Adobe's PostScript is the best known PDL.

⇨ Resolution

Most low-cost lasers still have a 300 × 300 dots per inch resolution (dpi). Which is very good, but not nearly as good as 1200 × 1200 dots per inch typeset used for standard publications. Several companies have developed systems to increase the number of dots to 600 dpi or better. The PrintSprint (Fig. 12-2) from Myriad Enterprise, at (714) 494-8165, can allow low-cost lasers to print at 600 × 600. It can also speed up the printer from 2 to 10 times faster. The PrintSprint uses a printer controller board that plugs into one of the slots on the motherboard and a small board that is installed in the laser options socket.

Figure 12-2

The PrintSprint can turn a 300-x-300-dpi laser printer into a 600-x-600. It can also speed up the printing.

The LaserMaster also has upgrade kits for the HP LaserJet III and LaserJet 4 that can increase the resolution to 1200 dpi. They also have several other upgrade kits. Call LaserMaster at (800) 327-8946 for details and brochures.

Most lasers print in the 8½"-×-11" A-size format. CalComp, a division of Lockheed, at (714) 821-2000, has developed a 600 × 600 high-resolution laser that can print in the 8½"-×-17" B-size format (Fig. 12-3). CalComp has also developed several color laser printers. Call them for brochures.

Figure 12-3

The CalComp CCL laser printer that outputs 600-×-600 print resolution. It can also print in the larger tabloid-size format.

Maintenance

Most of the lasers use a toner cartridge that is good for 3000 to 5000 pages. The cost of an original cartridge is about $75. Several small companies are now refilling the spent cartridges for about $30 each. It may be a good idea to keep an extra cartridge as a spare. The toner cartridge is sealed, so it lasts for some time on the shelf. I had a cartridge go out on a weekend when I was working on a tight deadline. Most stores that sell cartridges were closed. Since then, I keep a spare on hand.

Most laser printers keep track of the number of sheets that have been printed. If you have an H-P LaserJet, you can use the front panel buttons to run a self test. This tells you the configuration, how much RAM is installed, font cartridges installed, type of paper tray, how many pages have been printed, and several other tests.

When the toner gets low, most lasers display a warning message in the digital readout window. Or if the print is very light, the toner may be low. If you remove the toner cartridge and turn it upside down and shake it vigorously, sometimes you can get a few more copies out of it. This may help until you can get a replacement.

Of course, there are other maintenance costs. Since these machines are very similar to the repro copy machines, they have a lot of moving parts that can wear out and jam up. Most of the larger companies give a mean time between failures (MTBF) of 30,000 up to 100,000 pages. But remember that these are only average figures and not a guarantee. Most of the lasers are expected to have an overall lifetime of about 300,000 pages.

Paper

There are many different types and weights of paper. Almost any paper works in your laser. But if you use a cheap paper in your laser, it could leave lint inside the machine and cause problems in print quality. Generally speaking, any bond paper or a good paper made for copiers works fine. Colored paper made for copiers also works

fine. Some companies are marking copier paper with the word "Laser" and charging more for it. The lasers accept paper from 18 pound up to 24 pound easily. I have even used 67 pound stock for making up my own business cards. It is a bit heavy for wrapping around the drums and it jams once in a while. Some lasers use a straight-through path, so the heavier paper should not cause any problems in these machines.

Many of the laser printers are equipped with trays to print envelopes. Hewlett-Packard recommends envelopes with diagonal seams and gummed flaps. Make certain that the leading edge of the envelope has a sharp crease.

The Avery Company, at (818) 858-8245, and a few other companies make address labels that can withstand the heat of the fusing mechanism of the laser. There are also other specialty supplies that can be used with your laser. The Integraphix Company, (800) 421-2515, carries several different items that you might find useful. Call them for a catalog.

 # Color printers

There are several color printers that are available. They may cost from less than $1000 up to $15,000. These printers are often referred to as laser color printers, but at this time only QMS and Xerox actually uses the laser technology. The other companies use a variety of thermal transfer technologies using a wax or rolls of plastic polymer. The wax or plastic is brought into contact with the paper, then heat is applied. The melted wax or plastic material then adheres to the paper. Very precise points, up to 300 dots per inch, can be heated. By overlaying three or four colors, all of the colors of the rainbow can be created. The Fargo Electronics Company offers a color printer that uses the thermal wax for less than $1000. Of course, it does not have all of the goodies that you would find on the Tektronix Phaser or the CalComp ColorMaster.

Another type of color printer uses *dye-sublimation*, also called *thermal dye transfer* or *dye diffusion*. These systems use a ribbon with continuous series of four different color ink stripes across the ribbon. The paper that is to be printed is forced against the ink

ribbon. Dots of heat are applied to the various colors that cause the color to diffuse onto the paper. The higher the temperature, the more color that can be diffused. The dots of heat can be accurately controlled for up to 256 different shades for each color. The dye-sublimation provides the best resolution and can provide prints that are near photographic quality. But as you might suppose, these printers are also the most expensive. Again, the least expensive dye-sublimation printer is the Fargo.

The QMS ColorScript Laser 1000 is a true laser color printer. It blends four different color toners, black, cyan, magenta, and yellow to print out color. The drum is sensitized for each color and that color toner is transferred to it. Once all of the colors are applied to the drum, it then prints out on ordinary paper or on transparencies. The QMS ColorScript is still rather expensive at about $10,000, but it is still less than some high-end color lasers that may cost as much as $40,000.

The Xerox Corporation, at (716) 264-5482, has introduced a new true laser color printer. Call them for a brochure and pricing information.

Most of the color printers have PostScript, or they emulate PostScript. The Tektronix Phaser CP can also use the Hewlett-Packard Graphics Language (HPGL) to emulate a plotter. These color printers can print out a page much faster than a plotter.

One disadvantage of the color printers is the cost. Thermal wax may cost up to 45 cents per page, dye-sublimation may cost up to $2.75 per page. Most of this cost is for the ribbons and wax rolls that are used by the color machines.

The color printers are rather slow but the technology is improving. There will be several other color printers on the market soon. There is lots of competition so the prices are coming down.

Here are just a few of the companies who have color printers:

> CalComp, Lockheed   (800) 932-1212   Thermal transfer

> Fargo Electronics   (800) 258-2974   Thermal transfer and dye sublimation

> General Parametrics (800) 223-0999   Thermal transfer

➤ QMS ColorScript	(800) 631-2692	Thermal transfer
➤ Tektronix 200i	(800) 835-6100	Thermal transfer
➤ Tektronix Phaser III PXi	(800) 835-6100	Solid ink
➤ Tektronix Phaser II SDX	(800) 835-6100	Dye sublimation
➤ GCC Technologies	(800) 422-7777	Dye sublimation
➤ Kokak ColorEase	(800) 344-0006	Dye sublimation
➤ QMS Laser 1000	(800) 631-2692	Laser technology
➤ Xerox 4900	(716) 264-5482	Laser technology

One of the better printers is from CalComp, and I don't say that because I worked for Lockheed at one time. They build in excellent quality. On the downside, they are a bit expensive.

General Parametrics has a desktop film recorder attachment for their printer. This allows one to make 35mm color slides for presentations.

 # Plotters

Plotters can draw almost any two-dimensional shape or design under the control of a computer. The plotters are a bit like a robot. An arm selects a pen. The pen can be moved from side to side, while at the same time the sheet of paper may be moved from top to bottom. The computer can direct the pen to any point across the paper and can move the paper up or down for any point on an x-y axis. The motors are controlled by predefined x-y coordinates. They can move the pen and paper in very small increments so almost any design can be traced out.

Values can be assigned of perhaps 1 to 1000 for the y elements and the same values for the x or horizontal elements. The computer can then direct the plotter to move the pen to any point or coordinate on the sheet. Some of the newer plotters use ink jet technology instead of pens. This makes them faster. The different colored ink cartridges can be activated much quicker than moving an arm to a rack, selecting a pen, then replacing it, and selecting another.

Some less-expensive plotters use a thermal paper such as that used by fax machines. An advantage is that it may be much faster than the pen type plotters. A disadvantage is that this system does not provide any color. The resolution may also not be very good. The thermal paper also fades when exposed to light.

Plotters are ideal for such things as printing out circuit board designs, for architectural drawings, making transparencies for overhead presentations, graphs, charts, and many CAD/CAM drawings. All of this can be done in many different colors. The different colors can be very helpful if you have a complex drawing such as a multilayered motherboard. A different color could be used for each layer.

A plotter may have from one up to eight or more different colored pens. There are several different types of pens for various applications such as writing on different types of paper or on film or transparencies. Some pens are quite similar to ball point pens, others have a fiber type point. The points are usually made to a very close tolerance and can be very small so the thickness of the lines can be controlled. The line thicknesses can be very critical in some precise design drawings. The plotter arm can be directed to choose any one of the various pens.

There are several different sized plotters. Some desk top units are limited to only A and B sized plots. There are other large floor standing models that can accept paper as wide as four feet and several feet long. There are many very good graphics programs available that can use plotters. But there are several manufacturers of plotters and there are few or no standards. Just like the printers, each company has developed its own drivers. Again, this is very frustrating for software developers who must try to include drivers in their programs for all of the various brands.

Hewlett-Packard has been one of the major plotter manufacturers. Many of the other manufacturers now emulate the HP drivers. Almost all of the software that requires plotters includes a driver for HP. If you are in the market for a plotter, try to make sure that it can emulate the HP. One of the disadvantages of plotters is that they are rather slow. There are now some software programs that allow laser printers to act as plotters. Of course, they are much faster than a plotter, but except for the colored printers, they are limited to black and white.

 # Plotter sources

Here are a few of the plotter manufacturers. Call them for a product list and latest prices.

> ➤ Alpha Merics   (818) 999-5580
> ➤ Bruning Computer   (415) 372-7568
> ➤ CalComp   (800) 225-2667
> ➤ Hewlett-Packard   (800) 367-4772
> ➤ Houston Instrument   (512) 835-0900
> ➤ Ioline Corp.   (206) 775-7861
> ➤ Roland DG   (213) 685-5141

 # Plotter supplies

It is important that a good supply of plotter pens, special paper, film, and other supplies be kept on hand. Plotter supplies are not as widely available as printer supplies. A very high priced plotter may have to sit idle for some time if the supplies are not on hand. Most of the plotter vendors provide supplies for their equipment. One company that specializes in plotter pens, plotter media, accessories, and supplies is the Plotpro Company, at (800) 223-7568.

 # Installing a printer or plotter

Most IBM compatible computers allow for four ports, two serial and two parallel. No matter whether it is a plotter, dot matrix, or laser printer, it requires one of these ports. Most printers use the parallel port LPT1, most plotters use a serial port. Some printers have both serial and parallel connections.

If the serial port is used, the printer can be up to fifty feet from the computer. If the parallel is used, normally the cable can only be about ten feet. There are special devices that allow longer cables to be used.

The serial printers use an RS232C connector. The parallel printers use a Centronics type connector. When you buy your printer, buy a cable from the vendor that is configured for your printer and your computer.

 # Drivers

There are hundreds of printer manufacturers. Each manufacturer produces several different models. Every manufacturer and almost every model that is manufactured must have a unique software driver that tells the computer how to make it operate. The software drivers are special instructions for utilizing the various and unique capabilities of each printer model. There should be standards. Plotters must also have special software drivers.

If you don't have the proper driver for your printer or plotter, you may not be able to use it. Some printers and plotters can emulate some of the better known brands. Many laser printers emulate the HP LaserJet. Many dot matrix emulate the Epson models.

Windows has helped somewhat. The Windows software comes with the drivers of most printers. When the program is installed, you just point to your printer name and model and the driver is automatically installed.

 # Printer sharing

Ordinarily a printer sits idle most of the time. There are some days when I don't even turn my printer on. There are usually several computers in most large offices and businesses. Almost all of them are connected to a printer in some fashion. It would be a terrible waste of money if each computer had a separate printer that was only used occasionally. It is fairly simple to make arrangements so a printer or plotter can be used by several computers.

 # Sneaker net

One of the least expensive methods of sharing a printer is for the person to generate the text to be printed out on one computer,

record it on a floppy diskette, then walk over to a computer that is connected to a printer. If it is in a large office, a single low cost XT clone could be dedicated to running a high priced laser printer.

It doesn't matter whether the person carrying the floppy disk is wearing sneakers, brogans, or wing tips, the *sneaker net* is still one of the least-expensive methods of sharing printers.

 # Switch box

If there are only two or three computers, and they are fairly close together, it is not much of a problem. There are manual switch boxes that can allow any one of two or three computers to be switched on-line to a printer.

But with a simple switch box, if the computers use the standard parallel ports, the cables from the computers to the printer should be no more than 10 feet long. Parallel signals begin to degrade if the cable is longer than 10 feet and could cause some loss of data. A serial cable can be as long as 50 feet.

If an office or business is fairly complex, then there are several electronic switching devices available. Some of them are very sophisticated and can allow a large number of different types of computers to be attached to a single printer or plotter. Many of them have built-in buffers and amplifiers that can allow cable lengths up to 250 feet or more.

 # Printer-sharing device sources

Here are a few of the companies who provide switch systems. Call them for their product specs and current price list:

> ➤ Altek Corp.   (301) 572-2555
> ➤ Arnet Corp.   (615) 834-8000
> ➤ Belkin Components   (310) 515-7585
> ➤ Black Box Corp.   (412) 746-5530

➤ Buffalo Products	(800) 345-2356	Buffalo XL-256
➤ Crosspoint Systems	(800) 232-7729	
➤ Digital Products	(800) 243-2333	PrintDirector
➤ Fifth Generation	(800) 225-2775	Logical Connection
➤ Quadram	(404) 564-5566	Microfazer VI
➤ Rose Electronics	(713) 933-7673	
➤ Server Technology	(800) 835-1515	Easy Print
➤ Western Telematic	(800) 854-7226	

 # Green printers

The entire industry is under pressure to produce energy conservation products. The Federal Government will no longer buy computer products that do not meet Energy Star standards. Printers, especially laser printers, are notorious for being "energy hogs." Hewlett-Packard and most of the other manufacturers are designing newer models that go into a "sleep mode" after a period of inactivity. Ordinarily it takes from 20 to 30 seconds for a printer to warm up. Some of these models maintain a low voltage input so they can warm up almost instantly.

People with older printers can purchase a PC ener-g saver from the NEI Company, at (800) 832-4007. The printer, monitor, and keyboard can be plugged into this unit. After a period of inactivity, the printer and monitor shut down. You can set the period for any amount of time that you desire with the software.

The PC ener-g saver can pay for itself many times over in savings on electricity bills. Besides, you will be doing your part for energy conservation. Call them for brochures and details.

 # Progress

If Gutenberg were around today, you can bet that he would be quite pleased with the progress that has been made in the printing business. We have come a long way since 1436.

CHAPTER 13

CD-ROM

T ODAY, a CD-ROM drive is an essential part of your computer. Almost every computer sold within the next year will have a CD-ROM as standard equipment. It has become almost as necessary as a hard disk drive. Figure 13-1 shows a CD-ROM drive, a SCSI interface card, a sound card, and a SCSI hard disk.

A CD-ROM offers some very important benefits to the individual end user for entertainment, education, business, and industry. There are thousands and thousands of CD-ROM disc titles available.

A short time ago, CD-ROM disc titles were very expensive. But every day there is more and more competition. A CD-ROM title that cost $100 a few months ago can now be bought for less than half of that price. And the prices are still going down.

Figure 13-1

A CD-ROM drive with a SCSI interface card, a sound card, and a hard drive

CD-ROM and business

Some large businesses have huge databases of customers, invoices, prices, and other information. Businesses can use a single disc to replace large parts catalogs. A CD-ROM disc can store millions of part numbers, descriptions, drawings, costs, locations, and any other pertinent information.

In addition to paperwork records that are stored, some businesses keep important records on backup tape and floppy disks. Tape and floppy disks are only good for about 10 years before they start to deteriorate. A CD-ROM disc will last for 25 years or longer. It is much, much easier to search and find an item on a CD-ROM than on a backup tape or in a stack of paperwork.

If businesses replaced the millions of file folders and cabinets with CD-ROM discs, they could regain millions of square feet of office space. We could save thousands of trees if businesses saved documents electronically or on CD-ROM discs instead of putting everything on paper.

 # Home entertainment

A large number of the CD-ROM titles are designed for entertainment for both young and old. There are titles for arcade type games, chess, and other board games. There are titles for music, opera, art, and a large variety of other subjects to entertain you. Many of the titles are both educational and entertaining.

It takes a tremendous amount of memory to store digital images. Just one digitized frame of a movie may require over 25MB to store. At this rate, you could only store a few seconds of a movie on a standard CD-ROM disc. But new compression methods and new technologies will allow up to 3 hours of movies on systems that should be available by the time you read this.

 # Home library

At the present time, only one side of the CD-ROM discs are used for recording, but this single side can hold over 600MB of data. You can have a multitude of different programs on a single CD-ROM disc and a world of information at your fingertips. More books and information can be stored on just a few CD-ROM discs than you might find in an entire library. A 21-volume encyclopedia can be stored in just a fraction of the space on one side of a single CD-ROM disc. When data compression is used to store text, several hundred books can be stored on a single disc.

It may take only seconds to search through an entire encyclopedia or through several hundred books to find a subject, sentence, or a single word.

 # Easier way to learn

Text, graphics, sound, animation, and movies can be stored on CD-ROM discs. We have several avenues to the brain. The more avenues used to input information to our brain, the easier it is to learn and to remember. We can learn by reading. But we can learn much better if sound is added to the text. And we learn even better if graphics and motion are added. Rather than trying to remember just dry text, the many advantages of CD-ROM can make learning fun and pleasurable. Schools can use CD-ROM for teaching. Businesses can use CD-ROM to train their personnel.

 # Lawyers

Lawyers may have to spend hours and hours going through law books to find precedents, to find some of the finer points of the law, or to find loopholes. A few CD-ROM discs could replace several law clerks.

Health and medicine

The human body is a fantastic machine. There is more written about medicine and computers than any other subjects. There are several CD-ROMs published for the home user, such as the Family Doctor, published by Creative Multimedia Corp., (503) 241-4351, the Mayo Clinic Family Health Book, published by Interactive Ventures, (507) 282-2076, and several others.

A doctor must keep abreast of all of the scientific advances, new drugs, and treatments. A busy doctor can't possibly read all of the published papers. A CD-ROM can help. The American Family Physician is the official journal of the American Academy of Family Physicians. It is available from the Bureau of Electronic Publishing at (800) 828-4766.

The A.D.A.M. (for Animated Dissection of Anatomy for Medicine) Software Company, at (800) 755-2326, has developed several discs that show the various parts of the human anatomy. This CD-ROM is a very good tool for students and families wishing to learn about the human body. You are given an option of covering certain parts of the anatomy with fig leaves.

How CD-ROM works

CD-ROM is an acronym for *Compact Disc-Read Only Memory*. The system was first developed by Sony and Philips using lasers for recording and playing back music. (*LASER* is an acronym for *light amplification by stimulated emission of radiation*.) Almost all CD-ROM drives can also play the music compact discs. Most of the drives have a plug for ear phones and an audio connector on the back so it can be plugged into a sound card. You can set up a very good hi-fi system using a CD-ROM and a computer. Basically, the music compact disc systems are quite similar to the CD-ROM systems, but the CD-ROM drives are usually much more expensive.

When a CD-ROM disc is created, a powerful laser is turned on and off, in response to data 0s and 1s, which burns holes in the disc material. When the beam is turned to create a hole it is called a *pit*; when left off, the area of the track is called a *land*. When played back, a laser beam is focused on the track. The pits do not reflect as much light as the lands so it is easy to distinguish the digital data.

 # Laser color

As you know, white light encompasses all of the colors of the rainbow. Each color has its own frequency of vibration, the slower frequencies are at the dark red end. The frequencies increase as the colors move toward the violet end.

The particles that make up ordinary light are incoherent, that is, they are scattered in all directions. Lasers are possible because a single color of light can be sharply focused and amplified. All of the particles of one color are lined up in an orderly coherent fashion.

The laser effect can be obtained from several different gases and materials. Most of the present CD-ROM lasers use light at the lower frequency dark end of the spectrum, such as the red or yellow. The Samsung Company has developed a green laser. They claim that by using this laser and their proprietary compression techniques, they can store up to 110 minutes of the MPEG 2 video on a disc, five times as much as usual. (*MPEG* is an acronym for *Moving Pictures Experts Group*, which developed a set of methods for video compression.) Scientists are working to develop a blue laser that will have an even higher frequency. If they are successful, a CD-ROM with a blue laser will be able to store even more data on a disc than the green laser.

The data are recorded on a single spiral track that begins in the center and winds out to the outer edge. The track is divided into about 270,000 sectors, each sector with 2048 bytes. The sectors are numbered and given addresses according to the time in minutes, seconds, and hundredths of a second. For instance, the first sector is 00:00:00; the second sector is 00:00:01.

Remember that the hard disk has a head actuator that moves the head to the various tracks. The CD-ROM has a similar small motor that moves the laser beam to whatever sector on the track that is to be read. Figure 13-2 shows the CD-ROM disc spindle in the center. To the right is a slot with a white object that houses the laser beam. A small actuator motor moves the beam to whatever sector that is to be read.

Figure 13-2

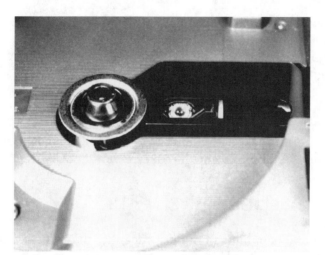

A CD-ROM drive that is partially disassembled to show the spindle in the center and the white object that houses the laser.

 # Rotational speed

If you remember your high school physics, the speed of a spinning disk or object is greater near the center than on the outer edge. If we took a track at the 2-inch diameter of the disk and stretched it out it would measure a little over 6 inches long ($\pi \times$ diameter = circumference, so $\pi \times 2$ inches = 6.28 inches). On the same disk, if a track at the 4-inch diameter is stretched out, it would measure over 12 inches long. At a constant speed, it is easy to see that an inner track passes beneath the head in about half the time that it takes for an outer track to pass beneath the head.

The CD-ROM uses a system that constantly changes the speed of the drive. The drive electronics speeds the disc up or slows it down depending on what area of the disk it is reading. When reading the inner portion the drive spins at about 200 rpm. When reading the outer portion, it spins at about 530 rpm. This is called *constant linear velocity (CLV)*.

The double speed CD-ROMs rotate at 400 rpm near the center and at 1060 rpm on the outer edge. The quad speed drives double these figures again. Plextor and several other companies have now introduced drives with 6 times the original speed.

I have used an old single speed drive with a proprietary interface for the last five years. It has worked fine for reading text, a few graphics, and sound. But I recently bought a Toshiba 3501 quad speed SCSI drive for my Pentium system. It makes a world of difference.

 # Transfer speed

From the early beginnings until just recently, the transfer speed, or the amount of time that it takes to read a track was 75 sectors per second. A sector is 2048 bytes (2K) times 75 is equal to 150K bytes per second.

Doubling the speed of the drive doubles the transfer rate to 300K bytes per second. A quad speed drive transfers data at 600K/s; the 6 times speed drives can transfer data at 900K/s. The faster transfer times allows video and motion to be displayed in a smooth fashion. The faster drives can read all of the CD-ROM discs that the slower drives can read, but read them faster.

The audio files must still be played back at the 150K rate. When playing audio the speed must drop down to the original speed of 200 to 530 rpm.

 # Data buffers and cache

The faster drives usually have a fairly large buffer system that also helps to smooth out video and motion. Data is read from the disc and

stored in a DRAM buffer, or cache, then downloaded to the PC at a very fast rate. The MPC specs call for a 64K buffer, but many of the newer systems have from 256K up to 2MB of DRAM memory buffers.

The Ballard Synergy Company, at (206) 656-8070, has developed software that can use a part of your hard drive for caching. Their d-Time[10] software can make almost any CD-ROM drive as fast as your hard disk drive. The software comes on a CD-ROM disc that has several utilities. Included is a Benchmark that measures the transfer speed of your CD-ROM drive and then measures the speed of your hard disk drive. I have an old Sony single speed CD-ROM installed on my 486DX2-66. This drive transfers data at 150K/s. It is very difficult to play back graphics or video. But if I run it with the d-Time[10], it can transfer data in 16-bit blocks at a rate of 840K/s, which is the speed of my older hard disk. I have a Toshiba quad speed CD-ROM on my Pentium. Using the d-Time[10] on this system, I can transfer data at a 1056K/s due to the faster hard disk drive.

The d-Time[10] software is very reasonable in cost. At the present time, it costs about one fourth of what a quad speed drive would cost and gives you almost all of the benefits.

 # Access or seek time

The access or seek time is the time necessary to find a certain block or sector on the track and begin reading it. The original MPC specification was that the drive should be able to find any block in 1000 milliseconds (ms) or 1 second. Most of the older drives had access times of 300 to 400 ms. Most of the newer machines now require about 200 ms.

 # CD-ROM differences

There are several different types of CD-ROM drives. Some mount internally, some are external, some use SCSI for an interface, some use an enhanced IDE interface, some use a proprietary interface, some are single speed, some double, triple, quad, or times 6 speed.

There are also a lot of different prices. The external drives may cost up to $100 more than an internal because they need a power supply and cables.

What you should buy depends on your needs.

 # Proprietary interface systems

If the CD-ROM drive uses a proprietary interface, it has a special card and ribbon cable. The interface card and cable may not be included in the price of the system. Read the ads carefully if you are buying by mail order.

The interface card should be plugged into one of the bus slots. Before plugging the card in, make sure that any jumpers or switches on the board are set properly. The board must be configured so it does not conflict with the address or interrupt (IRQ) of any of your other devices. Check your documentation. Always turn your computer off before unplugging or changing the settings of any card. Never plug in or unplug a card, cable, or device while the power is on.

Several of the sound cards, such as SoundBlaster, Pro Audio Spectrum, and Sound Galaxy, have built-in interfaces for certain CD-ROM drives. These 16-bit sound cards can control Panasonic, Sony, or Mitsumi drives. These proprietary interfaces save having to use an extra motherboard slot to control the CD-ROM drive. A CD-ROM can be difficult to set up and configure to work with your system IRQs and memory address locations. If the board conflicts with any other device in your system, it will not work. The sound board systems will usually check your system and tell you if there are any conflicts. It is usually fairly easy to set up a CD-ROM system that works off a sound card interface.

 # Enhanced IDE interfaces

The enhanced IDE interface can handle up to four devices. This can be any combination of EIDE hard drives and EIDE CD-ROMs or EIDE backup tape drives. The enhanced IDE interface and IDE CD-ROM drives are a bit less expensive than the SCSI interfaces and CD-ROM drives. The enhanced IDE systems seem to be equivalent to the SCSI in most areas.

SCSI interfaces

More and more companies are now manufacturing drives for the SCSI interface. If you have other SCSI products, such as a SCSI hard drive or tape backup, you already have an interface card. The SCSI interface cards can drive up to seven different devices. It is amazing how quickly the eight slots get used up. The SCSI can save having to install a separate interface for up to seven different devices. Most SCSI devices have two connectors, one for the input cable and an identical connector for the next item.

There are also several sound boards that have SCSI interfaces built-in, such as the Diamond Sonic Sound and the Adaptec Audio Machine. There are several different types of SCSI interfaces. Some of them are made for special-purpose SCSI devices and may not be able to completely control a hard disk. The Adaptec Audio Machine has complete control functions for hard disks and most other SCSI devices.

If you don't already have a SCSI interface, you may have to pay $100 to $200 extra for the interface.

Multiple drive systems

Even though you have over 600MB on a disc, there will be many times when it doesn't have the programs or information that you need at the moment. You will have to eject the disc, unload the caddy and put the new disc in. There are some systems that are similar to the audio CD players that have a carousel that holds five or six discs. They may be quite similar to the audio compact disc systems, but are usually much more expensive.

There are some systems that use a large number of CD-ROM drives in a system. The drives can be loaded with different discs, then any

file on any of the discs can be accessed. Again, at the present time these systems are very expensive, some as high as $20,000.

You can build your own system and save a bundle. The cost of CD-ROM drives is coming down every day. I have seen some double speed drives for less than $100. With an enhanced IDE interface, you could install up to four drives, or up to 7 or more with a SCSI interface. You would need a tower case with several bays. You can put together a multiple drive system for a very nominal sum.

Caddies

The more expensive CD-ROM drives require that the disc be placed in a caddy in order to run it. Some of the less expensive CD-ROM drives just have a tray to hold the disc. Most CD-ROM discs come in a plastic *jewel case*. You must open the jewel case, then transfer the disc to a caddy or to the tray. This requires a lot of handling of the disc, which can result in fingerprints, scratches, or other damage to the bright side of the disc.

If your drive uses a caddy, you can buy several caddies, load them up and not have to handle the discs thereafter. The caddies cost about $3.00 each and are available from several places. Look in the computer magazines.

CD-ROM recorders (CD-R)

CD-ROM recordings are ideal for data that should never be changed. CD-ROM discs are an excellent way to make backups, and to store and archive data. CD-ROM makes it very easy to share large files with other computers, across the room, the nation, or anywhere in the world. It can be shipped for a very nominal price and you won't have to worry too much about it being erased or damaged.

Ordinarily, a CD-ROM disc can store about 650MB, but the Young Minds and EWB Companies, at (909) 335-1350 or (619) 930-0440,

have developed a compression system that lets you store up to 4 gigabytes of data on a disc.

There are several companies who are now manufacturing CD-ROM recorders. When they were first introduced, they were very expensive at around $10,000. Some companies are now offering the CD-Recorders for less than $2000. The blank discs cost from $10 to $20 at this time.

Large organizations may have acres of file cabinets overflowing with paper. Some studies have shown that 90% of the files are never looked at again after they are stored, a terrible waste of space and paper.

There are systems that can be used to scan all of this information into a computer, which can then compress it. It can then be indexed, so any item can be quickly found and accessed, and then stored on a CD-ROM, a write once, read many (WORM), or other storage device. COLD is a recent acronym for *Computer Output to Laser Disk.* With the proper hardware and software, thousands of trees could be saved and millions of feet of file drawer floor space could be reclaimed. To learn more about this technology, subscribe to the following imaging magazines. They are free to qualified subscribers.

➤ *Imaging Business Magazine*, call (301) 343-1520 for a qualifying subscription application.

➤ *Advanced Imaging*, 445 Broad Hollow Rd., Melville, NY 11747-4722.

➤ *Managing Office Technology*, 1100 Superior Ave., Cleveland, OH 44197-8092.

If you are in any kind of business at all, you should be able to qualify. Several other magazines are listed in Chapter 17.

A group of hardware manufacturers, led by Philips, is working on a CD-Erasable (CD-E) format.

 # Kodak Photo CD

Eastman Kodak, at (716) 742-4000, has developed a system that displays photos on a television set or a computer monitor. A person can take a roll or film to a photo developer and have the photos copied onto a CD-ROM disc. The Kodak CD recorder is much too expensive for most small photo finishing labs so they have to send them out to be done. It usually takes about a week to get the disc back. It costs about $20 for a disk and the cost for putting 24 photos onto a CD disc is about $20. If later you decide to add more photos to the disc, just take it back to the lab and they will load them on.

One of the advantages of the Photo CD system is that the photos can be recorded at a resolution of 128×192 and up as high as 4000×6000 pixels. There are no televisions or even computers that would allow you to view the photos at 4000×6000. At this resolution, fewer than 100 photos in the 4" × 5" format can be recorded on a disc. The lower the resolution and the smaller the photo, the more photos that can be stored on a disc. Most photos are stored at 480×640. At a resolution of 128×192 as many as 6000 small thumbnail size photos can be stored on a disc. The 128×192 format is often used to make a small copy of each photo on the disc. These small copies are then used as an index or catalog for all photos on the disc. If you are using a computer, you can use a mouse to point and click on any of the small images to bring up the large photo.

The Kodak Photo CD player can be connected directly to a television or to a computer. The photos can be displayed and enlarged on a television screen, they can be rotated, mirrored, flipped, cropped, copied to a computer file, and can be printed out or exported.

The Kodak Photo CD player is a great tool for business presentations. It would be much more versatile than using a slide projector.

The Kodak Photo CD player is also a high fidelity player for audio CD.

You might ask why anyone would want to buy a Photo CD player when they could buy a camcorder for about the same price. But in

today's affluent society, why not have both? Each system has advantages that the other does not have.

Kodak has recently introduced a portable Photo CD player, the PCD 970. It is about the size of a VHS videocassette and operates with four AA size batteries. It can be connected to any television set or sound system. It also is a great tool for business presentations.

Multimedia upgrade kits

Many companies are offering multimedia upgrade kits or *bundles*. Many of them sport the MPC logo, which means that they conform to the MPC specifications for any of the products in the kit. Some of the kits may be a very good bargain. But you should check them out carefully. Be aware that some of the kits may have older CD-ROM drives and components. At the minimum, the kit should have a late model double or quad speed CD-ROM drive, a 16-bit audio sound board, a 22-kHz mono playback and 11-kHz recording (44 kHz-stereo playback and recording is better), Multivoice MIDI synthesizer (boards with the Wave Table are better), internal audio mixer for CD audio, MIDI and digitized sound, and MIDI and joystick ports.

Some of kits are good bargains. In addition to the hardware components, some vendors include several multimedia titles. In some cases, the list price of the titles alone exceeds the cost of the entire bundle. Some kits may even include speakers and a microphone.

Installing CD-ROM drives

Step 1: Remove the computer cover

There are three main types of CD-ROM drives at this time, proprietary, IDE, and SCSI. The first step in installing any of these drives is to remove the cover from your computer. Then, make sure that you have a standard 5¼" bay that is accessible from the front panel. Use two small screws on each side to mount the drive.

 # Step 2: Set any jumpers or switches

You should have received some sort of documentation and installation instructions with your drive.

✳ Proprietary drives

If you are installing a drive that uses a proprietary interface, it probably has a floppy disk with the installation drivers. The proprietary interface may also be a sound card. You probably have to set some jumpers or switches on the interface card so it doesn't interfere or conflict with any other IRQ or memory address. Many of the cards do a check of your system to determine if there are conflicts.

✳ IDE CD-ROM drives

If you are installing an IDE CD-ROM drive, it can be attached to a standard IDE interface. The standard IDE can interface with two devices, so if you only have one IDE hard drive, you can attach a CD-ROM drive. It would be much better though if you bought an Enhanced IDE (EIDE) interface, which is much faster than the standard IDE. The EIDE can also provide an interface for up to four devices. The IDE CD-ROM drives come with driver software, so they are fairly easy to install.

✳ SCSI CD-ROM drive

You may have up to seven SCSI devices installed, but each device must be assigned a logical unit number (LUN) between 0 and 6. The LUN is usually determined by a set of jumpered pins. Check your documentation. If you already have other SCSI devices installed, you must determine which LUNs are assigned to them and configure the CD-ROM drive for a number not being used.

 # Step 3: Install the interface board

After the jumpers are set, find an empty slot on the motherboard and insert the board.

 # Step 4: Install cables

For proprietary and IDE CD-ROM drives, you should have a flat 40-wire ribbon cable. For IDE drives, you may have to use the middle connector on the cable that is connected to your IDE hard drive.

For SCSI drives, you have a 50-wire ribbon cable that connects to the back of the CD-ROM and then to a SCSI interface board. Most SCSI interface boards have provisions for two cable connections. If you have more than two SCSI devices, you may need to buy a cable with two or more connectors in the center.

The flat ribbon cable has a different-colored wire on one side. This wire goes to pin one of the connectors. Some connectors may have a shell with a square slot on one side. The cable connector has a square elevation that fits in the slot so they can only be plugged in correctly. Otherwise, look for an indication of pin one on the CD-ROM drive and on the interface board.

Plug in one of the four-wire power cables to the drive. Most computer power supplies only have four cables. If all four cables are already being used, you may have to buy a small Y power cable, such as that shown in Fig. 13-3.

Figure 13-3

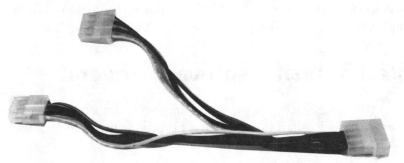

A Y power cable.

If you plan to use your CD-ROM drive with a sound card, and I strongly recommend that you do, you have to install a small audio cable. Figure 13-4 shows an audio cable connected to a Sound Blaster card. There is no standardization for the audio cables and sound cards. Since the CD-ROM drives and sound cards are made by

Figure 13-4

A CD-ROM drive, a sound board, and a two-wire audio cable. The audio cable plugs into the small white miniature connector at the extreme left.

different manufacturers, you must tell the vendor which sound card you are using to get the proper audio cable. Since there are so many variations, many vendors don't include the audio cable unless you specifically ask for it. The cable may cost an additional $5.

⇨ Step 5: Install software drivers

All of the drives should come with some sort of installation and driver software, usually on a floppy disk. The vendor may not provide it unless you ask for it.

If you have other SCSI devices already installed, then you probably have SCSI driver software, such as the Corel SCSI. If not, then you should contact your vendor for SCSI driver software. Once the SCSI software is installed, it automatically recognizes the new drive when you boot up.

 ## Step 6: Test the system

Test the system with a CD-ROM disc. If everything works, then replace the computer cover.

 # The LaserCard

The LaserCard Systems, at (415) 969-4428, has developed a card that is the same size and thickness as a credit card. They use about three-fourths of one side of the card to store up to 4.1MB of data. This data can be over 1200 pages of digital text, a photograph of the person, or the person's complete medical history, including charts, X-rays, and test results. It can also be used to store the person's financial records, which can be updated periodically.

The card, with a person's photo and fingerprints on it, can be used for security or access control. It can also be used for publishing large amounts of data, transaction systems, and almost any other type of records. A small reader/recorder is used to read or to update the card.

The card is a laser optical system, similar to that of the CD-ROM, so it is not affected by magnetic or electrostatic fields.

Eventually, almost everyone may carry a card like this with their medical history. It could even save one's life.

 # Sources

There are several companies and vendors for CD-ROMs and CD-ROM disc titles. Just look in any computer magazine and you will see dozens of ads. There are now several magazines that are devoted entirely to the CD-ROM technology.

CHAPTER 14

Computer sound and MIDI

S OUND can be an important part of your computer system. There are some Windows applications that can make great use of sound, but you need a sound board to take full advantage of the applications. The Windows 3.1 Sound Recorder is an included utility that lets you record, edit, insert, mix, and play sound files that are in the .WAV format. You can add sound annotations to documents such as spreadsheets, or to programs that support object linking and embedding (OLE).

Computers have made enormous contributions to the creation and playing of music. It has been said that music is the universal language. Everybody likes music of one kind or another. There are many different kinds of music and it can be used in many different ways. Music can be used to express just about every emotion known to man. There is music that makes us happy, elated, excited, and exhilarated. There is passionate music that can arouse you and make you feel amorous. There is music that can make you feel joyful, merry, and cheerful. There is music that is touching and sad and sorrowful. There is music that makes you feel sentimental and reminiscent. There is heartbreaking music of unrequited love that can make one feel so sad and forlorn. There is serious music that is solemn and sedate and dignified. And then there is rock-and-roll and heavy-metal music. All of this music can be played on your computer.

Not only can you play music through your computer, but even if you know nothing at all about music, you can use your Pentium to compose and create music. A computer is very good at converting text and graphics into digital data. Music can also be represented as digital data just as easily. Once music is digitized, you can edit it, rearrange it, add new sounds to it, remove certain sounds, or change it in hundreds of different ways. The Pentium is an excellent tool for this purpose.

 # Sound boards

A good audio board should be able to digitally record narration, sound, or music and store it as a *.WAV file. You should have the option of recording in mono or stereo and be able to control the sampling rate. The board should have chips to convert the stored digital signals for analog conversion (DACs). It should also have chips to convert analog sound to digital signals (ADCs).

A good board has a Musical Instrument Digital Interface (MIDI). With MIDI capabilities, you can use the board with MIDI instruments such as piano keyboards, synthesizers, sound modules, and other MIDI products.

The board should have an FM synthesis chipset that duplicates the 128 different MIDI voices and 46 percussion instruments. Instead of the synthesized sound, some of the more expensive cards may have samples of actual instruments and use a wave table for synthesis.

The board should have an audio mixer function that allows you to control the source and level of the audio signals. The better boards have tone controls for the bass and treble ranges. The board should also have a joystick port connector, a microphone input, and a speaker output jack.

Many of the boards have a proprietary interface for controlling CD-ROM drives. The interface may be able to control drives from three or four different manufacturers. There are a few who manufacture sound boards with a SCSI interface. The SCSI interface allows you to use any SCSI CD-ROM drive. The SCSI interface also controls up to six other devices.

 # Sound, microphones, and speakers

Sound is made by the pressure on air created by a vibrating object. The pressure of the vibrations causes the air to move back and forth creating sound. If a microphone is placed in the vicinity of the sound, it can capture an image of the sound and turn it into electrical impulses. There are several different types of microphones. One basic type has a diaphragm that vibrates due to the pressure of the sound waves. The diaphragm is attached to a coil of wire that moves in and out of the field of a permanent magnet. The movement of the coil of wire in the magnetic field produces an analog voltage that varies according to the vibration of the sound. We can record the electrical pulses, then using electronics to amplify the small signals, we can cause a loudspeaker to reproduce the original sound.

Basically, a loudspeaker is quite similar to the microphone. The speaker has a coil of wire that is attached to the speaker cone. The coil of wire is surrounded by a strong permanent magnet. Moving a coil of wire through a magnetic field produces a voltage; passing voltage through a coil of wire produces a magnetic field. The polarity of the magnetic field thus created varies plus or minus depending on the polarity of the voltage. As the positive and negative pulses of voltage are passed through the coil of wire, it alternately attracts and pulls the coil into the magnet or repels it pushing the coil and cone outward. The movement of the speaker cone produces pressure waves that are a replica of the original sound.

 # Digital sampling

Some large mainframe network computers operate by giving each person on a network a small slice of time, or time sharing. If the time was divided into millionths of a second, a person may receive a couple of slices, then the next person would get a few slices, then a few millionths of a second later the first person would get a few more slices of data. It would be done so fast that the person would not realize that the data was being received only part of the time.

Hundreds or even thousands of people could be on a single line, all receiving different data, at the same time.

Digitizing an analog voltage is somewhat similar to timesharing. Digital samples, or slices, are taken of the analog waves. If the number of digital samples per second is rather low, then there can be a lot of unrecorded space between each slice. When played back, the unrecorded space can usually be electronically reconstructed to some degree. But if the sample rate is fairly low, with wide spaces between each sample, the output sound is somewhat less than high fidelity. The higher the frequency of the sample rate, the more closely the output sound matches the original. Then why not take higher frequency samples? Because the higher the frequency of digital sample rate, the more space it requires to be stored or recorded. High fidelity digital sound requires a tremendous amount of disk space to store.

Sampling rates and bits

Sound can be digitized using 8-bit, or 1-byte, samples or 16-bit samples. An 8-bit system can chop a wave form into a maximum of 256 steps or 2^8. A 16-bit system (2^{16}) can save up to 65,000 pieces of information about the same wave form. As you can imagine, the 16-bit system offers much greater fidelity, but at a greater need for storage space.

Using an 8-bit mode with a sample rate of 11 kHz, you will be recording 11,000 bytes of data each second, or 660K per minute. If you were recording in 8-bit stereo at the same rate, the storage requirement would double to 1.32MB for one minute. To record in 16-bit stereo at 11 kHz, it would be twice the bits per second, or 2.64MB for one minute.

Most speech has a frequency range from about 300 Hz up to about 6 kHz. Sampling at 11 kHz and 8 bits is good enough for speech, but it would not be very good for high-fidelity music. Most systems are capable of sampling at 22 kHz and 44.1 kHz in both monaural and stereo modes. A sample rate for 44.1 kHz in monaural would be 88.2K bytes per second × 60 seconds = 5.292MB per minute. In stereo it would be doubled to 10.58MB per minute. One hour of

recording at this sample rate would require more than 630MB. Most audio CDs have about 630MB of storage space and can play for about one hour.

Standard digital sampling rates in the audio industry are 5.0125, 11.025, 22.05, and 44.1 kHz.

 # Why 44.1-kHz sample rate

If we had perfect hearing, we could hear sounds from 20 hertz (Hz), or cycles per second, up to 20 kHz. Most of us, especially older people, have a much narrower hearing range. So why should we worry about a 44.1 kHz sample rate? This is more than twice the frequency that we could hear even if we had perfect hearing.

Many instruments and other sounds have unique resonances and harmonics that go beyond the basic sounds they produce. These resonances and harmonics are what make a middle C note on a piano sound differently than the same note on a violin or trumpet. Many of the harmonics and overtones of sound are in the higher frequencies. In digital recording, the upper frequency must be at least twice of what you can expect when it is converted to analog. So 44.1-kHz digital signal produces a 22-kHz analog signal.

 # Resolution

We often speak of the resolution of our monitors. The more pixels displayed, the sharper the image and the higher the resolution. We also use resolution to describe digitized sound. The higher the sampling rate and the more bits of information about each sound wave, the higher the resolution and the better the fidelity. There is a limit to the resolution of an 8-bit system no matter how fast the sample rate. The maximum samples of a waveform that can be captured by an 8-bit system is 2^8 or 256. Some may think that a 16-bit system would only provide twice the resolution of an 8-bit system. Actually a 16-bit system can provide 256 times more resolution, or 2^{16} or 65,536. It is apparent that a 16-bit system can give much better resolution and fidelity than an 8-bit system.

Signal-to-noise ratio (SNR)

Analog audio is made up of voltage sine waves that vary up and down continuously. Noise and static is also made up of similar sine waves. Noise and static is everywhere. It is in the air, especially so during electrical storms. It is in our electrical lines and in almost all electronic equipment. It is very difficult to avoid it.

The signal-to-noise ratio is the ratio between the amplitude of the audio or video signal as compared to the noise component. The SNR is measured in dB, usually a minus dB. The larger the negative number the better.

Most sound boards, CD-ROM drives, and other sound systems list the SNR on their specifications. Most of the better systems have at least a –90 dB SNR. Since noise is analog voltage, a good digital system usually has less noise than the analog systems.

 # Digital signal processors (DSP)

One of the things that helps make it possible to get so much music from the sound board is a digital signal processor (DSP). It can be a very large task just to assemble and determine which notes to output from a single instrument. But it can be mind boggling to try to do it for several instruments.

The central processor unit (CPU) is the brains of your computer. Ordinarily, almost everything that transpires in your computer has to go through the CPU. But there are certain things such as intensive number crunching that can be speeded up with a coprocessor.

The digital signal processor (DSP) chips are quite similar in function to math coprocessors. A DSP can take over and relieve the CPU of much of its burdens. DSP chips can be configured and programmed for several specific tasks, such as high quality audio or complex graphics and video. The DSP can be used for musical synthesis and many special digital effects.

At one time, the DSP chips were rather expensive, but now the chips are quite reasonable. Since they add very little to the cost, more and more manufacturers are adding DSP chips to their sound boards. Before you buy a sound board, check the specifications.

Turtle Beach Systems was one of the first to design and implement the DSP technology on their MultiSound boards. Creative Labs followed soon after with their SoundBlaster 16 ASP. Several other companies are now manufacturing boards with the superior DSP technology. These chips add so much more function and utility to the sound board that eventually every manufacturer will be using them.

Which sound board should you buy?

It all depends on what you want to do and how much you want to spend. If you can afford it, I would suggest that you look for a 16-bit card with a DSP chip. For sources, look in any computer magazine such as *Computer Shopper, the New Media Magazine, PC World, PC Computing, PC Magazine*, and any of the several other computer magazines.

Installing a sound board

The CPU of your computer is always busy and can only be interrupted by certain devices that need its attention. The obvious reason for this is maintain order. If all of the devices tried to act at the same time, there would be total confusion. So computers have 16 interrupt or IRQ lines and each device is assigned a unique number. They are given a priority according to their ranking number. For instance, if the CPU received an interrupt request from the keyboard, which is IRQ 1, and a request from a mouse on IRQ 4, the keyboard request would be answered first.

If two devices are set for the same IRQ it will cause a conflict. You may have to set one or more jumpers or switches on your board before you install it.

Just as your house has a unique address, areas of RAM memory have distinct addresses. Certain devices use a certain portion of RAM to perform some of their processing. So you may have to set jumpers or switches for the input/output (I/O) address of the sound card. The default address, the one set by the factory, will probably be set to 220. This is the SoundBlaster standard and it is used by many others.

There may also be a set of jumpers to set the direct memory access (DMA) channel. On most PCs there are three or more DMAs and they don't usually cause a conflict if two or more devices are set to the same channel.

Many of the audio boards have built-in diagnostics that can detect a conflict with the IRQ or I/O settings. You may have trouble determining which other device is causing the conflict. If you have DOS 6.0 or later, you can use the Microsoft Diagnostics (MSD) command. It can show all of the IRQs and which components are using them.

Incidentally, the MSD command can be used to search for files or subjects and it also gives you a wealth of information about your computer. Besides the IRQs, it can show the memory usage, your autoexec.bat and config.sys and many other useful bits of information. You can view the information or have it printed out. Depending on what you have in your computer, it may take up to 20 pages to print it all out.

One of the benefits of CD-ROM is that it can play sound and music along with the text, graphics, and motion. You can play CD Compact audio discs on most CD-ROM drives. So it is necessary to be able to connect the CD-ROM to your sound board. Most CD-ROM drives have a small audio connector on the back panel. A special cable is then used to connect to the sound board. Unfortunately, the audio connector for the CD-ROM may be different on sound boards from different companies. Because there are so many variations, the audio cable is often not included with the sound board or with the CD-ROM drive. You may have to order it special. They cost about $5. Figure 13-4 in the previous chapter shows a CD-ROM drive, a sound board, and a two-wire audio cable. The audio plugs into the white miniature

connector on the extreme left of the CD-ROM drive. The other end plugs into a small connector on the sound board.

 # Speakers

Most of the sound cards have an output of about 4 watts. That isn't very much, but you're not going to be trying to fill a concert hall. You really don't need much for your computer. You can attach any small speaker, but several companies manufacture small speakers with a built-in amplifier. The speakers are powered by batteries or by a power supply. They may cost from $20 up to $100 for the larger ones. There are also high-end high fidelity systems available. Of course, high fidelity usually means high cost.

Just a few of the many companies that offer small computer speakers are Labtec, Media Vision, Koss, and Roland. Look through computer magazines for others.

If you use good sound boards and speakers, your computer can be a major component in an excellent high fidelity system.

 # Microphones

My SoundBlaster 16 ASP came with a microphone. The type needed for just voice annotations can be very inexpensive such as those available from Radio Shack for about $5.

If you expect to do any kind of high fidelity recording, then you definitely need a good mike. A sound system is only as good as its weakest link. A good mike may cost from $35 up to $500 or more.

There are two basic types of microphones. *Dynamic* uses a diaphragm and a coil of wire that moves back and forth in a magnetic field.

The other type is the *condenser*, or *capacitor*, microphone. A capacitor is made up of two flat plates. When voltage is applied to the

plates, a charged field, or a capacitance, exists between the plates. The capacitance depends on the voltage, the size of the plates, and the distance between the plates. If the plates are moved toward or away from each other the capacity changes. In a capacitor microphone, one plate is fixed and the other is a flat diaphragm. Sound pressure on the flexible diaphragm moves the one charged plate in and out, which causes a change in the capacity. Capacitor mikes can be made very small such as the lapel mikes.

Most professional type mikes sold today are the wireless kind. They have a small transmitter built into the mike that feeds the sound to a small receiver that is connected to an amplifier or recorder.

Microphones may also be classified as to their pickup directionality. The *omnidirectional* picks up sound from all directions. The *bidirectional* picks up sound from opposite sides of the mike. The *cardioid* picks up sound in a heart-shaped unidirectional pattern (*cardi* is a prefix for heart). The *unidirectional supercardioid* picks up sound on a very narrow straight-in path.

Unlike what you may see rock stars do to a microphone, you don't have to stick it in your mouth to have it pick up your voice.

 # Musical Instrument Digital Interface (MIDI)

Electronic circuits can be designed to oscillate at almost any frequency. The output of the oscillating circuit is a voltage that can be amplified and routed through a loud speaker to reproduce various sounds.

In the early 1970s, Robert Moog used voltage-controlled oscillators (VCOs) to develop the Moog synthesizer. With a synthesizer you can create synthetic musical sounds that imitate different instruments. The sounds from the early systems didn't sound much like real musical instruments.

Also in the early 1970s, John Chowning of Stanford University developed digital FM synthesis. The Yamaha Corporation licensed the technology from Stanford and introduced the first FM digital synthesizer in 1982. Since that time, there have been some tremendous technological advances. Today a person might not be able to discern whether a sound was synthesized or came from a real instrument.

In some instances, the music from a sound board does come from real instruments. Sample notes are recorded from instruments. Under computer control, any of the stored samples can be joined and played back. The notes can be held for a half note, or shortened to a quarter note, or for whatever the music requires. Samples from several instruments can all be playing at the same time. The music can sound as if it is being produced by a live hundred-piece orchestra. And it all comes from a chip that is about one inch square. It is absolutely amazing.

The early voltage-controlled oscillators (VCOs) were rather crude. The electronic industry was still in its infancy. There were no integrated circuits. As the electronic industry and technology evolved, newer and better VCOs were developed and incorporated into musical instruments.

The MIDI standard

There were no standards for the VCOs and new musical instruments. As usual, each vendor's product was a bit different than all others. In 1983 a group of companies got together and adopted a set of standards that they called the *Musical Instrument Digital Interface.* This was truly an historic agreement for the music industry. MIDI and the advances in electronic technology have made it possible to generate more new music in the last ten years than was generated in the last 100 years. Synthesized music is not only used for rock and roll, but for television commercials, movies and all types of music.

How MIDI operates

MIDI itself does not produce music. It is only an interface, or controller, that tells other devices, such as a synthesizer or a sampler, which

particular sound to produce. In some respects, MIDI is similar to the old style piano players that used a punched roll of paper to play.

Briefly, the MIDI specification says that a MIDI device must have at least two MIDI connectors, an input and an output. (These are DIN connectors that are the same type as that used for the computer keyboard connector on the motherboard.) A MIDI device may include adapter cards, synthesizers, piano type keyboards, various types of instrument pickups, digital signal processors, and MIDI controlled audio mixers. One of the great advantages of MIDI is that it allows many different electronic instruments to communicate with each other. When two MIDI instruments are connected, the devices exchange information about the elements of the performance, such as the notes played and how loud they are played. A master keyboard can be connected to two or more MIDI electronic keyboards, or other MIDI devices. Any note played on the master can be also played on the connected MIDI *slaves*. The electronic keyboards can emulate several different instruments. One person playing the master can use the slaves to make it sound as though a very large orchestra is playing. There are many options available, such as allowing you to record the notes played, then play them back or edit and change them.

General MIDI standard signals

There are 128 common instrument sound signals for MIDI control; each signal is numbered 1–128. (You may also see them numbered 0–127.) The standard was originated by the Roland Corporation and is now coordinated by the MIDI Manufacturers Association (MMA).

If the MIDI receives a signal and it is connected to a synthesizer, keyboard, or any MIDI instrument, it triggers the device to play a note corresponding to the signal number. For instance, a signal on number 3 would cause a honky-tonk piano sound, number 40 would be a violin. Note that there are 16 different instrument classifications. Every 8 numbers represents sounds from a basic class of instrument. For instance, the first 8 sounds are made by piano type instruments, the next 8 are made by chromatic percussion instruments, then organs, etc.

There are an additional 46 MIDI Note numbers for nonmelodic percussion instruments. These numbers include such things as drums, a cowbell, wooden blocks, triangles, and cymbals.

Synthesizers

The MIDI specification was primarily designed as a standard for controlling synthesizers. It did not specify how a synthesizer should create a sound or what sounds should be created.

The word *synthesize* means to combine or put together. Synthesizers can combine two or more wave forms to create new sounds. There are several types of sound waves or oscillations. Each musical note has a basic oscillation frequency. For instance, A2 has a frequency of 220 oscillations per second, or 220 Hz. Note E3 vibrates at 330 Hz, A4 at 440 Hz and E6 at 660 Hz. We could generate pure single frequency sine waves of each of these notes, but they would be rather dull and uninteresting. The actual notes are a combination of oscillation frequencies.

Even though it has the same basic frequency, if a note is played on different instruments, there will be a distinct difference in the sounds. The note A4 played on a trombone sounds quite different than A4 played on a guitar. They all sound differently because they are not pure single sine wave frequencies. The vibrations of a basic note causes other vibrations in the metal of a trombone or the wood of a guitar. These extra vibrations are the timbre that adds tonal color to a sound and distinguishes it from a note played on another instrument.

Harmonics

An important cause for difference in sounds are the harmonics created. A guitar string that is plucked to play A4 vibrates at 440 Hz. If you photographed the vibrating string with a high speed movie camera, then slowed it down, you could see a primary node of vibrations. But there would also be several smaller sized nodes on the

string. These smaller nodes would be vibrating at twice the frequency of the primary node and some would even be vibrating at four times the primary frequency. The sounds made at the higher frequencies blend with the primary sound to give it tone and color. These higher frequencies are called *harmonics*.

Harmonics are even multiples of the fundamental oscillation of a note or its basic pitch.

 # Envelope generator

Bob Moog determined that there were four main criteria in each sound. He identified them as *attack, decay, sustain, and release (ADSR)*. The attack determines how fast the initial sound rises. It may hold at the initial height for a while, then start to decay. Sustain determines how long the sound is audible while a key is held down. Release is the rate at which the sound intensity decreases to zero after the key is released.

The ADSR electronic envelope is used in synthesizers to describe almost any sound.

 # Wave tables

The FM synthesized sounds are usually not as good as the sound generated from an actual instrument. The more expensive sound cards and many of the better MIDI instruments use digital samples of real sounds. This requires some memory to store the samples, but actually not as much as you might think. For instance, a piano has 88 notes or keys. But it is only necessary to sample a few notes. Since they are all piano notes, the main difference is the pitch. Middle A or A4 has a frequency of 440 Hz. A2 has a frequency of 220 Hz. A sample of a single A can be electronically altered to make it sound like any A on the piano keyboard. So they only need a sample of an A, B, C, D, E, F, and G. With a small sample of each of these notes, any note of the 88 on the piano can be created. It also would not matter whether the note was a quarter note, half note, or whole note.

Once the note is simulated, it can be held for as long or as short a time as necessary.

The same type of system would be used to sample notes from other instruments. It would be a little simpler to store notes from other instruments because most of them don't have as many notes as a piano. A piano is one of the few instruments that allows more than one note to be played at the same time.

The samples are stored in ROM. When a note is called for, the sample is read from ROM, placed in RAM, electronically adjusted for whatever note is needed, then sent to an amplifier and loudspeaker.

The more instruments sampled and the more samples that are stored, the more memory that is required, both ROM and RAM. Some high-end keyboards may have 10MB or more of ROM and about 4MB of RAM.

 # Sequencers

Sequencers are a type of recorder that uses computer memory to store information about a performance. Like the MIDI, it does not record the sound itself, but just the information about the sound.

Even if you know nothing at all about music, you can write and compose music with a sequencer that is connected to a synthesizer or other electronic instrument. If you know a little bit about music, you can become an expert composer with a sequencer. Most sequencers are software programs that allow you to create, edit, record, and play back on a hard disk musical compositions in the MIDI message format.

A sequencer memorizes anything you play and can play it back at any time. They are similar to multitrack recorders, except that they are much faster because the tracks are on a computer. The computer also lets you do hundreds of things better, quicker, and easier than a tape recorder. A sequencer lets you edit music in thousands of ways that

are not possible with a tape machine. With a single MIDI instrument, an entire album could be recorded.

A sequence can be part of a song, a single track of a song, or the whole song. The sequences are laid down in tracks. Several tracks of different instruments can be laid down separately, then all played back together. A single track can be played back and edited or changed. Tracks can be recorded at different times, then blended together. A song or an album can be created by a group even though one may be in New York, one in Los Angeles, or others scattered all over the country. Each member of the group could record their part on a disk, then ship it to a studio where all of the tracks could be edited and blended together.

Some sequencers allow you to record channels while playing back existing channels. Tracks can be laid down over another track without erasing what is already there. Portions of a track can be erased and new material inserted. The editing capabilities are almost unlimited.

Some synthesizers and keyboards have a built-in hardware sequencer. The built-in sequencer allows one to do many of the same things that sequencer software allows. But a hardware sequencer would not have the capabilities of a computer.

Sequencer software, such as Cakewalk, lets you record in real time as an instrument is being played. Or you can use the step entry mode and enter one note at a time. The notes can be entered from a computer keyboard or a piano type MIDI keyboard that is connected to the computer.

The software is intelligent enough to take step entry notes, and combine them with the proper staff notation and timing. Some software even adds the proper chords to the step entry.

Some Windows sequencer software programs are Cakewalk Professional, Cadenza, Master Tracks Pro, and Midisoft for Windows. Many of the music software programs also print out music scores.

When you consider the modern technology that allows the editing and re-editing of a song until the cut is perfect, you just have to

admire the works of some of the early recording artists. They usually didn't get the opportunity to go back and change a mistake or to improve a lick here and there.

 # Keyboards

It is possible to use a computer keyboard to edit or create music. But it is a lot easier to work with an electronic piano keyboard. Many of the electronic keyboards have built-in synthesizers and MIDI connections.

If you are interested in music, one of the magazines that you should subscribe to is the *Electronic Musician*, (800) 888-5139. They have excellent articles about music and new devices. This magazine is of interest to professional musicians as well as amateurs and anyone who enjoys music. They also publish an annual *Digital Piano Buyer's Guide* that is available from the Mix Bookshelf, (800) 233-9604. The Mix Bookshelf specializes in books for musicians. One book that they carry is *The Musical PC*. It is an excellent book for anyone who wants to learn more about music and computers. Another book they carry is *Making Music With Your Computer.* It would be very helpful to anyone just getting into music. There are also articles in the book that would be of interest to the old pro.

Another magazine for musicians and anyone interested in music is called *Musician*, at (800) 347-6969. It is published primarily for the professional musician, but it is of interest to anyone who enjoys music and wants to keep up with what is happening in the music and entertainment field.

 # Catalogs

You will need music software for your PC. The *Soundware Catalog*, at (800) 333-4554, lists hundreds of music software programs. They have a comprehensive and detailed description of each program listed. Even if you don't intend to order the program, the descriptions

in the catalog can give you a good idea of what is available. Call them for a catalog.

The *Musician's Friend Catalog*, at (800) 776-5173, the *American Musical Supply Catalog*, at (800) 458-4076, and *Manny's Mailbox Music*, at (800) 448-8478, all have hundreds of musical instruments, supplies, videotapes for training, and books. Call them for catalogs.

 # Musician trade shows

Partly due to the success of the COMDEX shows, there are now lots and lots of trade shows. Here are a couple that you might be interested in attending.

The National Association of Music Merchants (NAMM) has two large shows each year, usually one near Los Angeles in the winter and one in Nashville during the summer. There are usually hundreds of exhibitors at these shows. You can find just about every imaginable musical product at these shows. They have dozens of rooms where they demonstrate amplifiers and loudspeakers. There will be hundreds of electronic keyboards on the floor, everything from the small toys up to the very expensive grand pianos. They will also have several old fashioned nonelectronic pianos all the way from the spinet up to the concert grand. If you are at all interested in music, this is the place to see all that is available.

To find out when and where the next NAMM show will be held you can call (619) 438-8001.

The Consumer Electronics Show (CES) also presents two large shows each year, a winter show held in Las Vegas during the first week in January and a summer show held in Chicago during the first week in June. This show also has several music and musical instrument exhibitors. To find out more about this show, call (202) 457-8700.

If you are interested in multimedia, you can order my book *Build Your Own Multimedia System and Save a Bundle* from McGraw-Hill, at (800) 822-8158. It is also available at most bookstores.

CHAPTER 15

Some applications

T HERE are many, many applications and ways to use your computer. I can't possibly list them all, but here are just a few uses:

For the kids

One of the better reasons to have a home computer is if you have children. If you don't have a computer for the kids, you should be ashamed of yourself. You are depriving them of one of the greatest learning tools of all time.

There are lots of software for the kids. One of the better magazines that offers and reviews this type of software is *KidSoft*, at 800-354-6150. Check other computer magazines for ads.

Home office

A new acronym, *SOHO*, has recently been created that means *Small Office, Home Office*. Many businesses can be operated from a home office. Several advantages in having a home office are no commuting, no high office rent, possibly taking care of young children at the same time, and setting own hours. More and more businesses are allowing their employees to work from home and telecommute. There are some jobs that can be done from home as easily as from an office.

There are several computer programs that let you connect your home computer to an office computer. A modem and almost any communications software such as CrossTalk, ProComm, or QModem lets you access another computer.

Deducting the cost of your computer

If you have a home office for a business, you may be able to deduct part of the cost of your computer from your income taxes. You may even be able to deduct a portion of your rent, telephone bills, and other legitimate business expenses.

Some IRS rules

I can't give you all of the IRS rules for a home office, but there are several deductions available if you use a portion of your home exclusively and regularly to operate your business. These deductions may include portions of your real estate taxes, mortgage interest, operating expenses (such as home insurance premiums and utility costs), and depreciation allocated to the area used for business. You may even be able to deduct a portion of the cost of painting the outside of your house or repairing the roof.

You should be aware that the IRS looks very closely at home office expenses. Before you deduct these expenses, I would recommend that you buy the latest tax books and consult with the IRS or a tax expert. There are many rules and regulations. And they change frequently. For more information, call the IRS and ask for publication #587, *Business Use of Your Home*. Look in your telephone directory for the local or 800 number for the IRS.

Here is another recommendation; whether you have a home office or not, keep good records. I have been rather sloppy in keeping records in the past. But after being audited twice for a home office, I am a changed man. I now use the askSam database program to keep track of all my expenses. The askSam for Windows system is very easy to use. Information can be entered as structured data or it can be entered much like you were using a word processor. The askSam Systems software is available from most large software companies or you can call them at (904) 584-6590.

 # Home office as a tax preparer

Congress and the IRS change the tax rules every year. Every year they become more and more complicated. It is almost impossible for the ordinary person to be aware of, comprehend, and understand all of the rules and regulations. Some of the rules are even difficult for the IRS. If you call several IRS offices with complicated questions, about 50% of the answers you get will be completely opposite.

If a person works at a single job and has a single source of income, the forms are fairly simple. But if you have several sources of income or a small business, preparing your taxes can be a nightmare. It is an impossible task for many people and they must hire a tax preparer. Many of the tax preparers charge from $50 to over $100 dollars an hour.

Since the tax rules change so often, and are so difficult for the average person to comprehend, being a tax preparer is almost like having a guaranteed income.

If you have any inclination for accounting and tax preparation, then you might consider taking a course to become a CPA or tax preparer. Many community colleges offer courses in accounting. But the H & R Block Company is probably the best place to learn tax preparation. They conduct several classes throughout the year in various locations.

 # Accountant

It is not absolutely necessary to be an accountant in order to be a tax preparer, but it helps a whole lot. Another reason to learn accounting is that many small businesses can't afford to hire full-time accountants. Many of them hire accountants on a part-time basis to keep their books and accounts in order. There are several good software programs that can be used for accounting. The ACCPAC accounting package from Computer Associates Company, at (516) 324-5224, is very good accounting program for both small and larger

businesses. Call them for brochures. Another low cost accounting package is Peachtree Accounting for Windows. This program is available from most software companies or from PC Zone mail order, at (800) 258-2088. Other accounting packages available from PC Zone are StageSoft Accounting for Small Business and One-Write Plus Accounting. Call them for a current catalog.

Tax programs

Since you have a computer, it may not be necessary for you to pay a tax preparer to do your taxes. There are several tax programs that can do the job for you. Unless you have a very complicated situation, your taxes can be done quickly and easily. In many cases, the cost of the program would probably be less than the cost of having a tax preparer do your taxes.

Besides doing your own taxes, most of these programs allow you to set up files and do the taxes of others. Many of the software companies offer tax preparation programs for professional tax businesses, but usually at a much higher price.

All of the programs operate much like a spreadsheet, in that the forms, schedules, and worksheets are linked together. When you enter data at one place, other affected data is automatically updated. Most of them have a built-in calculator so you can do calculations before entering figures. Many of them allow "what if" calculations to show what your return would look like with various inputs. Most of the companies also have software for state income taxes. Most of them allow you to print out IRS forms that are acceptable.

Here are brief reviews of just a couple of the better known programs:

TurboTax

ChipSoft Inc., 5045 Shoreham Place #100, San Diego, California 92122-3954, at (619) 453-8722. TurboTax is unique in that it offers modules for 41 states. It is an excellent program and is fairly easy to

install and learn. It starts out with a personal interview about your financial situation for the past year. It then lists forms that you might need. Based on the present year's taxes, it can estimate what your taxes will be for next year.

ChipSoft and the Intuit Company, at (415) 322-0573, have now merged. Quicken, from Intuit, is a financial software program that is an ideal adjunct to TurboTax. You can use Quicken to keep track of all of your financial records, then at the end of the year, the records can be directly imported into the TurboTax program.

J.K. Lasser's Your Income Tax

1 Gulf + Western Plaza, New York, New York 10023, at (800) 624-0023 or (800) 624-0024. It has several state modules. It has a scratch pad, calculator, and next year tax planner. The popular J.K. Lasser's Tax Guide is included with the package.

Electronic filing

The IRS is now accepting electronic filing from certain tax preparers and companies. Eventually you should be able to complete your taxes from one of the above listed programs, then use your modem to send it directly to the IRS. This, of course, saves you a lot of time and saves the IRS even more. Ordinarily the IRS has to input the data from your return into their computers by hand. Can you imagine the amount of time saved if they can receive it directly into their computers. So the IRS encourages electronic filing.

Electronic filing also offers advantages to you. Here are just a few:

> ➤ Faster refund (up to three weeks faster)

> ➤ Direct deposit of the refund

> ➤ More accurate return resulting in fewer errors

> ➤ IRS acknowledges receipt of the return

> ➤ It reduces paperwork

> ➤ Saves IRS labor, therefore taxpayers money

Some people have used electronic filing to file false claims for refunds. You can be sure that from now on the IRS agents will be checking to make sure that no one is filing refund claims for their cat or dog.

There are still some limitations. For more information call (800) 829-1040 and ask for the electronic filing coordinator. Or check with your local IRS office to see if electronic filing is possible in your area.

Other tools of the trade

The following items are some other tools that can go very well with your computer in business uses:

Point-of-sale terminals

Point-of-sale terminals (POS) are usually a combination of a cash drawer, a computer, and special software. It provides a fast customer checkout, credit card handling, audit and security, reduces paperwork, and provides efficient accounting. By keying in codes for the various items, the computer can keep a running inventory of everything that is sold. The store owner can immediately know when to reorder certain goods. A POS system can provide instant sales analysis data about which items sell best, buying trends, and of course, the cost, and the profit or loss.

There are several POS systems. A simple cash drawer with a built-in 40-column receipt printer, may cost as little as $500. More complex systems may cost $1500 and more. Software may cost from $175 up to $1000. But they can replace a bookkeeper and an accountant. In most successful businesses that sells goods, a POS system can easily pay for itself.

Here are a few of the POS hardware and software companies:

> ➢ Alpha Data Systems   (404) 499-9247
> ➢ CA Retail   (800) 668-3767
> ➢ Computer Time   (800) 456-1159

➢ CompuRegister	(314) 365-2050
➢ Datacap Systems	(215) 699-7051
➢ Indiana Cash Drawer	(317) 398-6643
➢ Merit Dig. Systems	(604) 985-1391
➢ NCR Corp.	(800) 544-3333
➢ Printer Products	(617) 254-1200
➢ Synchronics	(901) 761-1166

 # Bar codes

Bar codes are a system of black and white lines that are arranged much like the Morse code system of dots and dashes. By using combinations of wide and narrow bars and wide and narrow spaces, any numeral or letter of the alphabet can be represented.

Bar codes were first adopted by the grocery industry. They set up a central office that assigned a unique number, a *Universal Product Code (UPC)*, for just about every manufactured and prepackaged product sold in grocery stores. Different sizes of the same product have a different and unique number assigned to them. The same type products from different manufacturers also have unique numbers. Most large grocery stores now sell everything from automobile parts and accessories to drugs and medicines. Each item has its own bar code number.

When the clerk runs an item across the scanner, the dark bars absorb light and the white bars reflect the light. The scanner decodes this number and sends it to the main computer. The computer then matches the input number to the number stored on its hard disk. Linked to the number on the hard disk is the price of the item, the description, the amount in inventory, and several other pieces of information about the item. The computer sends back the price and the description of the part to the cash register where it is printed out. The computer then deducts that item from the overall inventory and adds the price to the overall cash received for the day.

A store may have several thousand items with different sizes and prices. Without a bar code system the clerk must know most of the prices, then enter them in the cash register by hand. Many errors are committed. With bar codes, the human factor is eliminated. The transactions are performed much faster and with almost total accuracy.

At the end of the day, the manager can look at the computer output and immediately know such things as how much business was done, what inventories need to be replenished, and what items were the biggest sellers. With the push of a button on the computer, he or she can change any or all of the prices of the items in the store.

Bar codes can be used in many other ways to increase productivity, keep track of time charged to a particular job, track inventory, and many other benefits. There are very few businesses, large or small, that cannot benefit from the use of bar codes.

There are several different types of bar code readers or scanners. Some are actually small portable computers that can store data, then be downloaded into a larger computer. Some systems require their own interface card that must be plugged into one of the slots on the computer motherboard. Some companies have devised systems that can be inserted in series with the keyboard so no slot or other interface is needed. Key Tronic has a keyboard with a bar code reader as an integral part of the keyboard.

If you are interested in the bar code and automatic identification technology, there are two magazines that are sent free to qualified subscribers. They are: *ID Systems*, 174 Concord Street, Peterborough, New Hampshire 03458, at (603) 924-9631, and Automatic I.D. News, P.O. Box 6158, Duluth, Minnesota 55806-9858.

Call or write for subscription qualification forms. Almost everyone who has any business connections can qualify.

⇨ Bar code printers

There are special printers that have been designed for printing bar code labels. Labels can also be printed on the better dot matrix and

on laser printers. There are several companies that specialize in printing up labels to your specifications.

Networks

The term *network* can cover a lot of territory. There are some networks that are worldwide. The telephone system is a good example of a worldwide type of network. There are some computer networks that connect only two or three computers, others that have thousands tied together.

Networks are made up of two major components, hardware and software. The hardware may consist of boards, cables, hubs, routers, and bridges. There are several different companies which supply network operating software (NOS). The main ones are Novell, Microsoft, and IBM.

There are a few standards so the hardware and software from the major companies are compatible. For instance, software from either Novell or Microsoft works on boards and systems from several different vendors and manufacturers.

There are several different types of networks, such as zero slot types, proprietary systems, peer-to-peer types, local area networks (LANs), and wide area networks (WANs). A local area network is usually a system within a single building, plant, or campus. A LAN may include several different types of systems.

A zero slot network is usually two computers tied together with a cable through their serial or parallel ports. Special software can allow access of the hard disk of each unit. Files can be viewed, copied, and transferred between computers. It is a very inexpensive way to share resources. A disadvantage is that it may be limited to a maximum of 115,000 bits per second, which is relatively slow. Another disadvantage is that the distance between the two computers may be limited to about 50 feet.

There are some companies that have proprietary systems for small networks and peer-to-peer systems. Moses Computer, at (408) 358-

1550, has several systems that are ideal for small networks. I have a MosesALL! IV! Computer network system in my office.

For small businesses or small groups, a proprietary system may be all that you need. They are usually inexpensive, yet can have many of the utilities and functions of the large systems.

I also have two other types of network interface cards (NICs) in my office. They are both Ethernet boards. I have several software programs that these boards work under, such as Microsoft LAN Manager, Novell's NetWare Lite, Windows for Workgroups, Windows 95, and Windows NT.

A disadvantage with using the proprietary systems is that they have their own nonstandard software and hardware. These proprietary systems may not work with the standard network operating software and hardware.

A peer-to-peer network may be rather sophisticated. It requires a network card in each computer and requires special software. Depending on the type of system, it may operate from 1 MHz up to 10 MHz or more.

A peer-to-peer network is distinguished from a client server network in that the computers on this type of network communicate with each other rather than with a large file server. They can share and transfer files and utilize the resources of all the computers on the network.

In a file server network, one computer is usually dedicated as the server. A Pentium type computer is ideal as a file server. It can have a very large hard disk that contains all of the company's files and records. The individual computers attached to the server are called *workstations*. The workstations can access the files and records and change or alter them as necessary.

A file server network offers several advantages to the company. They only have to buy software for one machine. They do have to pay for a license for each of the networked computers, but it costs much less than having to buy software for each machine.

A network can keep all of the records and data in one place. This can allow close control of the updating and revisions of the data. A network may allow communication among the networked computers. It may also allow the users to share a single printer, fax, modem, or other peripherals.

One disadvantage is that if the main server goes down, the whole system is down. The data and records must also be routinely backed up. For critical data, it may be necessary to have a redundant array of inexpensive disks (RAID) that would automatically make two or more copies of all data. A less expensive type system would be to use a couple of large IDE hard disks and a couple of SCSI hard disks. Since they use different interface controllers, there is less chance that both of them would fail.

For critical data, it is also necessary that the server be supplied with an uninterruptible power supply (UPS). A UPS is essential in areas where there are frequent lightning and electrical storms. It is also necessary in areas where there are wide variations in the electrical supply where there may be *brownouts*.

Of course, the company needs network operating software (NOS). Novell is the leader in both software and network interface cards (NICs) hardware. The Windows NT can also be used as a NOS.

There are several companies that provide NOS and NICs for small networks. Lantastic from the Artisoft Company, at (602) 670-7326, is one of the better known suppliers. Novell also has Novell Lite for small networks. The Microsoft Windows 95 can also be used for small networks.

There are three main methods, or topologies, of tying computers together, Ethernet, Token Ring, and Star. Each system has some advantages and disadvantages. The Ethernet system is the most popular.

If you would like to learn more about networks you might want to order the book *Build Your Own LAN And Save A Bundle* from TAB/McGraw-Hill. I highly recommend it. It was written by the same person who wrote the book you are reading.

Desktop publishing

If a company has to depend on outside printing for brochures, manuals, and documents, it may be quite expensive. Desktop publishing (DTP) may save the company a lot of money. There are some high-end DTP software programs, such as PageMaker and CorelDRAW Ventura, that are necessary if you expect to do a lot of DTP. But for many projects, Word for Windows 6.0, WordPerfect for Windows, or WordStar for Windows is all you need.

One of the better high end packages is CorelDRAW Ventura. Of course, Corel has several graphic and drawing packages. They have clip art and just about everything else that is needed for desktop publishing.

You may also need a good laser printer and scanner for DTP. If you plan to do any color work, you need a color printer and scanner.

DTP Direct, at (800) 395-7778 or (800) 325-5811, is a desktop publishing catalog. They list several DTP software packages. They also list several hardware DTP products. The ads in many of the computer magazines don't have much information about the product because the space is expensive. But many of the catalogs such as the DTP have a fairly good summary of the various features of the products. Call them for a copy of their catalog.

There are several good books on DTP. TAB/McGraw-Hill publishes several. Call (800) 822-8158 and ask for a catalog.

There are also several magazines that are devoted to DTP. Almost every computer magazine often carries DTP articles.

Presentations

The word *presentation* as used in this chapter has several meanings. A presentation can be used for sales and promotions, training employees, and for informing employees and other people of policies, benefits, events, changes, updates, news, and many other messages.

Presentations are not only for businesses. Almost any communication is a presentation. Even a discussion with your spouse about upgrading your computer is a presentation. Every time you have a conversation with a person, you are usually presenting ideas that you want the other person to *buy*. There may be no monetary reward if a person buys your ideas, but there may be a substantial reward and sense of satisfaction to your ego. Whether we realize it or not, most of us are nearly always presenting and selling our ideas. Usually for this type of presentation, we don't need a lot of software and hardware.

But for an old-fashioned type of presentation where a person stands up before a group with a projector and pointer, you may need software and hardware for text, graphics, sound, and video. A few years ago software and hardware to accomplish all of this would have required large studios full of equipment and would have cost many thousands of dollars. Today it can be done relatively inexpensively with a desktop multimedia PC. In the next sections, I talk about some of the tools that are available to help you make a better presentation.

The need for presentations

Presentations are very important business tools for sales, contract proposals, and all of the other things listed earlier. Business presentations are also used for reports. Businesses spend billions of dollars each year on presentations trying to get their message out. But a poor presentation can be a terrible waste of a company's valuable resources. Quite often, it is not the message that is at fault, but the messenger.

Designing a good presentation

It is not always the presenter's fault for giving a bad presentation. He or she may not have the proper tools to make a good presentation. There are several new electronic tools, but one of the more important tools is proper training. There are a few people who are born with the charisma that makes them the perfect silver-tongued orators. They don't need to be trained. But if you are like most of us, you may need to learn a few basic rules to become a better presenter.

The AskMe Multimedia Center, at (612) 531-0603, has an excellent software package, Super Show & Tell, for developing presentations. Michael O'Donnel, the company president, has written a booklet called "Making Great Presentations Using Your PC." The AskMe Company has also produced *A Guide To Multimedia On The PC*, a 52-page spiral-bound book that has a wealth of information. Call them for copies of these very helpful books.

⇨ Electronic notes

If you are giving a talk and need notes, put them on a laptop computer. Use a large type size. Have the notes arranged so each time you press page down new notes would roll up. Pressing Page Up would let you easily go back and review. Set the computer on the podium and you can glance down now and then at your notes.

Laptops have now become very inexpensive unless you are looking for one with color and an active matrix display. If you do much public speaking, notes on a laptop are much better than hand-written notes.

⇨ Displaying the presentation

The slide and the overhead projectors are still the most popular and most used. Of course, there is no sound or motion on these systems.

With an LCD panel any image that appears on a computer screen can be projected onto a wall or a large theater type screen. The output of a computer is plugged into the LCD panel, which is then placed on the bed of an overhead projector system. Whatever appears on the computer screen, appears on the LCD panel, which is then projected onto the screen.

If the computer has a soundboard and speakers, a complete presentation with color, sound, and motion is possible.

Some of the LCD panels can be connected to a TV, VCR, or a camcorder and project the output onto a large screen. Some of the LCD panel systems may be rather expensive. They have an active-matrix type

screen, the same type of screen used in the more expensive notebook computers. The active-matrix means that they require a separate transistor for every pixel in the panel, which may be several hundred thousand. One reason the active-matrix panels are so expensive is that a single defective transistor makes the whole display panel defective.

There are some less expensive LCD panels that are monochrome, but can display several shades of gray. The list prices for the LCD panels start at about $1000, but the color active-matrix may cost from $4000 and go as high as $10,000 or more.

Here are a few companies that manufacture LCD panels.

> In Focus Systems   (800) 327-7231

> nView Corp.   (800) 736-6439

> Proxima Corp.   (800) 447-7694

> Sayett Technology   (800) 678-7469

> Sharp Electronics   (201) 529-9636

> 3M Corp.   (800) 328-1371

 # Projection monitors

The NEC Company, at (800) 632-4636, has a couple of MultiSync Projection Monitors. These systems take the output from a computer, VCR, or other video source and project it onto a large screen. The systems use red, green, and blue projection lamps such as those used on very large screen television sets.

There are several other companies that make similar screen projection monitors.

 # Large screen TV

Several companies have developed small devices that allow the output of a computer to be plugged into a large screen TV. Advanced Digital Systems, at (310) 865-1432, has the VGA to TV Elite.

Consumer Technology, at (800) 356-3983, has The Presenter and The Presenter Plus, small pocket size devices that can connect a computer output to a TV. These devices can be used with a desktop PC or a small laptop. You can carry your presentation with you on a laptop and display it on a large television. The devices work with standard TVs or with the S-Video TVs.

The Comedge Company, (818) 855-2784, has the Audio/Video Key, a device that is similar to those listed above. It can be used to connect a computer to a TV, a VCR, or a camcorder. It has both standard video and S-VHS outputs.

Ordinarily there is a lot of loss and degradation when a video signal is copied. If you have ever seen a videotape copy of a copy you can see just how much is lost. Many of the newer VCRs and television sets are now equipped with the S-VHS or Super-video option. This option separates the chrominance signals from the luminance signals of composite video. The resulting signals are much cleaner with a lot less signal loss. If you are thinking of buying a new TV or VCR, look for the S-video input and output types.

Camcorder presentations

All three of the above devices can also be used to record a presentation from the computer to a VCR or camcorder. If you record your presentation on an 8mm tape recorder, you can easily take it with you. The palm-sized camcorders are small, relatively inexpensive, and can be connected to any TV. The 8mm tape cartridges can hold up to two hours of text, graphics, speech, or music. The cartridges are small enough to fit several in a coat pocket. The camcorders can run off a small battery so they don't have to have an external power source.

The Gold Disk Company, at (800) 465-3375, has VideoDirector. This software comes with cables that plugs into your computer, camcorder, or video recorder. You can use the software and cables to edit and record clips of your tapes. It works under Windows so it is very easy to use. The VideoDirector is ideal for editing home videotapes or for

professional editing for presentations. They have both DOS PC and Macintosh versions. A camcorder can be an excellent presentation tool.

We are all presenters and salespersons in almost everything we do. We can be much better salespersons if we communicate better.

Summary

There are thousands of different applications for your computer. It is a fantastic tool.

CHAPTER 16

Essential software

HIS chapter can save you hundreds of dollars on software. You cannot operate a computer without software. It is as necessary as hardware. Software programs are merely sets of instructions that tell the hardware what to do. Computers are dumb. Computers only do what the software tells them to do.

Off-the-shelf and ready-to-use software

A software upgrade may be one of the better things you can do to enhance your computer operations. There is more software, already written and immediately available, than you can use in a lifetime. The software companies are constantly revising and updating their software. There are off-the-shelf programs that can do almost everything that you could ever want to do with a computer.

There are several categories of programs that you need, such as a disk operating system (DOS), word processors, databases, spreadsheets, utilities, shells, communications, windows, and graphics. Depending on the uses you intend for your computer, there are hundreds of others for special needs.

List price vs. discount price

NOTE

I list prices several times in this chapter. Prices listed are for comparison only. They will be different by the time you read this, no doubt lower.

Software can be more expensive than the hardware. The prices may also vary from vendor to vendor. Quite often software has an inflated list price that is about twice what the discount price is. For instance, one of the catalogs listed below has a list price for Lotus SmartSuite 2.1 for $795. They have crossed out that figure and offer it at a discount for $449.95. WordPerfect 6.0 has a list price of $495, but the discount price from this company is $289.95. The software vendor can say, "Look at how much you are saving. We cut the price almost in half just for you." Most people are a bit wiser now so many of the companies have stopped listing an unreasonable price and just list a *discount* price. If you look through the catalogs listed below, you will find that the discount price is the same, or within just a few dollars, in almost all of the catalogs. However, there are a few that have prices that are considerably lower. Order all of the catalogs and do your own comparisons.

 # Software upgrades and surplus software

One of the best ways that I know of to save on software is to buy it from Surplus Software, at (800) 753-7877. Quite often there are quite a lot of software packages that have not been sold when a new version is released. The software business is somewhat like the soap business. The software and soap companies must come out with a new and improved version every year. Quite often the new and improved versions don't perform much better than the old ones did. Or it may do things that you have no need for. Like most people, I never use all of the capabilities of my software.

If you would like to save some money and don't mind using an older version software, call the Surplus Software and ask for a copy of their free catalog. It lists hundreds of surplus software packages still in their original shrink wrap.

The Surplus Software Company also carries several hardware components.

Live upgrade discounts

There is another important reason why you should order the Surplus Software catalog and that is for the trade-in value. You can buy Microsoft Word 2.0 for $29.95 from Surplus Software. This software can probably do just about all that you could ever want to do. But if you really must have the latest, Microsoft Word 6.0 is advertised in a discount software magazine for $299.95. But you can get it for about one third of this price with a *live* upgrade. A live upgrade is a previous version of the same product. This MicroWarehouse software magazine advertises that if you have any previous version of Word for Windows, you can trade it in for 6.0 and pay only $95.95 instead of $299.95. So if you buy Word 2.0 for $29.95 from Surplus Software, you can get Word 6.0 for a total cost of $125.90, a savings of $174.05.

 # Competitive upgrade discounts

You can get an even better deal if you trade in an older copy of one of Microsoft Word's competitors, such as WordPerfect, AMI Pro, or even WordStar. The cost of a competitive upgrade is $119.95, but you get a $30 rebate from Microsoft that brings the price down to $89.95. The Software Surplus catalog offers earlier versions of all of these packages.

Microsoft is not the only one which plays this game. WordPerfect 6.0 is listed for $289.95, but you can trade in any previous version of WordPerfect or any competitor's older version and get WordPerfect for only $69.95.

I hate to mention this, but the Software Surplus catalog lists WordStar 6.0 for only $25.95. This package also qualifies as a competitor to WordPerfect and Word for Windows for the reduced price. Incidentally, WordStar was once the number-one word processor in the world. Now many software companies don't even carry it. How the mighty have fallen.

If you bought a copy of WordStar 6.0 for $25.95 and traded it in for Microsoft Word 6.0, it would cost you $89.95 plus $25.95 for a total of $115.90, or a savings of $184.05 from the list price of $299.95.

Before you buy a major software product, you might call the software company and ask what would qualify for a competitive package to trade in for what you want to buy. There is usually quite a bit of latitude.

 # Proof of purchase for upgrade discount

For proof of purchase, they often ask for the title page from the original manual. The software companies have no use for the older used copies. It would just clutter up their stores. You can keep the old software and the rest of the manual. If you have a friend who has an older copy of a software package you want to buy, maybe your friend would give you the title page from his or her manual.

The proof of purchase varies among the different software publishers. You may be required to provide one or more of four general types of proof of purchase or ownership:

❶ The title page of the user manual.

❷ A copy of a sales receipt or invoice.

❸ The serial number of the software program.

❹ A photocopy of the original program disk.

If you are buying through mail order, you may mail or fax a copy of the required items.

Call the catalog companies and ask for a copy of their catalogs.

 # CD-ROM discs and multimedia

The Surplus Software Company also lists hundreds of low cost CD-ROM discs. The discs have hundreds of different kinds of software for business, graphics, education, science, games, entertainment, and other subjects. If you like beer, they even offer a CD that tells you how you can brew your own.

They list several multimedia kits with CD-ROM drives, sound boards, and titles for very low prices. The kits may have double speed CD-ROM drives. But if you used the low cost d-Time[10] CD-ROM drive accelerator software, from Ballard Synergy, at (206) 656-8070, it would provide about the same benefit that a more expensive quad speed drive would give you. The d-Time[10] uses your hard disk to cache data from the CD-ROM disc. Access and transfer rate then becomes essentially whatever the speed of your hard disk is.

 # Shareware and public domain software

Also remember that there are excellent free public domain programs that can do almost everything that the high cost commercial programs can do. Check your local bulletin board, user group, or the ads for public domain software in most computer magazines. There are also some excellent shareware programs that can be registered for a nominal sum.

 # Try before you buy

The Software Dispatch Company, at (800) 289-8383 can send you a CD-ROM disc that has several software programs on it. You can look at them and try them. If you find one that you would like to buy, just give them a call. Have your credit card ready. They will give you a password that you can use to unlock that particular program and download it to your hard disk. It has just about all the software that a person in a small office or home office (SOHO) would ever need.

⇨ Software catalogs

There are several direct mail discount software companies. If you are undecided about what you need, call the companies for a catalog, then decide. Many of the companies who send out catalogs sell both software and hardware. They usually have some very good descriptions of the software and hardware along with prices. I just don't have the available space to describe the software and hardware like the catalogs do. The catalogs are an excellent way to get the basic facts about software.

You should be aware that some of the companies are not exactly discount houses. You might find better prices at your local store or in some of the computer magazines.

You should also note that some of the catalogs do not have a date on them. They usually have some sort of unintelligible code near the mailing address. If you order from one of the catalogs, they will ask you for the code. They then charge you the price listed in that particular catalog. Prices of software and hardware change almost overnight. So if you don't have the latest catalog and you order, you may not be paying the latest price. Here are just a few of the companies who will send you their software catalogs:

➢ Computer Discount Warehouse (CDW)   (800) 330-4239

➢ DellWare   (800) 847-4051

➢ Desktop Publishing (DTP Direct)   (800) 325-5811

➢ Elek-Tek   (800) 395-1000

➢ Global Software & Hardware   (800) 845-6225

➢ J&R Computer World (mostly Mac)   (800) 221-8180

➢ JDR Microdevices   (800) 538-5000

➢ Insight CD-ROM   (800) 488-0002

➢ MicroWarehouse   (800) 367-7080

➢ PC Connections   (800) 800-5555

> ➤ PowerUp! Direct   (800) 851-2917
> ➤ Shareware Express   (800) 346-2842
> ➤ The PC Zone   (800) 258-2088
> ➤ Tiger Software   (800) 888-4437

Essential software

I can't possibly list all of the thousands of software packages available. The computer magazines listed in Chapter 17 often have detailed reviews of software. And of course, they usually have many advertisements for software in every issue. Briefly, here are some of the essential software packages that you need.

Operating systems software

DOS to a computer is like gasoline to an automobile. Without it, it won't operate. DOS is an acronym for *Disk Operating System*. But it does much more than just operate the disks. In recognition of this, OS/2 has dropped the D.

If you are new to computers, DOS should be the first thing that you learn. DOS has over 50 commands, but the chances are that you will never need to know more than 15 or 20 of the commands. DOS 6.2 has a very poor manual, but it has very good on-line help. At the prompt, just type help [command name] or help ?.

✻ MS-DOS
You won't need DOS with Windows 95. But Windows 95 can only be used on 386DX systems and up. There are still millions of people with older XTs, 286s, and 386SXs that still need DOS. There are many people who will not move up to Windows 95, so Microsoft will continue to offer MS-DOS. But it is doubtful that they will be updating it as often as in the past.

✻ IBM PC DOS
IBM claims that their PC-DOS 7.0 is smaller, faster, and has several features not found in MS-DOS 6.22. PC-DOS 7.0 can be loaded in

on top of any DOS that you may already have. It automatically updates and replaces those files and commands that have the same name. Some of the files in PC-DOS 7.0 have a similar function, but different names, such as RAMBOOST, which is better than Memmaker at providing free memory. Like Microsoft, IBM went to outside companies and licensed some of the features such as the Stacker compression software. To match MS-DOS, they also used Central Point's backup software and several other very useful utilities.

PC-DOS 7.0 also has support for the PCMCIA technology, for PenDOS, CD-ROM support, and much more.

❊ Novell DR DOS

DR DOS can do everything that MS-DOS does and some things even better. But Novell may also stop upgrading and revising DR DOS.

❊ OS/2 WARP

OS/2 Warp breaks the 640K barrier and can seamlessly address over 4 gigabytes of RAM. It can do true multitasking and run several programs at the same time. If one program crashes, it does not affect the other programs. It can run all DOS software and any of the software that has been developed for Windows.

OS/2 also has Adobe Type Manager (ATM) that allows scalable fonts for Windows and for printing. It has several other excellent utilities and goodies. Version 3 has BonusPak that allows Internet Connection, Fax software, multimedia, and much more. They even include a few games such as Solitaire and Chess if you have nothing else to do.

OS/2 Warp is a 32-bit system. It can be run on 16-bit 286 systems, but developers recommend a 386SX or higher. They also recommend at least 4MB of RAM, but it would be better to have 8MB or more.

OS/2 Warp is very easy to install and comes with an on-disk tutorial for easy learning.

At the time of this writing, there is speculation that IBM is working on an OS/2 version 4 that will meet or exceed all of the features found in Windows 95.

✳ Windows 95

Windows 95 is the revision of Windows 3.1. It does away with the need for DOS. It does everything that DOS and Windows 3.1 did and more. Windows 3.1 could be run on the 16-bit 286 and 386SX, but Windows 95 is 32-bit software, so it requires a 386DX as a minimum. It runs with only 4MB of RAM, but 8MB is recommended, better yet would be at least 16MB.

Windows 95 will go a long way toward making Plug-and-Play a reality. Programs that are developed to run under Windows 95 are supposed to meet the Plug-and-Play specifications set out by Microsoft.

✳ Windows NT

At the time this is being written, Microsoft is doing a revision of Windows NT. There are many things in Windows 95 that will be in the new Windows NT. But this is high-end software that will be used primarily on servers and large systems. Many of the high-end RISC systems use Windows NT. The new version should be available by the time you read this.

Word processors

The most-used of all software is word processing. There are literally dozens of word processor packages, each one slightly different than the others. It amazes me that they can find so many different ways to do the same thing. All of the major word processor programs come with a spelling checker and a thesaurus that can be very handy. They usually also include several other utilities, such as a calculator, communications programs for your modem, outlines, desktop publishing, print merging, and many others.

✳ WordStar

I use WordStar. I am almost ashamed to admit it because I am afraid that people will laugh at me behind my back. At one time, WordStar was the premier word processor and number one in its field. But it has lost a lot of its luster and has been displaced by others, such as WordPerfect and Microsoft Word.

I started off with WordStar 3.0 on my little CP/M Morrow with a hefty 64K of memory and two 140K single-sided disk drives. It took me some time to learn it. I have been using it for so long that it is like second nature to me. I have tried several other word processors and found that most of them would require almost as much time to learn as WordStar did originally. Learning to use a new word processor is almost like learning a new language. It is a proven fact that the older one gets the more difficult it is to learn a new language. I don't have a lot of free time. WordStar does all I need. In fact, WordStar, like most other programs, has lots of utilities and functions that I have never used. WordStar has both DOS and Windows versions.

Most word processors come with a dictionary and thesaurus, but they are usually quite limited. WordStar publishes the up-to-date and very comprehensive *The American Heritage Dictionary* on ten high-density disks. The installation requires about 15MB of disk space. The 3rd edition is designed to work under Windows. It is a reference that helps you simplify and streamline your writing tasks. Some of the features are a full dictionary with over 200,000 words. It has *Roget's II Thesaurus* with over 500,000 synonyms. You can use Word Hunter to find words that you might not know how to spell or words that you can't quite recall. If you type in just portions of a word, it can help in solving crossword puzzles and much more.

WordStar also publishes *Correct Quotes* and several other writing aids.

WordStar International can be reached at (800) 227-5609 or (800) 843-2204.

WordStar has an educational division that offers an excellent discount to schools, both for site licenses and for student purchases. The educational division is at (800) 543-8188.

✳ WordPerfect

This is one of the hottest-selling word processors, so it must be doing something right. WordPerfect has the ability to select fonts by a proper name, has simplified printer installation, the ability to do most desktop publishing functions, columns, import graphics, and many other useful functions and utilities. WordPerfect 6.0 for DOS is

probably their last upgrade for DOS. They will concentrate on WordPerfect for Windows for future upgrades and improvements.

WordPerfect also has several other software products such as WordPerfect Presentations; WordPerfect Office for e-mail, scheduling, and calendaring; DataPerfect, a database; and WordPerfect Works, an integrated software package.

WordPerfect has now merged with Novell, which should make it a bit easier for them to compete with Microsoft Word.

✳ **Microsoft Word for Windows**

Microsoft Word for Windows lets you take advantage of all of the features and utilities of Windows. If you have previously learned a different word processor, such as WordPerfect, Word for Windows lets you use the WordPerfect commands. Besides being an excellent word processor, Word for Windows does just about everything that is needed for such things as desktop publishing, generating reports, making charts, drawings, and presentations. It does columns, imports graphics, can import data from databases, spreadsheets, and other files. It even has a corrector for people like me who constantly type *teh* instead of *the*. It has many more features than I would *ever* use, even if I could learn them all.

✳ **PC-Write**

PC-Write 4.0 is the least-expensive of all the word processors. It is shareware and if copied from an existing user, they ask for a $16 donation. Full registration with manual and technical support is $89. It is easy to learn and is an excellent personal word processor.

It is available from Quicksoft Inc., at (206) 282-0452.

There are many other good word processors. Look for ads and reviews in computer magazines.

Grammar checkers

You may be the most intelligent person alive, but you might not be able to write a simple intelligible sentence. There are several

grammar checking programs that can work with most of the word processors. They can analyze your writing and suggest ways to improve it. Here are just a couple of them.

> ➤ Right Writer from Que Corp.   (800) 992-0244
> ➤ Grammatik from Reference Software (800) 872-9933

⇨ Database programs

Database packages are very useful for business purposes. They allow you to manage large amounts of information. Most programs allow one to store information, search it, sort it, do calculations, make up reports, and several other very useful features.

At the present time, there are almost as many database programs as there are word processors. Some of them allow the interchange of data from one program to another.

The average price for the better-known database packages is almost twice that of word processors.

✳ dBASE 5.0

dBASE II was one of the first database programs for the personal computer. It has gone through several revisions and improvements. The most current version is dBASE 5.0 for Windows. There is also a dBASE 5.0 version for DOS. It is a very powerful program and has hundreds of features. Previous versions were highly structured and could be a bit difficult to learn. The new Windows version is very easy to use, in many cases, just point and click, or click and drag. You can create forms or design reports very quickly and easily. It has excellent built-in help and tutorials.

dBASE 5.0 is downward-compatible, so the 7 million users who have databases generated by the older versions can still use their old data.

The MicroWarehouse catalog has a list price of $339.95, or $189.95 with an upgrade trade-in. The price will no doubt be lower by the time you read this. dBASE is one of the Borland family of products.

✳ Paradox

Paradox is fairly easy to learn and use, and is fast and powerful. It is designed for both beginners and expert users. It is a full-featured relational database that can be used on a single PC or on a network. The main menu has functions like View, Ask, Report, Create, Modify, Image, Forms, Tools, Scripts, and Help. Choosing one of these items brings up options that are associated with that item. Extensive use is made of the Function keys. There are Paradox versions for both DOS and Windows.

The query by example is very helpful for beginners and experts alike. Paradox has a very powerful programming language, PAL. Experienced programmers can easily design special applications.

It's a product of Borland International, at (408) 438-5300.

✳ askSam

The funny looking name is an acronym for *Access Knowledge via Stored Access Method*. It is a free-form, text-oriented database management system. It is very much like a word processor. In fact, if you can use a word processor, you will have no trouble using askSam. Data can be typed in randomly, then sorted and accessed. Data can also be entered in a structured format for greater organization. It is not quite as powerful as dBASE 5 or Paradox, but it is much easier to learn and use. It is also much less expensive. It is ideal for most business database needs. It is also great for personal records needs such as expenses.

The Windows version even has a spell checker and hyperlink. A hyperlink in a document can link up with other parts of a document, open a new document or report, and several other useful functions.

They also have a discount program for students. Students can get a very good discount when they buy the program if the order is placed by an instructor. Any instructor who places an order for 10 or more copies gets a free copy. They also have a very low price to upgrade from a previous version.

This product is from Seaside Software, at (800) 800-1997.

✳ FoxPro

FoxPro is very easy to use. It has windows and can be controlled by a mouse or the keyboard. It has several different windows. A View Window is the master control panel to create databases, open files, browse, set options, and other functions. You don't have to be a programmer to type commands into the Command Window to operate FoxPro. The Browse Window lets you view, edit, append, or delete files. It also has Memo Fields, a built-in editor, allows you to create Macros, has extensive context sensitive help, and much more.

FoxPro is a part of Microsoft.

 # Spreadsheets

Spreadsheets are primarily number crunchers. They have a matrix of cells in which data can be entered. Data in a particular cell can be acted on by formulas and mathematical equations. If the data in the cell that is acted on affects other cells, recalculations are done for the other cells as well. Several of the tax software programs use a simple form of spreadsheet. The income and all the deductions can be entered. If an additional deduction is discovered, it can be entered and all the calculations will be done over automatically.

In business, spreadsheets are essential for inventory, expenses, accounting purposes, forecasting, making charts, and dozens of other vital business uses.

There are a large number of spreadsheet programs. Here are just a few.

✳ Lotus 1-2-3

Lotus was one of the first spreadsheets. The current version for Windows is a spreadsheet, database, and graphics package all in one. It is still one of the most powerful and popular spreadsheets.

The discount price listed in several catalogs is $309.95. The upgrade price is $95.95. Any previous version of 1-2-3 can be used for a live upgrade.

Competitive spreadsheets such as Excel, Quattro, Quattro Pro, or SuperCalc can qualify for a competitive upgrade.

Check through any of the catalogs listed earlier or call Lotus Development, at (617) 577-8500.

✳ Microsoft Excel

Microsoft Excel is a very powerful spreadsheet program, with pull down menus, windows, and dozens of features. It can even perform as a database. It has a long list of other features. Excel is one of the products that makes up Microsoft Office.

Several catalogs have a discount price for Excel of $299.95. A live upgrade is only $89.95; a competitive upgrade is $119.95.

✳ Quattro Pro

The Quattro Pro spreadsheet looks very much like Lotus 1-2-3. In fact, Lotus sued Borland because it has the "look and feel" of 1-2-3. After dragging through the courts for several years and costing hundreds of thousands of dollars, a judge has ruled against Lotus.

Quattro Pro has better graphics capabilities for charts, calculates faster, has pull down menus, can print sideways, and has several features not found in Lotus 1-2-3. It is fully compatible with Lotus 1-2-3 spreadsheet files. It is very easy to learn, it has Object Help, Interactive Tutors, and Experts.

Like most of the other major software packages, earlier versions of Quattro are available from Surplus Software for a very low price.

The Quattro division is now a part of Novell. They have recently updated and revised the program.

There are many other spreadsheet programs. Check the ads and reviews in computer magazines.

Suites

Several companies are now bundling several software packages together as a suite. The suites usually have a word processor, a database, a spreadsheet, and perhaps one or two other packages. The software in the suite packages is integrated so all the functions work together. A suite usually costs much less than buying each package separately.

Here are just a few of the more popular suites.

Microsoft Office

Microsoft Office has several different versions. One version includes Microsoft Word 6.0 for word processing, Excel 5.0 for spreadsheets, PowerPoint for presentations, and Mail for E-mail and fax systems. Another version includes all of these plus Access 2.0, for databases.

Novell PerfectOffice

The Novell PerfectOffice Suite includes six major software packages. They are WordPerfect 6.1, Quattro Pro 6.0, Presentations 3.0, InfoCentral 1.1, Envoy 1.0, and GroupWise 4.1. The packages work together so data from any one program can be moved back and forth to any other one.

WordPerfect, of course, is about the most popular word processor in the world. Quattro Pro is one of the better spreadsheets. Presentations is one of the better programs for designing your own presentations. Envoy is an electronic document publisher and lets you view documents that may have been created in fonts that you don't have. GroupWise is an integrated package for E-Mail, calendaring, scheduling, and task management.

PerfectOffice works on almost all networks such as NetWare, Windows for Workgroups, Windows NT, Banyan Vines, and others.

 Lotus SmartSuite

Lotus SmartSuite includes AMI Pro for word processing, Lotus 1-2-3 for Windows for spreadsheets, Lotus Approach for database, Lotus Organizer, a personal information manager, and Freelance Graphics for creating presentations.

CorelDRAW 5

The Corel Corporation has now acquired Ventura Publisher from the Xerox Corp. Ventura is one of the premier desktop publishing software packages. Corel has added several of their graphics and other features to the Corel Ventura Publisher. Ventura is sold separately, or it can be purchased along with CorelDRAW as CorelDRAW 5. This package includes over 22,000 clip art images, 825 fonts, and 100 royalty-free photos on CD-ROM. Graphics, text, and other materials can be imported under the Windows OLE and placed in Ventura files.

Microsoft Works

Microsoft Works could be called a poor man's suite. It has a word processor, a spreadsheet, database, communications, charting, and drawing all in one package. A discount house is offering this software package for $79.95. The same discount house offers other suites for prices from $279 up to $559. So you know that the Microsoft Works package cannot be nearly as powerful or have as many goodies as the full-featured suites. Depending on what you want to do, the Microsoft Works may be all you need.

Phoenix Ultimate Utilities Suite

The Phoenix Company, at (800) 452-0120, was one of the first companies to make a legitimate clone of the IBM BIOS. This allowed the clone makers to manufacture IBM compatible PCs. Phoenix still designs BIOS chips, but it has also diversified into the software

329

business. Phoenix doesn't have that many software packages so it went to four other companies and included their software to make up a suite of five Ultimate Utilities for Windows. Here are the excellent and useful utilities.

✳ Eclipse Find from Phoenix

Eclipse Find is a text retrieval program that lets you find and view files in less than three seconds. It lets you view, archive, copy text to clipboard, or print.

✳ Dashboard from HP

Dashboard is similar to the dashboard of an automobile. You can set up favorite icons just like presetting the stations in your car radio. You can work with several screens or switch or launch any one of them. It has several other very useful and time-saving features.

✳ Folderbolt from Kent Marsh

Folderbolt is a security utility that offers several options for files. You can designate some read only or full password protection. You can prevent access, copying, alteration, or deletion of files.

✳ Uninstaller from MicroHelp

Every time you install a Windows program, it loads bits and pieces of the files in many nooks and crannies. If you decide to delete the file, you may leave several of the bits and pieces behind. Every time you run Windows from then on you may get error messages. Uninstaller can search your system and find all of the bits and pieces that were left behind and delete them. This program alone is worth the price of the package.

This package can also be purchased as a standalone package. It is discussed in more detail later.

✳ SuperQueue from Zenographics

When printing a long document, SuperQueue takes over and feeds the document to a special file on disk. It then returns control to you and feeds the file to the printer in the background. It also allows you to batch print several documents. It handles the multiple documents while you go about doing more productive work.

Utilities

Utilities are essential tools that can unerase a file, detect bad sectors on a hard disk, diagnose, defragment, sort, and do many other things. Norton's Utilities was the first, and is still foremost, in the utility department.

SpinRite and Disk Technician are excellent hard disk tools for defragmenting and for detecting potential bad sectors on a hard disk. They are essential tools for hard disk preventive maintenance.

Norton Utilities

This is a program that everybody should have. It has several excellent utilities that can save you time and money. The Norton Disk Doctor (NDD) file can automatically repair disk problems, both hard and floppy. The Norton Disk Editor lets you explore and repair sectors of a hard disk. The File Fix lets you repair data files. The Unerase command is great for recovering accidentally erased files. (This utility is so important that Microsoft now includes a similar utility in MS-DOS 6.0 and later versions.) Norton also has Norton Commander, a shell program, and Norton Backup, a very good hard disk backup program. They have a Norton Backup for DOS and one for Windows.

The latest version of the Norton Utilities at this time is 8.0. It improves many of the old standard features and adds several new ones. It has added several new Windows utilities that can help in diagnosing, troubleshooting, and repairing problems in Windows.

One of the excellent features is that when you install it, you are given the option to have your Autoexec.bat file changed. If you agree, Norton automatically checks all of your hard drives for cross-linked files, fixes any corrupted files and asks if you want to make out a report. It then makes a mirror image of the FAT and stores it in a second location. If the primary FAT is damaged, you will still be able to access your data from the second FAT.

This is a product of Symantec, at (408) 253-9600 or (800) 441-7234.

⇨ PC Tools Pro

This is an excellent program that just about does it all. It has data recovery utilities, hard disk backup, a DOS shell, a disk manager, anti-virus, and lots more.

Central Point Software, at (503) 690-8090, is now a part of Symantec.

⇨ SpinRite 3.1

SpinRite 3.1 has several new features that were not in the original versions. It performs the most rigorous hard disk tests of any other software. It can detect any marginal areas and move the data to a safe area. SpinRite can maximize hard disk performance and prevent hard disk problems before they happen.

Gibson Research, at (714) 362-8800, produces SpinRite.

⇨ Disk Technician Gold

Disk Technician, at (619) 274-5000, does essentially the same type of tests that SpinRite does, but not quite as rigorously. Disk Technician also has several automatic features and can now detect most viruses. It can be installed and will work in the background to detect any errors as they may happen when writing to a hard disk.

⇨ CheckIt PRO: Analyst

CheckIt PRO: Analyst for Windows from TouchStone Software Corp., at (714) 969-7746, is a program that quickly checks and reports on the configuration of a computer, the type of CPU it has, the amount of memory, the installed drives, and peripherals. It runs

diagnostic tests of the installed items and can do performance benchmark tests.

Directory and disk-management programs

There are dozens of disk management programs that help you keep track of your files and data on the hard disk, find it, rename it, view it, sort it, copy, delete it, and many other useful utilities. They can save an enormous amount of time and make life a lot simpler.

XTreePro Gold and XTree for Windows

XTree from the XTree Company, at (805) 541-0604, was one of the first and still one of the best disk management programs available. I use it to view my files then delete unnecessary ones. I also use it to copy and back up files from one disk or directory to another. It also lets you order the files by date or alphabetically. I often look at the date stamp so I know which files are the latest. It has many other features. I don't know how anyone can get along without XTree.

XTree is now a part of the Central Point and Symantec Companies.

Norton Commander

Norton Commander from Symantec Corp., at (800) 441-7234, is a shell program that offers speed and convenience for file management, file viewing, PC-to-PC file transfer, and even electronic mail. It lets you view many different database programs, spreadsheets, word processors, graphics, and compressed files. It lets you edit, copy, rename, move, or delete files. It is very easy to learn and use.

 # Computer-aided design (CAD) programs

Most CAD programs are high-end programs that require very good high resolution monitors and powerful computers. The Pentium is an ideal computer for computer aided design.

 ## AutoCAD

AutoCAD from the Autodesk Company is a high end, high cost design program. It is quite complex with an abundance of capabilities and functions. But it is also rather expensive at about $3000.

Autodesk is the IBM of the CAD world and has more or less established the standard for the many clones that have followed. Autodesk, Inc., at (415) 332-2344, produces AutoCAD.

 ## Generic CADD

Autodesk has several modules and other programs that cost less than the full blown AutoCAD. One of them is Generic CADD 6.0, from (800) 228-3601, extension 803.

Home Series

Autodesk has a set of five low cost programs they call the Home Series. These programs are HOME, KITCHEN, BATHROOM, DECK, and LANDSCAPE. You don't have to be an architect to design your dream home, design an up-to-date kitchen, or bathroom, a deck, or plan your landscape. Each of the five programs has a list price of $59.95. The programs come with a library of professional symbols such as doors, outlets, furniture, fixtures, and appliances that you can import and place in your drawing. The program tracks the materials specified in your drawing and automatically creates a shopping list.

3D PLAN

Autodesk recently added 3D PLAN, a program that lets you look at any of the plans that were created in the HOME, KITCHEN, BATHROOM, DECK, and LANDSCAPE programs in three dimensions. Surfaces are shaded to add a realistic appearance.

I would recommend these programs to anyone who plans to design a home or do any remodeling on an older home. They can save you hours of time and lots of money. Autodesk is at (800) 228-3601, extension 803.

DesignCAD 2D and DesignCAD 3D

These CAD programs do just about everything that AutoCAD does, and they cost less. DesignCAD 3D allows you to make three-dimensional drawings. Call American Small Business Computers at (918) 825-4844.

There are several other companies that offer CAD software. Check the computer magazines.

Miscellaneous software programs

There are many programs for things such as Accounting, Statistics, Finance, Graphics, and many other applications. Some are very expensive, some very reasonable.

CorelDRAW

CorelDRAW can be used for such things as drawing, illustration, page layout, charting, animation, desktop publishing, and presentations. It has word processing, OCR, over 5000 drag and drop symbols and shapes, over 18,000 clip art images, over 750 fonts, and many other features and utilities. This is all in CorelDRAW version 3. It comes on a 600MB CD-ROM disc. They have also added more fonts, features,

and functions to CorelDRAW and released it as CorelDRAW 4. It comes on two CD-ROM discs. Both releases are available.

Corel has several other excellent software packages. Call them for a brochure at (613) 728-3733.

 # CorelSCSI

CorelSCSI is a program that has software and several SCSI drivers that work with most major SCSI host adapters such as Always, DPT, Ultrastor, and Adaptec. It also has SitBACK, a software program for unattended backup, and Corel Tape Backup software. It also has several other programs and utilities.

This is available from Corel Corp., at (613) 728-3733.

 # Stacker

Stacker from Stac Electronics, at (619) 431-7474, is an excellent compression program for software. Software programs keep getting bigger and bigger. No matter how big your hard drive is, it never seems to have enough empty space. Most software has a lot of empty space in between the 0s and 1s. Some time ago engineers figured out how to compress the software and squeeze it down. Software compression would be somewhat like taking all the text on this line and pushing it together to eliminate the space between the words. There would also be special symbols for the most frequently used letters such as e and s. The software can have a 2:1 or even higher compression ratio. At that rate, you could store 200MB on a 100MB hard disk.

Software compression has been around for some time. The Bulletin Boards have been using it for several years, but it was quite a bit of trouble to compress and decompress the data. A few years ago, Stac Electronics came up with a system that did the compressing and decompressing seamlessly and automatically. It is great. It can double your disk storage. It is just like adding another hard disk, except that it is considerably less expensive and less trouble to install.

I have been using Stacker compression software since it was first introduced. I have installed it on several hard disks. I have not had any problems whatsoever.

With Stacker you can also use data compression on floppy disks. You can store 2.88MB on a 1.44MB floppy and even configure it so it can be used on any other system, even those that do not have Stacker installed.

MS-DOS and IBM PC DOS have the Stacker utility included.

 # Uninstaller for Windows

When a program for Windows is installed on your computer, it copies pieces and portions into several different areas. If you decide later that you don't want that application, you can use DOS to delete the program. But it will not delete all references to the program. Every time you load Windows, it may hunt for that program, then tell you that it can't find it. Even some Demo programs load themselves into several areas that are difficult to clean out. Use the DOS EDITOR and look at the WIN.INI sometime. You may find references there to programs that you erased months ago. These leftover bits and pieces can clutter up your disk considerably.

The Uninstaller from MicroHelp can track down all of the different parts of a Windows program and delete them. Even if you are a Windows pro, the Uninstaller can save you time.

You can call MicroHelp, Inc., at (404) 516-0899, for more information.

 # StreetSmart

StreetSmart from Charles Schwab Company, at (800) 334-4455, lets you use your computer and modem to trade stocks, options, mutual funds, and bonds. It lets you research Dow Jones News and Dow Jones databases, use MarketScope for S&P database and news, stock ratings, and buy/sell recommendations, use Company Reports to do

comprehensive research on earnings and financials. You can create your own performance graphs, import and export critical financial data, and customize your portfolio reports. If you have any interest in the stock market, then you should have a copy of StreetSmart.

Money Counts

This is a very inexpensive program that can be used at home or in a small business. With it you can set up a budget, keep track of all of your expenses, balance your checkbook, and several other functions. From Parsons Technology, at (800) 223-6925, this program costs very little.

It's Legal

This software, also from Parsons Technology, helps you create wills, leases, promissory notes, and other legal documents.

The Random House Encyclopedia

This program puts a whole encyclopedia on disk and allows you to find any subject very quickly. It is available from Microlytics at (716) 248-9150.

WillMaker

WillMaker from Nolo Press, at (510) 549-1976, is a low cost program that can help you create a will. Everyone should have a will, no matter what age you are or how much you own. Many people put it off because they don't want to take the time. Or they don't want to pay a lawyer a large fee. This inexpensive software can help you easily create a will that can prevent many family problems.

We don't like to think about this sort of thing, but it happens to everyone, sooner or later.

 # Living Trust Maker

Living Trust Maker from Nolo Press, at (510) 549-1976, is a program that *every* family should have. Even if you have a will, it is possible that it could end up in probate court. You may have heard some of the horror stories about how probate can take several years to settle and the costs can completely eat up all of a large estate. A living trust can avoid probate and its lengthy and costly processes.

Ordinarily, a living trust requires a lawyer and can be relatively expensive. With the Nolo Press Living Trust Maker, you can create your own living trust without a lawyer. The program allows you to fashion the trust to your unique needs. The software guides you through the process, but it comes with a large user guide and legal manual that can explain and answer most of your questions. Nolo Press has free technical support if you have any problems.

 # Software for kids

One of the big reasons to have a home computer is for the kids. If you have children and you don't have a computer, then they are being handicapped. In today's society, a child needs all the help he or she can get in order to make it as an adult. A computer is absolutely essential to help in the very important early training. There are thousands of software programs, commercial, shareware, and public domain, that have been developed for children. Most of the software catalogs listed above have children's software listings.

A good example of a children's educational program is the Smithsonian Institution Dinosaur Museum from the Software Marketing Corporation, at (602) 893-2042. Many of the programs such as this come on CD-ROMs. This one comes on five 1.44MB floppies. The program is in 3-D so a pair of plastic 3-D Video Glasses comes with it.

The *KidSoft Magazine*, at (800) 354-6150, has reviews of dozens of software programs for kids.

 # Software training

Most software manuals are very poorly written. You can usually tell how bad the manuals are by the number of books written telling you how to use the software. Microsoft is the largest software publisher in the world. They also have a very large book publishing house, the Microsoft Press. They publish hundreds of books each year to help people learn to use the software they publish. A cynical person might suspect that Microsoft publishes poor manuals so they can sell more books.

There are also several companies who conduct training classes and seminars for learning some of the most popular software. These seminars may cost several hundred dollars for a one or two day session. I can't learn enough in one or two days to justify the cost of some of the seminars. If you pay five or six hundred dollars for a software package, you shouldn't have to spend another five or six hundred dollars to learn how to use it.

One of the better ways to learn software is by using videotapes. The ViaGrafix Company, at (800) 842-4723, has about 200 different videotape courses. They have tapes on all of the most popular software and even some that is not so popular. You should be able to find a tape for almost any program imaginable. They even have instructional tapes on networking, telecommunications, programming, and much more. You can view the tapes at your leisure and learn at your own pace. Call them for a catalog.

 # LapLink for Windows

If you do any traveling, it is almost essential that you have a laptop computer. Or if you work in an office, it is very convenient to copy data from a desktop PC to a laptop to bring work home. But it is sometimes a problem transferring files and data from the PC to the laptop and then back to the PC. For many years, Traveling Software, at (800) 343-8080, has been foremost in providing software and cables specifically for this purpose. They have now developed several new utilities that make the file transfer faster and easier. You can now

use it with a modem to tie into the office PC, a network so you can work at home, or update your files or access your E-mail while traveling.

You can connect two PCs with the supplied cables by using the LPT1 parallel printer ports, the COM serial ports, by modem, by wireless devices or over a network such as Novell. Using the cables and software, two computers can be tied together in a very low-cost type of network. If you own a laptop, or work in an office with two or more computers, you could probably save a lot of time with LapLink for Windows.

 # Summary

I can't possibly mention all of the fantastic software that is available. There are thousands and thousands of ready-made software programs that can allow you to do almost anything with your computer. Look through any computer magazine for the reviews and ads. You should be able to find programs for almost any application.

CHAPTER 17

Component
sources

HOW much you save by doing it yourself depends on what components you buy and where you buy them. You have to shop wisely and be fairly knowledgeable about the components in order to take advantage of good bargains.

⇨ Computer shows and swap meets

I have done a lot of my buying at computer shows and swap meets. There is at least one computer show or swap almost every weekend in the larger cities. If you live in or near a large city, check your newspaper for ads.

To set up a computer swap, an organizer usually rents a large building, such as a convention center or a large hall. Booth spaces are then rented out to the various local vendors. Most of the booths will have good reputable local business people. Most of the shows have a circus-like atmosphere about them and I often go just because of this.

One of the best features of the swap meets is that almost all of the components that you need are there in one place on display. Several different booths will have similar components for sale. I usually take a pencil and pad with me to the shows. I walk around and write down the prices of the items that I want to buy and compare prices at the various booths. There can be quite a wide variation in the prices. I bought a good printer at one show. One dealer was asking $995 for it in one booth. About 50 feet away, another dealer was offering the same printer for $695.

You can also haggle with most of the dealers at the shows, especially when it gets near closing time. Rather than pack up the material and lug it back to their stores, many will sell it for a lower price.

The Interface Company, at (617) 449-6600, puts on the biggest computer shows in the country. They have the Computer Dealers Exposition (COMDEX) in Atlanta in the spring and a Fall COMDEX in Las Vegas. The attendance goes up every year. When I first started attending in 1984, they only had about 60,000 people at Las Vegas. They now attract over 200,000. Every hotel room in Las Vegas is usually sold out six months before the show. They have now started a New Media Expo that will be held in Los Angeles in the spring. The Interface Company also puts on international shows in several foreign countries.

Your local store

Most of the vendors at the swaps are local business people. They want your business and will not risk losing you as a customer. But there may be a few vendors from other parts of the country. If you buy something from a vendor who does not have a local store, be sure to get a name and address. Most components are reliable. But there is always a chance that something might not work. You may need to exchange it or get it repaired. Or you may need to ask some questions or need some support to get it working.

Again, computers are very easy to assemble. Once you have bought all of the components, it will take less than an hour to assemble your computer. But it is possible to make a mistake. Most components are now fairly reliable. However, there is a possibility that a new part that you buy and install could be defective. Most of the dealers will give you a warranty of some kind and will replace defective parts. If there is something in the system that prevents it from operating, you may not be able to determine just which component is defective. Besides that, it can sometimes take a considerable amount of time to remove a component like a motherboard and return it to someone across town. Or even worse, someone across the country. So if at all

possible, try to deal with a knowledgeable vendor who will support you and help you with any problems.

⇨ Magazines and mail-order

Every computer magazine carries pages and pages of ads for compatible components and systems that can be sent to you through the mails. If you live in an area where there are no computer stores, or shows, you can buy by mail.

One of the biggest magazines in size and circulation is the *Computer Shopper*. It usually has over 1000 tabloid-sized pages. About 90% of the magazine is made up of full page ads for computer components and systems. They do manage to get a few articles in among the ads. For subscription information, call (800) 274-6384. The *Shopper*, and some of the other magazines, have a categorized list of all the products advertised in the magazine and what page the product is on. This makes it easy to find what you are looking for.

Another reason to use mail-order is because it may be less expensive than the local vendors. The local vendors usually have their stores in a fairly high rent district; the mail-order people may be working out of their back bedroom. Most local vendors have to buy their stock from a distributor. The distributor usually buys it from the manufacturer or a wholesaler. By the time you get the product, it may have passed through several companies that each have made some profit. Most of the direct marketers who advertise by mail have cut out the middlemen and passed their profit on to you.

Without computer magazines, there would be no mail-order and without mail-order there would be no computer magazines. Ads are the life blood of magazines. The subscription price of a magazine doesn't even come close to paying for the mailing costs, so they must have ads to exist.

Most mail-order vendors are honest. But a few bad advertisers can ruin a magazine. *PC World* has a regular Consumer Watch column. If

you have a problem with a mail-order vendor that you can't resolve, write to them. They can usually get it resolved. For *PC World* subscription information call (800) 234-3498. The magazines have formed the Microcomputer Marketing Council (MMC) of the Direct Marketing Association, 6 East 43rd Street, New York, New York 10017. They have an action line at (212) 297-1393. They police the advertisers fairly closely.

You should be sure of what you need and what you are ordering. Some of the ads aren't written very well and may not tell the whole story. Ads are expensive so they may abbreviate or leave out a lot of important information. If possible, call them up and make sure. Ask what their return policy is for defective merchandise. Also ask how long before the item will be shipped. And ask for the current price. The ads are usually placed about two months before the magazines are delivered or hit the stands. The way prices are coming down, there could be quite a change in cost at the time you place your order. Of course, if you send them the advertised price, I am sure that they will not refuse it. A $2 or $3 phone call could save you a lot of time, trouble, grief, and maybe even some money.

Ten rules for ordering by mail

Here are some brief rules that you should follow when ordering by mail.

Rule 1: Look for a street address

Make sure the advertiser has a street address. In some ads, they give only a phone number. If you decide to buy from this vendor, call and verify that there is a live person on the other end with a street number. But before you send any money, do a bit more investigation. If possible, look through past issues of the same magazine for previous ads. If the vendor has been advertising for several months, then it is probably okay.

 # Rule 2: Compare other vendor prices

Check through the magazines for other vendors prices for this product. The prices should be fairly close. If it appears to be a bargain that is too good to be true, then . . . you know the rest.

 # Rule 3: Buy from MMC members

Buy from a vendor who is a member of the Microcomputer Marketing Council (MMC) of the Direct Marketing Association (DMA), or other recognized association. There are now about 10,000 members that belong to marketing associations. They have agreed to abide by the ethical guidelines and rules of the associations. Except for friendly persuasion and the threat of expulsion, the associations have little power over the members. But most of them realize what is at stake and put a great value on their membership. Most that advertise in the major computer magazines are members.

The Post Office, Federal Trade Commission, magazines and legitimate businessmen who advertise have taken steps to try to stop the fraud and scams.

 # Rule 4: Do your homework

Read the ads carefully. Advertising space is very expensive. Many ads use abbreviations. Many ads may not be entirely clear. If in doubt, call and ask. Know exactly what you want, state precisely the model, make, size, component, and any other pertinent information. Tell them which ad you are ordering from, ask them if the price is the same, if the item is in stock, and when you can expect delivery. If the item is not in stock, indicate whether you will accept a substitute or want your money refunded. Ask for an invoice or order number. Ask the person's name. Write down all of the information, the time, the date, the company's address and phone number, description of item, and promised delivery date. Write down and save any telephone conversations, the time, date, and the person's name. Save any and all correspondence.

 Rule 5: Ask questions

Ask if the advertised item comes with all the necessary cables, parts, accessories, software, etc. Ask what the warranties are. Ask about the seller's return policies and refund policies. With whom should you correspond if there is a problem?

Rule 6: Don't send cash

You will have no record of it. If possible, use a credit card. If you have a problem, you can possibly have the bank refuse to pay the amount. A personal check may cause a delay of three to four weeks while the vendor waits for it to clear. A money order or credit card order should be filled and shipped immediately. Keep a copy of the money order.

Rule 7: Ask for delivery date

If you have not received your order by the promised delivery date, notify the seller.

Rule 8: Try the item out as soon as you receive it

If you have a problem, notify the seller immediately, by phone, then in writing. Give all details. Don't return the merchandise unless the dealer gives you a return material authorization (RMA). Make sure to keep a copy of the shipper's receipt, packing slip, or some evidence that the material was returned.

Rule 9: What to do if it is defective

If you believe the product is defective or you have a problem, reread your warranties and guarantees. Reread the manual and any documentation. It is very easy to make an error or misunderstand how

an item operates if you are unfamiliar with it. Before you go to a lot of trouble, try to get some help from someone else. At least get someone to verify that you do have a problem. There are many times when a problem will disappear and the vendor will not be able to duplicate it. If possible, when you call try to have the item in your computer and be at the computer so you can describe the problem as it happens.

Rule 10: Try to work out your problem with the vendor

If you cannot, then write to the consumer complaint agency in the seller's state. You should also write to the magazine and to the DMA, 6 East 43rd Street, New York, New York 10017.

Federal Trade Commission rules

Here is a brief summary of the FTC rules:

Rule 1: Must ship within 30 days

The seller must ship your order within 30 days unless the ad clearly states that it will take longer.

Rule 2: Right to cancel

If it appears that the seller cannot ship when promised, the seller must notify you and give a new date. The seller must give you the opportunity to cancel the order and refund your money if you desire.

Rule 3: Must notify if order can't be filled

If the seller notifies you that your order cannot be filled on time, the seller must include a stamped self-addressed envelope or card so you can respond to this notice. If you do not respond, the seller may assume that

you agree to the delay. The seller still must ship within 30 days of the end of the original 30 days or cancel your order and refund your money.

 # Rule 4: Right to cancel if delayed

Even if you consent to a delay, you still have the right to cancel at any time.

 # Rule 5: Must refund money if canceled

If you cancel an order that has been paid for by check or money order, the seller must refund the money. If you paid by credit card, your account must be credited within one billing cycle. Store credits or vouchers in place of a refund are not acceptable.

 # Rule 6: No substitutions

If the item you ordered is not available, the seller may not send you a substitute without your express consent.

Sources of knowledge

There are several good magazines that can help you gain the knowledge needed to make sensible purchases and to learn more about computers. These magazines usually carry some very interesting and informative articles and reviews of software and hardware. They also have many ads for computers, components, and software.

Some of the better magazines that you should subscribe to are the *Computer Shopper, Byte, PC Computing, PC World* and *PC Magazine*. Most of these magazines are available on local magazine racks. But you will save money with a yearly subscription. Besides, they will be delivered to your door.

If you need a source of components, you only have to look in any of the magazines listed above to find hundreds of them. If you live near a large city, there will no doubt be several vendors who advertise in your local paper.

Many of the magazines, such as *Computer Shopper* and *PC Computing*, have a section that lists all of the products advertised in that particular issue. The components and products are categorized and listed by page number. It makes it very easy to find what you are looking for.

Another source of computer information can be found in the several good computer books published by McGraw-Hill.

There are hundreds of computer and computer related magazines. If you read *every* one of them, you still will not be able to keep up with the flood of computer information.

 # Recommended computer magazines

Here are just a few of the magazines that can help you keep abreast to some degree.

Audio-Forum
96 Broad St.
Guilford, CT 06437

Black Box Corp.
P.O. Box 12800
Pittsburgh, PA 15241

Byte
P.O. Box 558
Hightstown, NJ 08520

CD-I World
P.O. Box 1358
Camden, ME 04843-1358

CD-ROM Multimedia
720 Sycamore St.
Columbus, IN 47201
(800) 565-4623

CD-ROM Today
Subscription Dept.
P.O. Box 51478
Boulder, CO 80321-1478

CD-ROM Professional
462 Danbury Rd.
Wilton, CT 06897-2126

Compute!
P.O. Box 3245
Harlan, IA 51593-2424

ComputerCraft
76 N. Broadway
Hicksville, NY 11801-9962

Computer Currents
5720 Hollis St.
Emeryville, CA 94608

Computer Graphics World
P.O. Box 122
Tulsa, OK 74101-9966

Computer Pictures
Knowledge Industry Publications, Inc.
Montage Publishing, Inc.
701 Westchester Ave.
White Plains, NY 10604

Computer Shopper
P.O. Box 51020
Boulder, CO 80321-1020

Computer World
P.O. Box 2044
Marion, OH 43306-2144

Desktop Video World
P.O. Box 594
Mt. Morris, IL 61054-7902

Digital Imaging
Micro Publishing
21150 Hawthorne Blvd., #104
Torrance, CA 90503

Digital Video Magazine
P.O. Box 594
Mt. Morris, IL 61054-7902

Electronic Musician
P.O. Box 41525
Nashville, TN 37204-9829

High Color
P.O. Box 1347
Camden, ME 04843-9956

Home & Studio Recording
Music Maker Publications, Inc
7318 Topanga Canyon Blvd.
Suite 200
Canoga Park, CA 91303

Home Office Computing
P.O. Box 51344
Boulder, CO 80321-1344

Imaging Magazine
1265 Industrial Hwy.
Southampton, PA 18966
(800) 677-3435

Insight Direct Inc.
1912 W. 4th St.
Tempe, AZ 85281

International Spectrum
10675 Treena St.
Suite 103
San Diego, CA 92131

Internet
P.O. Box 713
Mt. Morris, IL 61054-9965

KidSoft Magazine
718 University Ave., #112
Los Gatos, CA 95030-9958
(800) 354-6150

LAN Magazine
P.O. Box 50047
Boulder, CO 80321-0047

MicroComputer Journal
Classified Dept. 76
N. Broadway
Hicksville, NY 11801

MicroTimes Magazine
5951 Canning St.
Oakland, CA 94609

Musician's Friend
P.O. Box 4520
Medford, OR 97501

Nuts & Volts
430 Princeland Ct.
Corona, CA 91719-1343

Open Computing
P.O. Box 570
Hightstown, NJ 08520-9328

PC Computing
P.O. Box 50253
Boulder, CO 80321-0253

PC Magazine
P.O. Box 51524
Boulder, CO 80321-1524

PC Novice
P.O. Box 85380
Lincoln, NE 68501-9807

PC Today
P.O. Box 85380
Lincoln, NE 68501-5380

PC World Magazine
P.O. Box 51833
Boulder, CO 80321-1833

PRE-
8340 Mission Rd., #106
Prairie Village, KS 66206

Publish!
P.O. Box 51966
Boulder, CO 80321-1966

Video Magazine
Box 56293
Boulder, CO 80322-6293
(800) 365-1008

Videomaker Magazine
P.O. Box 469026
Escondido, CA 92046
(800) 334-8152

Voice Processing Magazine
P.O. Box 6016
Duluth, MN 55806-9797

Windows Magazine
P.O. Box 58649
Boulder, CO 80322-8649

 # Free magazines to qualified subscribers

The magazines listed as free are sent only to qualified subscribers.
The subscription price of a magazine usually does not come anywhere
near covering the costs of publication, mailing, distribution, and other
costs. Most magazines depend almost entirely on advertisers for their
existence. The more subscribers that a magazine has, the more it can
charge for its ads. Naturally, they can attract a lot more subscribers if
the magazine is free.

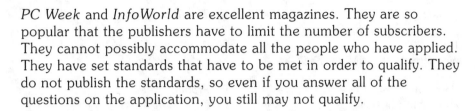

PC Week and *InfoWorld* are excellent magazines. They are so popular that the publishers have to limit the number of subscribers. They cannot possibly accommodate all the people who have applied. They have set standards that have to be met in order to qualify. They do not publish the standards, so even if you answer all of the questions on the application, you still may not qualify.

To get a free subscription, you must write to the magazine for a qualifying application form. The form asks several questions, such as how you are involved with computers, the company you work for, whether you have any influence in purchasing the computer products listed in the magazines, and several other questions that give them a very good profile of their readers.

I wouldn't tell you to lie. But it might help you qualify if you exaggerate just a bit here and there, especially when it asks what your responsibilities are for the purchasing of computer equipment. I am pretty sure that they will not send the FBI out to verify your answers.

One way to qualify for most of these free magazines is to become a consultant. There are very few rules and regulations as to who can call themselves a consultant. (You should be particularly aware of this fact if you decide to hire a consultant.)

The list of magazines below is not nearly complete. There are hundreds of trade magazines that are sent free to qualified subscribers. The Cahners Company alone publishes 32 different trade magazines. Many of the trade magazines are highly technical and narrowly specialized.

Advanced Imaging
445 Broad Hollow Rd.
Melville, NY 11747-4722

Automatic I.D. News
P.O. Box 6158
Duluth, MN 55806-9870

*AV Video Production &
Presentation Technology*
701 Westchester Ave.
White Plains, NY 10604
(914) 328-9157

Beyond Computing (An IBM Magazine)
1133 Westchester Ave.
White Plains, NY 10604

California Business
P.O. Box 70735
Pasadena, CA 91117-9947

CD-ROM News Extra
462 Danbury Rd.
Wilton, CT 06897-2126

Client/Server Computing
Sentry Publishing Company
1900 W. Park Dr.
Westborough, MA 01581-3907

Communications News
2504 Tamiami Trail N.
Nokomis, FL 34275
(813) 966-9521

Communications Week
P.O. Box 2070
Manhasset, NY 11030

Computer Design
Box 3466
Tulsa, OK 74101-3466

Computer Products
P.O. Box 14000
Dover, NJ 07801-9990

Computer Reseller News
P.O. Box 2040
Manhasset, NY 11030

Computer Systems News
600 Community Dr.
Manhasset, NY 11030

Computer Tech. Review
924 Westwood Blvd., #65
Los Angeles, CA 90024

Computer Telephony
P.O. Box 40706
Nashville, TN 37204-9919
(800) 677-3435

Data Communications
P.O. Box 477
Hightstown, NJ 08520-9362

Designfax
P.O. Box 1151
Skokie, IL 60076-9917

*Document Management &
Windows Imaging*
8711 E. Pinnacle Peak Rd., #249
Scottsdale, AZ 85255

EE Product News
P.O. Box 12982
Overland Park, KS 66212

Electronic Design
P.O. Box 985007
Cleveland, OH 44198-5007

Electronic Manufacturing
P.O. Box 159
Libertyville, IL 60048

Electronic Publish & Print
650 S. Clark St.
Chicago, IL 60605-9960

Electronics
P.O. Box 985061
Cleveland, OH 44198

Federal Computer Week
P.O. Box 602
Winchester, MA 01890

Identification Journal
2640 N. Halsted St.
Chicago, IL 60614-9962

ID Systems
P.O. Box 874
Peterborough, NH 03458

Imaging Business
Phillips Business Information, Inc.
P.O. Box 61130
Potomac, MD 20897-5915
(301) 343-1520

InfoWorld
P.O. Box 1172
Skokie, IL 60076

LAN Times
122 E. 1700 S
Provo, UT 84606

Lasers & Optronics
301 Gibraltar Dr.
Morris Plains, NJ 07950

Machine Design
P.O. Box 985015
Cleveland, OH 44198-5015

Managing Office Technology
1100 Superior Ave.
Cleveland, OH 44197-8092

Manufacturing Systems
P.O. Box 3008
Wheaton, IL 60189-9972

Medical Equipment Designer
29100 Aurora Rd., #200
Cleveland, OH 44139

Micro Publishing News
21150 Hawthorne Blvd., #104
Torrance, CA 90503

Mini-Micro Systems
P.O. Box 5051
Denver, CO 80217-9872

Mobile Office
Subscription Dept.
P.O. Box 57268
Boulder, CO 80323-7268

Modern Office Technology
1100 Superior Ave.
Cleveland, OH 44197-8032

Mr. CD-ROM
MAXMEDIA Distributing Inc.
P.O. Box 1087
Winter Garden, FL 34787

Network World
161 Worcester Rd.
Framingham, MA 01701
(508) 875-6400

New Media Magazine
P.O. Box 1771
Riverton, NJ 08077-7331
(415) 573-5170

Network Computing
P.O. Box 1095
Skokie, IL 60076-9662

The Network Journal
600 Harrison St.
San Francisco, CA 94107
(800) 950-0523

Office Systems
P.O. Box 3116
Woburn, MA 01888-9878

Office Systems Dealer
P.O. Box 2281
Woburn, MA 01888-9873

PC Week
P.O. Box 1770
Riverton, NJ 08077-7370

Photo Business
1515 Broadway
New York, NY 10036

The Programmer's Shop
5 Pond Park Rd.
Hingham, MA 02043-9845

Quality
P.O. Box 3002
Wheaton, IL 60189-9929

Reseller Management
Box 601
Morris Plains, NJ 07950

Robotics World
6255 Barfield Rd.
Atlanta, GA 30328-9988

Surface Mount Technology
P.O. Box 159
Libertyville, IL 60048

Scientific Computing
301 Gibraltar Dr.
Morris, Plains NJ 07950

Sun Expert
P.O. Box 5274
Pittsfield, MA 01203-9479

Software Magazine
Westborough Office Park
1900 W. Park Dr.
Westborough, MA 01581-3907

STACKS
P.O. Box 5031
Brentwood, TN 37024-5031

Component and software catalogs

Several companies publish special catalogs for components and software through direct mail. Even IBM has gotten into the act. You should be aware that most of these companies charge a bit more than those who advertise in the major magazines. But ads cost a lot of money so there usually isn't too much information about an advertised product in the major magazines. The direct mail-order companies usually have room in their catalogs to give a fairly good description and lots of information about the product. The catalogs are free. Here are just a few:

CompuClassics
P.O. Box 10598
Canoga Park, CA 91309

Data Cal Corp.
531 E. Elliot Rd.
Chandler, AZ 8522-1152

Compute Ability
P.O. Box 17882
Milwaukee, WI 53217

Dell Direct Sales L.P.
11209 Metric Blvd.
Austin, TX 78758-4093

Computers & Music
647 Mission St.
San Francisco, CA 94105

Digi-key Corporation
701 Brooks Ave. S.
P.O. Box 677
Thief River Falls, MN 56701-0677

DAMARK
7101 Winnetka Ave N.
P.O. Box 29900
Minneapolis, MN 55429-0900

DTP direct
5198 W. 76 St.
Edina, MN 55439

Edmund Scientific Company
101 E. Gloucester Pike
Barrington, NJ 08007-1380

Global Computer Supplies
11 Harbor Park Dr.
Dept. 48
Port Washington, NY 11050

Global Office Products
11 Harbor Park Dr.
Dept. 30
Port Washington, NY 11050

Hello Direct
5884 Eden Park Place
San Jose, CA 95138-1859

IBM PC Direct
P.O. Box 12195
Bldg. 203/Dept. WN4
Research Triangle Park, NC 27709-9767
(800) 426-2968

JDR Microdevices
2233 Samaritan Dr.
San Jose, CA 95124

KidSoft Software Catalog
(800) 354-6150

MAILER'S Software
970 Calle Negocio
San Clemente, CA 92673

MicroWarehouse
1720 Oak St.
P.O. Box 3014
Lakewood, NJ 08701-3014

Momentum Graphics, Inc.
16290 Shoemaker
Cerritos, CA 90701-2243

Mr. CD-ROM
P.O. Box 1087
Winter Garden, FL 34787
(800) 444-6723

Multimedia World
P.O. Box 58690
Boulder, CO 80323-8690

One Network Place
4711 Golf Rd.
Skokie, IL 60076

Paper Catalog
205 Chubb Ave.
Lyndhurst, NJ 07071

Pasternack Enterprises
P.O. 16759
Irvine, CA 92713

PC Connection
6 Mill St.
Marlow, NH 03456

Personal Computing Tools
90 Industrial Park Rd.
Hingham, MA 02043

Power Up!
P.O. Box 7600
San Mateo, CA 94403-7600

PrePress
11 Mt. Pleasant Ave.
East Hanover, NJ 07936-9925

Presentations
Lakewood Building
50 S. 9th St.
Minneapolis, MN 55402-9973

Processor
P.O. Box 85518
Lincoln, NE 68501
(800) 334-7443

Projections
Business Park Dr.
Branford, CT 06405

Queblo
1000 Florida Ave.
Hagerstown, MD 21741

Software Labs
100 Corporate Pointe, #195
Culver City, CA 90230-7616

Soundware
200 Menlo Oaks Dr.
Menlo Park, CA 94025

South Hills DATACOMM
760 Beechnut Dr.
Pittsburgh, PA 15205

TENEX Computer Express
56800 Magnetic Dr.
Mishawaka, IN 46545

Tiger Software
800 Douglas Tower
7th Floor
Coral Gables, FL 33134
(800) 888-4437

Tools for Exploration
4460 Redwood Hwy.
Suite 2
San Rafael, CA 94903

United Video & Computer
724 Seventh Ave.
New York, NY 10019
(800) 448-3738

UNIXREVIEW
P.O. Box 420035
Palm Coast, FL 32142-0035

Public domain and shareware software

There are several companies that provide public domain, shareware, and low cost software. They also publish catalogs listing their software. Some may charge a small fee for the catalog.

> Computer Discount Warehouse   (800) 330-4CDW

> Computers International   (619) 630-0055

> Industrial Computer Source   (800) 523-2320

> International Software Library   (800) 992-1992

> J&R Computer World   (800) 221-8180

> Jameco Electronic Components   (415) 592-8097

> Micro Star   (800) 443-6103

➤ MicroCom Systems	(408) 737-9000
➤ MMI Corporation	(800) 221-4283
➤ National PD Library	(619) 941-0925
➤ Numeridex	(800) 323-7737
➤ PC Plus Consulting	(818) 891-7930
➤ PC-Sig 1030D	(800) 245-6717
➤ PrePress Direct	(800) 443-6600
➤ PsL News	(800) 242-4775 (cost $24 year)
➤ Public Brand Software	(800) 426-3475
➤ Selective Software	(800) 423-3556
➤ Shareware Express	(800) 346-2842
➤ Software Express/Direct	(800) 331-8192
➤ Softwarehouse	(408) 748-0461
➤ The Computer Room	(703) 832-3341
➤ The PC Zone	(800) 258-2088
➤ Zenith Data Systems	(800) 952-3099

 # Computer books

There are several companies that publish computer books. One of the larger companies is TAB/McGraw-Hill, Blue Ridge Summit, PA 17294-0850, (800) 822-8158. Another good source for computer books is Osborne/McGraw-Hill at (800) 227-0900. Call them for a current catalog listing of the many books that they publish. I admit that I am a bit prejudiced, but I recommend them highly.

CHAPTER 18

Troubleshooting and repairing your PC

THIS is one of the longest chapters in this book, but I must tell you that you may not be able to find the answer to your problems in this chapter. There are thousands and thousands of little things that can go wrong in a computer, in both hardware and software. This chapter could be ten times as long and still not cover every possible problem. However, this chapter covers most of the major problems that you might experience.

When speaking of troubleshooting, most people think of hardware problems. But I have had far more trouble with software problems than with hardware. Software problems may be even more difficult to solve than hardware problems.

Finding the cause of the problem is the first step in fixing it. There are several hardware and software diagnostic tools available that can help you find and fix the problems. A few of them are discussed.

Computer basics

Troubleshooting is a little easier if you know just a little of the electronic basics. Computers are possible because of electricity. Under the control of software and hardware, small electric on/off signal voltages are formed when we type from the keyboard or when data is read from a disk or other means of input. This voltage is used to turn transistors on and off to perform various tasks.

An electric charge is formed when there is an imbalance or an excess amount of electrons at one pole. The excess electrons flow through whatever path they can find to get to the other pole. It is much like water flowing downhill to find its level.

Most electric or electronic paths have varying amounts of resistance so work or heat is created when the electrons pass through them. For instance, if a flashlight is turned on, electrons pass through the bulb, which has a resistive filament. The heat generated by the electrons passing through the bulb causes the filament to glow red hot and create light. If the light is left on for a period of time, the excess electrons from the negative pole of the battery pass through the bulb to the positive pole of the battery. Electrons continue to flow until the amount of electrons at the negative and positive poles are equal. At this time, there will be a perfect balance and the battery will be dead.

A computer is made up of circuits and boards that have resistors, capacitors, inductors, transistors, motors, and many other components. These components perform a useful function when electricity passes through them. The circuits are designed so the paths of the electric currents are divided, controlled, and shunted to do the work that we want done. The transistors and other components can force the electrons to go to the memory, or to a disk drive, the printer, or wherever the software and hardware directs it to go.

If an electronic circuit is designed properly, it should last several life times. There is nothing in a semiconductor or transistor to wear out. But occasionally, too many electrons may find their way through a weakened component and cause it to heat up and burn out. Or for some reason the electrons may be shunted through a path or component where they shouldn't go. This may cause an intermittent, partial, or complete failure.

Electrostatic voltage

Before you touch any of the components or handle them, you should ground yourself and discharge any electrostatic voltage that may have built up on your body. It is possible for a person to build up a charge

of 4000 volts or more of electrostatic voltage. If you walk across some carpets and then touch a brass door knob, you can sometimes see a spark fly and often get a shock. If you should touch a fragile electronic component, this high voltage can be discharged through the component. It may weaken the component or possibly ruin it. Most electronic assembly lines have the workers wear a ground strap whenever they are working with any electrostatic discharge sensitive components. You can discharge yourself by touching an unpainted metal part of the case of a computer or other device that is plugged into a wall socket. The computer or other grounding device does not have to be turned on.

 # Document the problem

The chances are if a computer is going to break down, it will do it at the most inopportune time. This is one of the basic tenets of Murphy's immutable and inflexible laws.

If it breaks down, try not to panic. Ranting, cussing, and crying may make you feel better, but they won't solve the problem. Instead get out a pad and pencil and write down everything as it happens. It is very easy to forget. Write down all the particulars, how the cables were plugged in, the software that was running, and anything that might be pertinent. You may get error messages on your screen. Use the PrtSc (for Print Screen) key to print out the messages if possible.

If you can't solve the problem, you may have to call someone or your vendor for help. If you have all the written information before you, it helps. Try to call from your computer, if possible as it is acting up. If it is a software problem, have your serial number handy. Most organizations ask for that before anything else.

 # Instruments and tools

For high levels of troubleshooting, a person would need some sophisticated tools and expensive instruments to do a thorough analysis of a system. You would need a good high frequency

oscilloscope, a digital analyzer, a logic probe, and several other expensive pieces of gear. You would also need a test bench with a spare power supply, spare disk drives, and plug-in boards.

It would be very helpful to have a diagnostic card, such as the POST-PROBE or the Ultra-X, and several of the diagnostic and utility software programs such as those discussed later in this chapter.

It would be helpful to have a known good computer with some empty slots so you could plug in suspect boards and test them.

You would also need a voltohmmeter, some clip leads, a pair of side cutter dikes, a pair of long-nose pliers, various screwdrivers, nut drivers, a soldering iron, and solder.

You would need a good work bench with plenty of light over the bench and a flashlight, or a small light to light up the dark places in the computer case.

Besides the expensive tools and instruments needed for high level troubleshooting and repair, you would need quite a lot of training and experience.

Fortunately, we don't need the expensive and sophisticated tools and instruments for most of our computer problems. Just a few simple tools and a little common sense is all that is needed for the majority of the problems. Here are some tools that you should have around. It is good to have these tools even if you never have any computer problems:

❶ You should have a pad and pen near your computer so you can write down all of the things that happen if you have a problem.

❷ You should have several sizes and types of screwdrivers. A couple of them should be magnetic for picking up and starting small screws. You can buy magnetic screwdrivers, or you can make one yourself. Just take a strong magnet and rub it on the blade of the screwdriver a few times. The magnets on cabinet doors will do, or the voice coil magnet of a loudspeaker. Be very careful with any magnet around your floppy diskettes. It can erase them.

❸ You should also have a small screwdriver with a bent tip that can be used to pry up ICs. Some of the larger ICs are very difficult to remove. One of the blank fillers for the slots on the back panel of the computer also makes a good prying tool.

❹ You should have a couple pairs of pliers. You should have at least one pair of long-nose pliers.

❺ You should have a set of nut drivers. Many of the screws have slotted heads for screwdrivers as well as hexagonal heads for nut drivers. Using a nut driver is usually much easier to use than a screwdriver.

❻ You may need a pair of side cutter dikes for clipping leads of components and cutting wire. You might buy a pair of cutters that also have wire strippers.

❼ By all means buy a voltohmmeter. There are dozens of uses for a voltohmmeter. They can be used to check for the wiring continuity in your cables, phone lines, switches, etc. You can also use a voltohmmeter to check for the proper voltages in your computer. There are only two voltages to check for, 12 volts and 5 volts. The newer DX4 and Pentium 90, 100 and 120 MHz CPUs require 3.3 volts, but usually a voltage regulator on the motherboard or on the CPU socket reduces the 5-volt supply to the required 3.3 volts.

You can buy a relatively inexpensive voltohmmeter at any of the Radio Shack stores or an electronic store.

❽ You need a soldering iron and some solder. You shouldn't have to do much soldering, but you never know when you may need to repair a cable or some other minor job.

❾ You should also have several clip leads. Clip leads are insulated wires with alligator clips on each end. You can use them to extend a cable, for shorting out two pins, and hundreds of other uses. You can buy them at the local Radio Shack or electronic store.

❿ You need a flashlight for looking into the dark places inside the computer or at the cable connections behind the computer.

Chances are that you will never need most of these tools. Still it is nice to have them available if you ever do need them.

Solving common problems

For many common problems, you won't need a lot of test gear. Often a problem can be solved using our five senses: eyes, ears, nose, touch, and taste. Actually, we won't be using our taste very often.

Eyes—If we look closely, we can see a cable that is not plugged in properly. Or a board that is not completely seated. Or a switch or jumper that is not set properly. And many other obvious things, such as smoke.

Ears—We can use our ears for any unusual sounds. Ordinarily, those little electrons don't make any noise as they move through your computer at about two thirds of the speed of light. The only sound from your computer should be the noise of your drive motors and the fan in the power supply.

Smell—If you have ever smelled a burned resistor or a capacitor, you will never forget it. If you smell something very unusual, try to locate where it is coming from.

Touch—If you touch the components and some seem to be unusually hot, it could be the cause of your problem. Except for the insides of your power supply, there should not be any voltage above 12 volts in your computer so it should be safe to touch the components, even when the power is on. Before touching a component, be sure that you have discharged yourself of any electrostatic voltage.

 # The number one cause of problems

If you have added something to your computer or done some sort of repair and the computer doesn't work, something may not have been plugged in correctly or some minor error was made in the installations. If you have added a component, remove it to see if the computer works without it. Never install more than one item at a

time. Install an item, then check to see if it works, then install the next one.

By far the greatest problem in assembling a unit, adding something to a computer, or installing software, is not following the instructions. Quite often it is not necessarily the fault of the person trying to follow the instructions. I am a member of Mensa and have worked in the electronic industry for over 30 years, but sometimes I have great difficulty in trying to decipher and follow the instructions in some manuals. Sometimes a very critical instruction, or piece of information, may be inconspicuously buried in the middle of a 500-page manual.

 # The importance of documentation

You should have some sort of documentation or manuals for all of your computer components and peripherals. You should have a written record of the switch and jumper settings of each of your boards. It is also very important that you have the drive type and the CMOS information of your hard disk drives written down with your records or on a special floppy disk. If for some reason your system fails, you may not be able to access your hard drive and its data if you don't know the drive type listed in your CMOS configuration. You should know what components are inside your computer and how they are configured.

Norton Utilities lets you make a Rescue disk that has a copy of your CMOS, Boot Record, Partition Tables, Autoexec.bat, and Config.sys. This disk is bootable, so it can be used any time that you may lose your CMOS or any of the other vital information. PC Tools also lets you make an Emergency disk similar to the Norton Rescue disk.

 # What to do if it is completely dead

There are several software diagnostic programs. They are great in many cases. But if the computer is completely dead, the software

won't do you any good. If it is completely dead, the first thing to do is to check the power outlet. If you don't have a voltmeter, plug a lamp into the same socket and see if it lights. Check your power cord. Check the switch on the computer. Check the fan in the power supply. Is it turning? The power supply is one of the major components that frequently becomes defective. If the fan is not turning, the power supply may be defective. However, the fan may be operating, even though the power supply is defective. Does any of the panel lights come on when you try to boot up? Does the hard disk motor spin up?

If there is a short anywhere in the system, the power supply will not come on, the fan won't turn, and none of the drives will come on. The power supply has built-in short circuit protection that shuts everything down when the output is shorted.

If a SIMM or memory chip is not completely seated, the computer may not boot up. You may not get any kind of error message or warning.

You can check any of the cables from the power supply with a voltohmmeter. The power supply will not work unless it has a load, so have at least one disk drive plugged in. There should be +12 V between the yellow and black wires and +5 V between the red and black. If there is no voltage, then you probably have a defective power supply.

If you hear the fan motor and the panel lights come on, but the monitor is dark, check the monitor's power cord, the adapter cable, and the adapter. The monitor also has fuses, but they are usually inside the monitor case. You should also check the monitor's brightness and contrast controls. If you have just installed the monitor, check the motherboard or adapter for any switches or jumpers that should be set. Check your documentation. You should also check your CMOS setup to make sure that the BIOS knows what type of monitor you have.

Remove all of the boards except for the monitor adapter and disk controller. Also, disconnect all peripherals. If the system works, then add the boards back until it stops. Be sure to turn off the power each

time you add or remove a board or any cable. If you have spare boards, swap them out with suspected boards in your system.

 # Config.sys and autoexec.bat

If you have just added a new piece of software and your system doesn't work or it doesn't work the way it should, check your autoexec.bat and config.sys files. Many programs change these files as they are being installed. These files may have commands and statements that conflict with your new software or system. I try out a lot of different software and systems. I have had problems where a statement or command was left in the autoexec.bat or config.sys file from a system no longer being used. It may ask the computer to perform a command that is not there. It will go off in never-never land and keep trying to find the command or file. You usually have to reboot to get out.

You may get an error message that says, "Unrecognized command in Config.Sys." It may then have an additional message: "Bad or missing file, driver or path." You could have a misspelled word in the Config.Sys file, or you may have left out a back slash or forward slash. It is quite easy to type in the wrong slash, such as a / instead of a \. The structure of the Config.Sys is rather strict and doesn't provide much room for error.

Whenever you make a change to your Autoexec.bat or Config.Sys, always keep the old one as a backup. You can rename them with the DOS REN command. You can call the old files Config.old, or Autoexec.1 or whatever. If your new Autoexec.bat or Config.Sys doesn't work, you can always go back and rename the old files back to their original names.

If you have a long Autoexec.bat file that doesn't work, you might try editing out parts of it, then reboot and retry it. (Use the DOS EDIT command that uses ASCII text. Don't use a word processor because it adds symbols and characters that confuse the system.) You can temporarily change lines in your Autoexec.bat or Config.sys files by adding a REM (for REMARK) at the beginning of a line that you don't want to be executed.

If you press F8 while booting up, DOS 6.2 and PC-DOS 7.0 let you look at each line of the Autoexec.bat and Config.sys file and ask if you want to load it. If you say "no" to a certain line, and the system then works, you have found the problem.

You should always have a "clean" boot disk that has a very lean autoexec.bat and config.sys on it. There may be times when you don't want any TSRs or anything in your RAM memory in order to run a special program. If you have a lot of TSRs or other things in your 640K of RAM memory, you may not be able to run some programs. Use the DOS MEMMAKER or the IBM PC-DOS 7.0 RAMBOOST program to create more free memory.

 # Beep error codes

Every time a computer is turned on, or booted up, it does a power on self test (POST). It checks the RAM, the floppy drives, the hard disk drives, the monitor, the printer, the keyboard, and other peripherals that you have installed. If everything is okay, it gives a short beep then boots up. If it does not find a unit, or if the unit is not functioning correctly, it beeps and displays an error code. It may beep two or more times depending on the error. If the power supply, the motherboard, the CPU, or possibly some other critical IC is defective, it may not beep at all.

You can check the beep system by holding a key down while the system is booting up. You may hear a continuous beep. After the boot is complete, the system may give two short beeps and display the message, "Keyboard error. Press F1 to continue."

There are several other beep error codes that are in the system BIOS. Each BIOS manufacturer may use slightly different codes for some of the errors it finds. Some of the beep codes are for fatal errors that cause the system to hang up completely. The beeps are arranged so you may get a beep, a pause, another beep, then three beeps close together, or 1-1-3. This code would indicate that there was a failure in the CMOS setup system. One long and two short beeps, accompanied by a POST code of 400, 500, 2400 or 7400, could mean that there is an error in

the CMOS RAM, a motherboard switch setting, or defective video card. A 1-1-4 would indicate that there was an error in the BIOS itself. A continuous beep or repeating short beeps could indicate that the power supply or the motherboard had a fault.

POST codes

The POST codes start with 100 and may go up to 20,000. Ordinarily, the codes are not displayed if there is no problem. If there is a problem, the last two digits of the code will be something other than 00s. Each BIOS manufacturer develops its own codes so there are some slight differences, but most of them are similar to the following:

101 Mother board failure.
109 Direct Memory Access test error.
121 Unexpected hardware interrupt occurred.
163 Time and date not set.
199 User indicated configuration not correct.
201 Memory test failure.
301 Keyboard test failure or a stuck key.
401 Monochrome display and/or adapter test failure.
432 Parallel printer not turned on.
501 Color Graphics display and/or adapter test failure.
601 Diskette drives and/or adapter test failure.
701 Math Coprocessor test error.
901 Parallel printer adapter test failure.
1101 Asynchronous Communications adapter test failure.
1301 Game control adapter test failure.
1302 Joystick test failure.
1401 Printer test failure.
1701 Fixed disk drive and/or adapter test failure.
2401 Enhanced Graphics display and/or adapter test failure.
2501 Enhanced Graphics display and/or adapter test failure.

POST cards

Several companies have developed diagnostic cards (Fig. 18-1) or boards that can be plugged into a slot on the motherboard to display

Figure 18-1

Two diagnostic POST cards

the POST codes. If there is a failure in the system, it can tell you immediately what is wrong.

If you have eliminated the possibility of a defective plug-in board or a peripheral, then the problem is probably in your motherboard. If the power supply is okay, you could use a diagnostic card, such as the POST-PROBE from Micro 2000, at (818) 547-0125, or the R.A.C.E.R. II from Ultra-X, at (800) 722-3789. These two cards are quite similar in the tests that they perform. They can be plugged into a computer that is completely dead except for the power supply, and they check every chip and component on the motherboard. Each card has a small digital display that lights up a code for the condition of each component.

These cards work on any ISA or EISA machine, XT, 286, 386, 486, or Pentium. The POST-PROBE comes with a Micro Channel Architecture (MCA) adapter so it can also be used on IBM PS/2

systems. The R.A.C.E.R. II has a separate board that was designed for the MCA PS/2 systems.

R.A.C.E.R. is an acronym for *Real-time AT/XT Computer Equipment Repair*. This card can be used on any ISA machine, XT, 286, 386, or 486 to diagnose and find faults in the computer hardware. There are several other POST cards on the market, but most of them are not very sophisticated. The Ultra-X R.A.C.E.R. II has several ROMs that can run over 70 diagnostic tests. Besides displaying the test codes on the plug-in board, the progress of the tests can be displayed on a monitor. If there is a failure in one of the tests, a fault tree is displayed that lists in order which chips might be at fault. In a computer where several chips interact, it is often difficult to determine exactly which chip might be at fault. The Ultra-X can narrow it down to a very few. At the end of the test, a report can be printed out.

Businesses can lose a lot of money when a computer is down. The R.A.C.E.R. II and POST-PROBE diagnostic cards are tools that every professional repair shop and every computer maintenance department should have. It might also be well worth the money for an individual to buy one. If you have to take your computer to a repair shop, at $50 to $100 an hour, the repair could be rather expensive. You also have to give up some of your time and some trouble just to take the computer in to the shop. If the shop is busy, it may be some time before you get your computer back.

QuickPost-PC

The QuickPost-PC from Ultra-X, at (800) 722-3789, is a low-cost card that can do many of the diagnostic tests done by the R.A.C.E.R. II, except that it is not as sophisticated. It monitors the POST as the computer boots up and displays the code for any fault.

Both Micro 2000 and the Ultra-X Company have several other diagnostic products, both hardware and software. Call them for a brochure.

Diagnostic and utility software

There are several excellent diagnostic software programs available. Some of the utilities and tests are quite similar in some of the programs. Most of them test and report on your system configuration and your system memory. Many of them do a test on your hard drives. Some of them, such as SpinRite and Disk Technician, are primarily designed for hard disk tests and preventive maintenance.

Most BIOS chips have many diagnostic routines and other utilities built-in. These routines allow you to set the time and date, tell the computer what type of hard drive and floppies that are installed, the amount of memory, the wait states, and several other functions. The AMI and DTK BIOS chips have a very comprehensive set of built-in diagnostics. They can allow hard and floppy disk formatting, check speed of rotation of disk drives, do performance testing of hard drives, and several other tests.

MS-DOS MSD command

If you own a copy of MS-DOS 6.0 or later, you have an MSD (Microsoft Diagnostics) command. This utility can be used to search for files or subjects, and it also gives you a wealth of information about your computer. It can show you the IRQs, the memory usage, your autoexec.bat and config.sys, and many other useful bits of information. You can view the information or have it printed out. Depending on what you have in your computer, it may take up to 20 pages to print it all out.

Norton Utilities

Norton Utilities, from Symantec Corp. (408) 253-9600, includes several diagnostic and test programs and essential utilities. One of the programs is Norton Diagnostics (NDIAGS). This tests the memory, the CPU, the DMA controllers, the real time clock, CMOS tests, and the serial and parallel ports.

Software cannot recognize and test the serial and parallel ports unless you have a loopback plug installed. These are 9- and 25-pin connectors that plug into the serial and parallel sockets. Some of the pins in these connectors are shorted out so the software can recognize them. There is a coupon in the back of the Norton Utilities manual for a loopback set. Symantec sells them for $19.95. Call them for more information.

Of course, Norton Utilities has all of the standard utilities, most of which are periodically updated and improved with new releases. Some of the standard utilities are Unerase, Disk Doctor, Disk Test, Format Recover, Directory Sort, and System Information.

 # PC Tools

PC Tools from Central Point Software, at (503) 690-8090, has even more utilities than the Norton Utilities. PC Tools can diagnose and repair disk partitions, boot records, FATs, lost clusters, and other disk problems. It also lets you create an Emergency Disk, similar to the Norton Rescue disk. It has a utility that can recover data from a disk that has been erased or reformatted. It has several other data recovery and DOS utilities. It can also be used for hard disk backup. It can also detect well over 1000 different viruses. PC Tools has now been merged with Symantec.

 # MicroScope

MicroScope from Micro 2000, at (818) 547-0125, is an excellent diagnostic software tool. It can test the CPU, IRQs, DMAs, memory, hard disk drives, floppy drives, video adapters, and much more. It can search for Network cards and display its I/O and node address. It shows IRQ and I/O addresses. It tests memory and displays available memory space. It displays CMOS contents and lets you run CMOS setup. It can run video tests for memory and character sets. It can do a read, write, and random seek test of the hard drives. It even allows you to edit sectors of the hard drive. It can be set up to run any or all of the tests continuously. It can be set to halt on an error or to log the error and continue.

QAPlus/FE

QAPlus/FE from DiagSoft, at (408) 438-8247, is a very sophisticated software program. Among its many functions is the ability to diagnose problems on the disk systems, memory, video, IDE and SCSI drives and interfaces, interrupts, BIOS, serial, and parallel ports. To test the serial and parallel ports, you need loopback plugs. The loopback plugs come free with QAPlus/FE diagnostic software.

If a semiconductor or system is going to fail, it usually does so within the first 72 hours of use. Many vendors do a burn-in on their products to find any such systems before they are shipped. But many vendors may not have the time nor the software to properly exercise the units. The QAPlus/FE can perform rigorous and continuous tests on systems for burn-in. If you buy an expensive system or component, it may be well worth the cost of buying a copy of QAPlus/FE just for the burn-in capability. If you find a defective component early, it can usually be sent back to the dealer or replaced at no cost.

 # CheckIt PRO: Analyst for Windows

CheckIt PRO: Analyst for Windows from TouchStone Software, at (800) 531-0450, is a` comprehensive analysis tool that can be used by ordinary personnel as well as advanced users. It can collect configuration and performance data, test hardware integrity, evaluate a system to compare performance with other systems, determine upgrade needs, and assess compatibility of hardware and software.

CheckIt was developed several years ago, then they improved it and called it CheckIt PRO. CheckIt PRO: Analyst has been improved again and several new features have been added. It is a very good software tool.

 # The Troubleshooter

The Troubleshooter from AllMicro, at (800) 653-4933, has its own self-booting operating system that bypasses DOS. It can test the

motherboard, run memory tests, test the hard disks and floppy disk drives, check and test the serial and parallel ports, test the video adapter, keyboard, and mouse. It can identify the system hardware and print out a report. It is a good low-cost software tool.

WinSleuth Gold Plus

WinSleuth Gold Plus from Dariana Software, at (714) 236-1380, is another good low-cost diagnostic software tool. It even has an 800 technical support line, which is something unheard of today. They also have a BBS number for technical support. WinSleuth Gold Plus can check hardware configuration, give you BIOS information, CMOS settings, perform CPU tests, keyboard tests, and many more tests. It is a very good tool to have in your library.

WINProbe

WINProbe is from the Landmark Company, at (800) 683-6696. The PC Certify program that comes with WINProbe can save a lot of time and trouble. PC Certify can also be used to test all types of hard drives, floppy drives, and the controllers.

Besides the drives, PC Certify does complete diagnostic tests on the whole computer. It tests the memory, the serial and parallel ports, the BIOS, the video adapter, the monitor, keyboard, and printer. The tests can be run continuously as many times as you desire. These tests are ideal for burning in a computer. The program even prints out a form for a technician to fill out. The form shows what tests were run and has a space for the technician to verify and sign.

The WINProbe portion also has the following diagnostic utilities: audio for sound tests, communications for serial ports, floppy drive rpm test, floppy drive surface analysis, hard drive surface analysis, keyboard tests, math coprocessor, motherboard CPU function tests, mouse driver tests, printer cable test, RAM chip test and video mode tests. The WINProbe also comes bundled with a DOS for Windows program. This is a very low-cost package that everyone should have.

First Aid for Windows Users and PC 911

First Aid for Windows Users from CyberMedia, at 800-721-7824, is a low-cost program that can spot problems, diagnose them, and then fix most of them automatically. For those it can't fix automatically, it can help you fix them manually. It fixes problems with printing, multimedia, bad INI files, path problems, missing application components, networks, and many others. The software is optimized for several of the well-known brand name programs such as Microsoft Office, Word, Excel, Corel Draw, Quicken, Paradox, and many others. In addition, they offer free upgrades to the program that can be downloaded from CompuServe.

PC 911 is a low-cost companion program to First Aid for Windows from CyberMedia. PC 911 keeps track of all changes made to your PC's setup files. Several times in the past I have installed programs that automatically changed my autoexec.bat and Config.sys files to where my system would no longer operate. Recently, a program changed my files so that I was not able to use my word processors. It took me a couple of hours to find the problem. PC 911 could have saved me that time. PC 911 can also help you with conflicts in IRQs, DMAs, and other problems when installing multimedia and other cards.

First Aid and PC 911 can be bought separately or you can save about one third by buying them as a bundle. They are well worth it.

 # Which one should you buy?

If I could only afford one program, I would be hard pressed to choose one. All of them are good tools. Many of them have a few similar utilities, but there are also different utility features in every one of them. I can't possibly list all of the features of the products here. I suggest that you call each company and ask for literature on their products.

I can't even list all of the diagnostic products that are available. New ones are being developed daily. Check computer magazines for ads and reviews.

Spares

One of the easiest ways to check a part is to have a good spare handy. If you suspect a board, it is very easy to plug in a known good one. It is a good idea to have a few spare boards and components on hand, especially if your computer is critical to your business and you cannot afford any down time. I would suggest that you have a spare floppy disk drive, a floppy disk controller board, and a spare keyboard. These items are all fairly inexpensive. Depending on how critical your business is and how important your computer is to it, you might even want to have spares of all your components such as a motherboard, power supply, and all of your plug-in boards.

You may have some very expensive video adapters, VL Bus IDE, PCI bus interfaces, or other boards that may cost hundreds of dollars. But there are usually some equivalent inexpensive boards for all of the boards in your system. For instance, a good VL-Bus interface with caching may cost from $150 to $200 or more. You can buy a simple IDE interface for less than $10. A good graphics high resolution monitor adapter may cost $300, but you can buy an adapter that doesn't have all of the goodies for about $30. A low-cost board can help pinpoint the problem. If your monitor doesn't light up, but it works with a replacement adapter, then you know the probable cause of the problem.

DOS error messages

DOS has several error messages if you try to make the computer do something it can't do. But many of the messages are not very clear. Don't bother looking in the MS-DOS manual for error messages, they are not there. If you are using the IBM PC-DOS and you get an error message, just type help n, where n is the first letter of the error message, and an explanation pops up.

I have dozens of books on DOS but few of them make any reference to the DOS error messages. One of the better books I have is *DOS, The New Complete Reference* by Kris Jamsa, published by Osborne-McGraw-Hill, at (800) 227-0900. He has written several books for Osborne-McGraw-Hill. His *DOS Secrets, Solutions, Shortcuts* is another good book on DOS. He explains the DOS commands in great detail and the DOS error commands and what to do about them. These reference books should be in your library.

Some common DOS error messages

✳ Access denied

You may have tried to write on or erase a file that was protected. The file may have been hidden or protected by an ATTRIBUTE command. Use the Attribute command to change it.

✳ Bad command or file name or File not found

You may have made a mistake in typing in the command, or the command or file does not reside in the current directory.

✳ CHKDSK errors

You should run CHKDSK often. Some people put CHKDSK/F in their autoexec.bat so it is run every time the system is booted up. (Disk Technician can do it for you.) The CHKDSK may give you an error that says:

```
nnn lost clusters found in n chains
Convert lost chains to files Y/N
```

Reinvoke CHKDSK with the /F (for fix) and the lost clusters will be converted to FILE000n.CHK. These are usually incomplete files. When you delete a file, sometimes portions of it may be left in a sector. Or something may have caused an error in the FAT and caused portions of two different files to be written in a single sector or cluster. The files created by CHKDSK/F are usually incomplete. In most cases, they can be deleted. MS-DOS 6.22 has ScanDisk, which does a better job than CHKDSK.

✳ **General failure reading or writing drive n:, Abort, Retry, Fail**
The disk may not be formatted. It is also possible that track 0 on the disk, which stores the FAT, has become defective. It might be possible to restore the disk by using Norton's Disk Doctor (NDD) file on it.

✳ **Invalid directory**
If you do a CD (Change Directory) from the root directory, all you have to type is cd norton, or any directory you want to change to and it changes immediately. If you happen to be in the WordPerfect directory and you type cd Norton, it will say that it is an invalid directory. If you are in any directory except the root directory, you have to type cd \norton or whatever directory. If you type cd /norton, using the forward slash instead of the back slash, you get the same error message.

✳ **Nonsystem disk or disk error.**
Replace and strike any key when ready
You had a nonbootable disk in drive A:.

✳ **Not ready error reading drive A: Abort, Retry, Fail**
You may have asked the computer to go to drive A: and it was not ready or there was no disk in the drive.

⇨ Software error messages

Most software packages have their own error messages. In many cases, the manual does not tell you what the error message means. You will probably have to call the software company to get an answer.

⇨ Glitches

There are times when something may go wrong for no apparent reason and the computer may hang up. Glitches can happen when you are running almost any kind of program. Sometimes you can get out of them with a warm boot (pressing Ctrl, Alt, Del). At other

times you may have to turn off the computer, wait a few seconds, then turn it back on.

You should remember that anything that you are working on is in memory. If you are working on a file that is on your disk, then you still have a copy on the disk, but if it is something that you have just typed in, when you turn off the computer or reboot, anything in memory is gone forever. By all means, try to save your work before rebooting.

Power supply

The power supply is one of the most frequent causes of problems. Most of the components in your computer are fairly low power and low voltage. The only high voltage in your system is in the power supply and it is pretty well enclosed. So there is no danger of shock if you open your computer and put your hand inside it. But you should **NEVER EVER** connect or disconnect a board or cable while the power is on. Fragile semiconductors may be destroyed if you do so.

Semiconductors have no moving parts. If the circuits were designed properly, the semiconductors should last indefinitely. Heat is an enemy and can cause semiconductor failure. The fan in the power supply should provide adequate cooling. All of the openings on the back panel that correspond to the slots on the motherboard should have blank fillers. Even the holes on the bottom of the chassis should be covered with tape. This forces the fan to draw air in from the front of the computer, pull it over the boards and exhaust it through the opening in the power supply case. Nothing should be placed in front of or behind the computer that would restrict air flow.

If you don't hear the fan when you turn on a computer, or if the fan isn't running, then the power supply could be defective. Table 18-1 lists the pin connections and wire colors from the power supply.

Table 18-1   **Power Supply Connections**

Disk drive power supply connections

Pin	Color	Function
1	Yellow	+12 Vdc
2	Black	Ground
3	Black	Ground
4	Red	+5 Vdc

Power supply connections to the motherboard

P8	Pin	Color	Function
	1	White	Power good
	2	No connection	
	3	Yellow	+12 Vdc
	4	Brown	−12 Vdc
	5	Black	Ground
	6	Black	Ground

P9	Pin	Color	Function
	1	Black	Ground
	2	Black	Ground
	3	Blue	−5 Vdc
	4	Red	+5 Vdc
	5	Red	+5 Vdc
	6	Red	+5 Vdc

The 8-bit slotted connectors on the motherboard have 62 contacts, 31 on the A side and 31 on the B side. The black ground wires connect to B1 of each of the eight slots. B3 and B29 has +5 Vdc, B5 −5 Vdc, B7 −12 Vdc, and B9 has +12 Vdc. These voltages go to the listed pins on each of the eight plug-in slots.

Most of the other contacts on the plug-in slots are for address lines and data input/output lines. They are not often involved in problems.

 # Intermittent problems

Intermittent problems can be most frustrating and maddening. They can be very difficult to find.

If you suspect a cable or a connector, try wiggling it to see if it goes away or gets worse. I once spent several hours trying to find the cause of a floppy disk problem. It turned out to be a loose wire in the connector. It was just barely touching the contact. A slight vibration could cause the disk drive to become erratic. A wire or cable can be broken and still make contact until it is moved.

You might also try unplugging a cable or a board and plugging it back in. Sometimes the pins may be slightly corroded or not seated properly. Recently, I turned on one of my computers that hadn't been used for about a month. I got a message that the FDC (floppy disk controller) had an error. This board also controls my hard disks so I was a bit concerned. I unplugged the controller board and cleaned the contacts and plugged it back in. (The copper contacts on a plug-in board may become corroded. You can clean them with an ordinary pencil eraser.) But I still got the FDC error message.

I got out another FDC and prepared to plug it in. But I had to change the setting of a shorting bar on the controller board. On a hunch, I slipped the shorting bar on and off my original controller a few times, then tried the board again. The floppy drives worked perfectly. The shorting bar and the pins had become corroded during the time it was not used.

The contacts of the edge connectors on floppy drives and plug-in boards can also become corroded. Sometimes just unplugging and plugging them back in several times can wipe away the corrosion.

Before unplugging a cable, you might put a stripe on the connector and cable with a marking pen or nail polish so you can easily see how they should be plugged back in.

You may even have a problem in the contacts of a DIP switch. You might try turning it on and off a few times.

WARNING Again, always write down the positions before touching any switch. Make a diagram of the wires, cables, and switch settings before you disturb them. It is easy to forget how they were plugged in or set before you moved them. You could end up making things worse. Make a pencil mark before turning a knob or variable coil or capacitor so it can be returned to the same setting when you find out that it didn't help. Better yet, resist the temptation to reset these types of components. Most were set up using highly sophisticated instruments. They don't usually change enough to cause a problem.

If too much current flows through a chip, it can get hot and fail. It may only fail at certain times when you are running a particular program. If you suspect a chip and it seems to be warmer that it should be, you might try using a hair dryer to heat it up. If it fails due to the extra heat, then you have found the problem. Be careful that you do not heat up a good chip and cause it to fail.

If a component seemed to be too hot, at one time we could spray a coolant on it such as Freon. Because of environmental concerns, you may no longer be able to buy Freon. You might try using ice water in a plastic bag. This will cool it. If the component then works properly, you have found your defect.

Some of the diagnostic software runs a system in an endless loop to try to force the system to fail.

 # Serial ports

Conflicts in setting up serial port devices can cause a lot of problems. Like the parallel ports, pins for the serial ports are available on any of the bus plug-in slots. The serial ports may be available as a group of ten pins on the motherboard. Or it may be on a multifunction plug-in board. The serial port may be a male DB25 connector with pins, or there may be a male DB9 connector. The original RS232 specification called for 25 lines. But most systems only use four or five lines, so the DB9 connector with 9 pins is more than sufficient. Many of the mice sold today have the DB9 connector, so if your

system has the DB25 connector you need to order an adapter. The adapter costs about $3.

The serial ports are most often used for a mouse or other pointing device, for modems, FAX boards, for plotters, scanners, and several other devices. DOS supports four serial ports, COM1, COM2, COM3, and COM4. But DOS only has two Interrupt Request (IRQ) lines for the serial ports, IRQ4 for COM1 and IRQ3 for COM2, so COM3 and COM4 must share the IRQ lines with COM1 and COM2. You need special software in order to permit sharing. They can share because it is not likely that all four IRQ lines would be used at the same time.

If two devices are set for the same COM port, it causes a serious conflict. Neither device will operate properly. When installing a mouse, modem, or FAX board, the interface plug-in boards must be configured so none of the devices use the same port. If you have devices already installed on your system, you may not know which port they are set for.

There are several programs that can help you determine which ports are being used. One of the better ones is a low-cost shareware program called Port Finder. It is available from James McDaniel of mcTRONic Systems, at (713) 462-7687.

 # Software problems

I have had far more trouble with software than I have had with hardware. Quite often it is my fault for not taking the time to completely read the manuals and instructions. But I don't usually have the time to read and study every page in the manual when I install a program. Many of the programs are getting easier to run. Plug and Play will eliminate a lot of problems. But there will still be lots of software problems that you will probably run into. Many vendors have support programs for their products. If something goes wrong, you can call them. Some companies charge for their support. Some have installed a 900 telephone number. You are charged a certain fee for the amount of time on the phone. It can cost a lot of money to maintain a support staff.

If you have a software problem, document, or write down, everything that happens. Before you call, try to duplicate the problem, or make it happen again. Carefully read the manual. When you call, it is best to be in front of your computer, with it turned on and the problem on the screen if possible. Before you call, have the serial number of your program handy. One of the first things they will probably ask is for your name and serial number. If you have bought and registered the program, it will be in their computer.

Most software programs are reasonably bug-free. But lots of things can go wrong if the exact instructions and procedures are not followed. In many cases, the exact instructions and procedures are not very explicit. It seems that most software manuals are written by people who know the software very well. But they seem to forget that the person using it for the first time does not know it.

Software companies could save millions of dollars if they produced manuals that were better written to make installation and usage easier. If you spend a lot of money on a program, you shouldn't have to spend a lot more to learn how to use it.

 # User groups

There is no way to list all of the possible software or hardware problems. Computers are dumb and very unforgiving. It is very easy to plug a cable in backwards or forget to set a switch. There are thousands of things that can go wrong. Sometimes it can be a combination of both software and hardware. Often there is only one way to do something the right way, but ten thousand ways to do it wrong. Sometimes it is difficult to determine if it is a hardware problem caused by software or vice versa. There is no way that every problem can be addressed.

One of the best ways to find answers is to ask someone who has had the same problem. One of the best places to find those people is at a Users Group. If possible, join one and become friendly with all the members. They can be one of your best sources of troubleshooting. Most have had similar problems and are glad to help. Many local

computer magazines list User Groups in their area. The nationally distributed *Computer Shopper* alternates with a listing of Bulletin Boards one month and User Groups the next.

Thank you for buying my book. I wish you all the best. I hope all your problems are easy ones.

Index

Illustrations are indicated in **boldface.**